Philosophical Theory and the Universal
Declaration of Human Rights

Philosophical Theory and the Universal Declaration of Human Rights

Edited by William Sweet

A C T E X P R E S S

University of Ottawa Press

University of Ottawa Press gratefully acknowledges the support extended to its publishing programme by the Canada Council and the University of Ottawa.

We acknowledge the financial support of the Government of Canada through the Book Publishing Industry Development Program (BPIDP) for our publishing activities.

National Library of Canada Cataloguing in Publication

Philosophical Theory and the Universal Declaration of Human Rights / edited by William Sweet.

(Actexpress)
Includes bibliographical references and index.
ISBN 0-7766-0558-5

1. Human rights—Philosophy. 2. United Nations. General Assembly. Universal Declaration of Human Rights. I. Sweet, William, 1955– II. Series.

JC571.P52 2003   323'.01   C2003-901090-2

 UNIVERSITY OF OTTAWA
UNIVERSITÉ D'OTTAWA

Books in the ACTEXPRESS series are published without the University of Ottawa Press's usual editorial intervention. The editorial process for *Philosophical Theory and the Universal Declaration of Human Rights* has been insured by the editor and his contributors.

Proofreading: Käthe Roth

Cover illustration: The drawing is by Walter Crane and appeared in *Cartoons for the Cause* published in 1896, captions subsequently modified.

ISBN 0-7766-0558-5

© University of Ottawa Press, 2003
542 King Edward, Ottawa, Ont. Canada K1N 6N5

press@uottawa.ca   http://www.uopress.uottawa.ca

Printed and bound in Canada

CONTENTS

Preface   vii

Introduction: Theories of Rights and Political and Legal Instruments   1
William Sweet

PART I. THEORIES OF RIGHTS

1. Natural Law and Natural Rights   19
   Howard P. Kainz

2. The Ethical Background of the Rights of Women   27
   Sarah Hutton

3. Economic Rights and Philosophical Anthropology   41
   Leslie Armour

4. T. H. Green on Rights and the Common Good   71
   Rex Martin

5. A Postsecular Exchange: Jacques Maritain, John Dewey, and Karl Marx   83
   Thomas M. Jeannot

PART II. THE UNIVERSAL DECLARATION AND
THE PRACTICE OF HUMAN RIGHTS

6. Human Rights: Fifty Years Later   99
   Mostafa Faghfoury

7. The Universal Declaration of Human Rights, Maritain, and the Universality of Human Rights   109
   Bradley R. Munro

8. The Universal Declaration of Human Rights
    in the Supreme Court of Canada   127
    Jack Iwanicki

9. Human Rights and the Survival Imperative:
    Rwanda's Troubled Legacy   143
    Philip Lancaster

PART III: RIGHTS AFTER THE UNIVERSAL DECLARATION

10. Reconciling Individual Rights and the Common Good:
    Aquinas and Contemporary Canadian Law   155
    Paul Groarke and J.L.A. West

11. Moderating the Philosophy of Rights   171
    Ralph Nelson

12. MacIntyre or Gewirth? Virtue, Rights, and the Problem
    of Moral Indeterminacy   183
    Gregory J. Walters

13. Universal Human Rights, Concepts of Ownership, and
    Aboriginal Land Claims   201
    David Lea

14. Solidarity and Human Rights   213
    William Sweet

Contributors   233

Index   237

PREFACE

The twentieth century was the century of human rights – of their massive violation, but also of humanity's increased recognition of them. From the Déclaration des droits internationaux de l'homme (Declaration of the international rights of man, adopted by the Institute of International Law during its session at New York on 12 October 1929) to the recent discussion of the establishment of an International Court of Justice, the notions of "right" and "human rights" can no longer be said to be creatures of rarefied philosophical discourse. They are part of the basic vocabulary of people and peoples throughout the world – particularly those who struggle against tyranny and oppression.

Today's human rights discourse and documents reflect over two centuries of philosophical discussion, but there has been a reciprocal influence of charters, declarations, and international conventions on the way people think about human rights. This volume investigates some of these interrelationships between philosophical theory and human rights documents.

This volume is dedicated to Léon Charette (1935–1996), a longtime member and former President of the Canadian Jacques Maritain Association. An alumnus and professor of philosophy at the University of Ottawa, Léon was a defender of the thought of one of the twentieth century's principal architects of philosophical thinking about human rights, Jacques Maritain. Léon's sense of justice and compassion and his dedication to the cause of human dignity were evident in both his research and his relations with his students and colleagues. It is appropriate that he be acknowledged in a lasting way in a volume of studies on the philosophical discussion of human rights.

I wish to thank the Social Sciences and Humanities Research Council of Canada and the Fr. Edo Gatto Chair of Christian Studies (St. Francis Xavier University) for financial support that made the preparation of this volume possible. I also wish to thank Ms Marcy Baker for secretarial support and Ms Monica MacKinnon for carefully copyediting the text.

William Sweet
St Francis Xavier University

Introduction

THEORIES OF RIGHTS AND POLITICAL AND LEGAL INSTRUMENTS

William Sweet

1. Introduction

In his famous lecture "The Rights of Man,"[1] the French philosopher Jacques Maritain draws attention to a remarkable event which occurred shortly after the end of the Second World War. Despite the diversity of interests, histories, cultures, politics, and ideologies, nations from every part of the planet were able to agree on a list of universal human rights. And for the more than fifty years since, the United Nations Universal Declaration of Human Rights (UDHR) of 1948 and the rights it enumerates have played a central role in calls for justice, equality, and the respect of human dignity throughout the world.

The Universal Declaration explicitly identified well over two dozen "human rights." Aside from the principal rights to "life, liberty and security of person" (Article 3), freedom of conscience and thought and expression (Article 19), and freedom of peaceful assembly and association (Article 20), the "dignity and the free development of [human] personality" entailed cultural and economic rights: the right to participate freely in the cultural life of the community (Article 27); to social security (Article 22), including the right to work; and to just remuneration, including the right to equal pay for equal work (Article 23). Further, people had a "right to rest and leisure" (Article 24), a "right to a standard of living adequate for the health and well-being" (Article 25), and a right to education (Article 26). The range of rights enumerated in the UDHR was impressive.

Maritain thought a complete account of human rights required a philosophical theory. He argued that while rational justifications were "*powerless* to create agreement among men," they nevertheless "are *indispensable*."[2] Without a foundation, the list of rights would soon be "inflated,"[3] and people would not be sure that what they assented to was "true and rationally valid."[4] With the wrong foundation, rights would be "bankrupt"[5] and the proper object of criticism and scepticism. Maritain admitted that the quest for an underlying theory is not easy – that it "brings into play the whole system of moral and metaphysical (and anti-metaphysical) certainties to which each individual subscribes,"[6] and that even if we find the right foundation, knowledge of it may be "obscure" and "unsystematic."[7] Still, he thought the "practical agreement" on the "practical truths"[8] expressed in the UDHR was a great achievement, and he was confident that "a new age of civilization" would "recognize and define the rights of the human being in his social, economic, and cultural functions."[9]

Yet in the years since the adoption of the UDHR, respect for the rights it proclaims has been at best limited. Once-stable societies have collapsed into bloody civil war, totalitarian and single-party states abound, colonialism has often been replaced only by more subtle forms of imperialism, and the gap between the rich and poor has never been greater. Appeals to rights have often been ineffective. Some critics reject the rights listed in the UDHR altogether, and even defenders of human rights have had difficulty accepting several of the articles of the UDHR as stating genuine "rights." Nor have the old objections of Burke, Bentham, and Marx to universal human rights – that they are ahistorical, vague, imprecise, insensitive to cultural differences, metaphysically problematic, and serve to reinforce the status quo – lost their influence.[10]

Today we may ask whether the circumstances and grounds which led to the formulation of theories of rights, bills of rights, the UDHR, and other declarations are still relevant. What do we make of "human rights" more than half a century after the Universal Declaration – a declaration for which many, like Maritain, had so much hope? How does the contemporary practice of rights fit with traditional theories of rights? What has been the effect of political and legal instruments such as the UDHR? What have events of the recent past shown us about these theories and declarations? It is to such questions that the essays in this volume seek to provide an answer.

2. Theories of Rights

How does philosophical theory bear on the existence of rights and, specifically, on the rights enumerated in the UDHR? To answer this, we need to consider both the context in which the contemporary discussion of human rights has arisen, and why philosophical theories of rights have been challenged.

A principal challenge to human rights is that the term "human rights" is vague and ambiguous. For some, the term refers to those freedoms or powers that are or can be claimed by human beings, which are derived from the dignity and worth inherent in (or ascribed to) human persons, and which enable them to engage in activities essential to their growth and development. These rights are said to be universal and, generally, include rights to life, liberty, the security of the person, property, equal protection of the law, freedom of conscience and thought, free religious practice and expression, peaceful assembly and association, and to take part in government.

But others see human rights as fundamentally "equality rights" or rights of "non-discrimination." Here, proponents focus on the cultural and economic sphere – the rights of linguistic, racial, and visible minorities, of the poor and the marginalized, and of the disabled. They are particularly concerned with addressing "abuses," such as denying education or participation in culture, or economic development. Some advocates see these "abuses" to include"business practices that limit access to loans, mortgages, bank accounts, telephone services, and other services for people who are on welfare or are unemployed."[11]

This vagueness or ambiguity in the term "human rights" is reflected in the differences concerning the origin of rights. For some, rights are principles "discovered" in nature, which serve as a basis for individuals to challenge the arbitrary authority of the state. For others, however, rights have their home in political and legal instruments – such as charters, declarations, constitutions, international agreements, conventions, and protocols – which presuppose the existence and support of communities and states.

How can we account for these different understandings of the concept of rights? The history of the "discourse" of human rights is fairly well known. While the existence of "natural rights" is implied in works of antiquity, it is only in the Middle Ages that we begin to see an acknowledgment of rights as distinct from "the right."[12] For St. Thomas Aquinas, rights are a product of law.[13] What we call human rights is a product of a law immanent in nature – specifically, in the end or *telos* of the being concerned – which derives its force from its relation to a transcendent order, divine reason, or the eternal law. Rights are, then, subordinate to "law," and are ascribed so far as they are conducive to a being's end or *telos*.

It is not, however, until the seventeenth century (with Hugo Grotius [1583–1645] in *De Jure Belli Ac Pacis* [*The Rights of War and Peace,* 1625]) that the term "rights" is carefully unpacked. Grotius and others recognized that rights cannot be separated from the concrete, even if they are abstract and general. And it quickly became clear that a discourse of rights must take account of both the social environment and the characteristics of human beings. As the understanding of "nature" and "human nature" developed, so did the notion of "right."

"Nature" can be understood in different ways, and so "rights" came to be approached in correspondingly different ways as well. For many seventeenth- and eighteenth-century authors, "nature" was an order that was self-subsistent; its laws were necessary and had force intrinsically. Philosophers no longer had to refer to an underlying divine reason or eternal law. The natural law was "written in our hearts," and natural rights in their entirety were logically derived from it.

A second view – one that has had a strong influence in political thought in the Anglo-American world – is found in Hobbes and Locke and their successors. While there is a natural moral law, its status is unclear; the notions of a human *telos* and a common good recede from view. The fundamental natural law of self-preservation is soon understood as equivalent to an individual's right to life. "Natural rights," then, take on a role of their own. With the focus on individual rights, social life is no longer seen as fundamental, but as conventional – a means to the preservation of the lives of individuals. Political and legal authority is regarded as a product of contractual arrangements that people voluntarily engage in. Thus, natural rights are prior to the state and serve as limitations on the state.

On both of the above "modern" views, however, rights are "natural" to human beings and, thus, are absolute and inalienable. And once it was recognized that individuals may determine their own good for themselves, the purpose of rights was no longer just to enable them to pursue the good, but to prevent undue interference from others. Rights were "negative."

Through the late eighteenth and nineteenth centuries, rights play an increasingly important role in political, social, and philosophical thought. We see movements demanding freedom of conscience, religious toleration, the rights of women and of those without property, the elimination of slavery, and the extension of the franchise. At each step, the recognition of "new" rights was concomitant with changes in the understanding of nature and of the human person. The discourse of rights reflected our view of nature – of the world – as a whole.

The "new" discourse of rights did not go unopposed. As human beings came to be understood more and more in purely naturalistic terms, and as nature came to be seen as malleable or as something that has changed and continues to change, we encounter more and more challenges to rights. While acknowledging that natural rights were "sacred,"[14] Edmund Burke considered rights to be a "Metaphysical abstraction,"[15] and "rights talk" to be inflammatory rhetoric – one of the "pretexts" of the "troublous storms that toss / The private state, and render life unsweet."[16] Burke held that "pride, ambition, avarice, revenge, lust, sedition, hypocrisy, ungoverned zeal, and all the train of disorderly appetites" hid behind talk of rights,[17] and that this discourse was responsible for the "havoc" of the French Revolution.[18] Jeremy Bentham also considered "universal human rights" to be unnecessary, vague, anarchical, and dangerous.[19] Karl Marx had a more benign, but still critical, view. In his *Critique of the Gotha Program* (1875), he argued that human or "equal rights" were "ideas which in a certain period had some meaning but have now become obsolete verbal rubbish,"[20] and that the discourse of human rights simply served class interests. For all these reasons, and more, some critics wished to consign the language of "human rights" to the "museum of antiquities." And these objections have been extended in our own days in different ways by Margaret MacDonald, Raymond Aron, Richard Rorty, and Alasdair MacIntyre.[21]

Does this mean that the circumstances and grounds that led to the formulation of theories of rights – and rights themselves – are no longer relevant? Despite these challenges, the discourse of rights has not lost its power, and several philosophers have attempted to address the criticisms raised above.

Defences of natural human rights are found in authors as diverse as Mary Wollstonecraft, Immanuel Kant, Herbert Spencer, many of the leading figures of nineteenth- and twentieth-century American jurisprudence, H.L.A. Hart and, today, Alan Gewirth, John Finnis, Tibor Machan, Ronald Dworkin, and Robert Nozick. In general, their argument is that for personhood to be possible – or for "person" to be a moral term – rights are logically required.

Others responded to the late-eighteenth- and nineteenth-century challenges to rights by attempting to reformulate rights. Inspired by Rousseau and Hegel, and aspiring to unite rationalist and empiricist traditions, the idealist T.H. Green (1836 –82) and his student Bernard Bosanquet (1848–1923)[22] argued for a "thick" notion of human nature and for the inseparability of individuals from their social context. Rights, then, are properties of individuals which reflect the functions or positions they have in communities. Rights are natural, but not inalienable or absolute.

More recently, we have "pragmatic" defences of the existence of universal human rights. Jack Donnelly, for example, points to the fact that human rights have "become a ... well established part of international relations."[23] He notes that the "ideal of equal and autonomous individuals pursuing ... their own conceptions of the good life, [has become] deeply embedded as a regulative political ideal in contemporary international society." Thus, almost everywhere we look we find "a basic moral commitment to the idea that all human beings, simply because they are human, have the equal and inalienable individual rights recognized in The Universal Declaration and Covenants."[24]

In these defences, rights are both values and indicators of value – they not only reflect moral principles, but constitute socially recognized, quasi-legal claims. And so, despite the changes in meaning and the present ambiguities in the term, the discourse of rights and theorizing about rights remain important. Demands for justice and equality continue to be made in terms of rights. This discourse has also come to have a place in many non-Western countries, and has shaped the ways in which these cultures understand themselves.

Human rights, then, exist as a practice at both the national and international levels. But for such a practice to continue and thrive requires, on the one hand, recognition and the possibility of enforcement and, on the other, as clear as possible an account of what rights are, what their moral weight is in relation to other values, and how they might be explained and defended. The task of philosophical theory is still far from complete.

3. Political and Legal Instruments

Having rights is of little consequence unless they are recognized as rights and unless some sanctions are in place. A discussion of rights is not complete, then, without some comments on the place of political and legal instruments related to human rights. But we have other reasons for looking at these political and legal instruments. Recognition in national and international law of human rights and of the "practice" of rights has obviously influenced people to use the discourse of rights. And some scholars would add that changes in circumstances and in how we speak about rights, particularly since 1948, have affected our theories of rights. Does seeing rights as a "practice" in national and international law affect how we think about and attempt to explain or justify them?

The concept of rights has long been recognized in law and constitutions. The American Declaration of Independence (1776) and its Bill of Rights (1791), the

Polish Bill on Government (1791), and the French Declaration of the Rights of Man and the Citizen (1789) are early examples. The American and French documents in particular affirm both that the well-being of the people is a good and that the authority of the state is based on the will of the people. These explicit recognitions in law of a set of basic human rights and liberties, together with the recognition of the universal applicability of law, gave momentum to extending rights to all human beings.

The history of Britain and its dominions, France, and the United States, in the nineteenth century reveals a gradual extension of a core set of rights. Yet only with the twentieth century did rights become generally understood to extend internationally. After the horrors of the First World War and subsequent political realignments, attempts were made to formulate declarations of international law and human rights, such as the Declaration of the International Rights of Man of 12 October 1929.[25] But not until the Second World War and the recognition of what had been perpetrated during that war, did the call go forth for the "recognition of the inherent dignity ... of all members of the human family" and for a declaration of human rights.

The key moment in the international political and legal recognition of human rights is the Universal Declaration of 1948. The rights it enumerates have been appealed to by almost every democratic movement since. These rights have been elaborated and developed in a number of covenants and protocols, such as the International Covenants on Economic, Social and Cultural Rights (1966) and on Civil and Political Rights (1966), and the Optional Protocol to the International Covenant on Civil and Political Rights (1966). As noted earlier, these rights include not only fundamental rights to life, liberty, and security of the person; to freedom of conscience; and to freedom of association. There were also cultural and economic rights, deemed necessary for the dignity and free development of one's personality.

The rights of the Universal Declaration and of its Covenants and Protocols are not just rights of the United Nations. They are (and have been) a model for a number of other international charters, such as the American Declaration of the Rights and Duties of Man (1948), the European Convention on Human Rights (1950), the European Social Charter (revised 1996), and the African Charter on Human and Peoples' Rights (1981). Through the latter half of the twentieth century, individual countries (such as Canada) followed suit and adopted charters or bills of rights, or gave explicit constitutional guarantees of certain basic rights. And in turn agencies and national and international judicial bodies have come to be involved in the implementation and enforcement of human rights. Human rights issues are sometimes treated by the International Court of Justice, the principal judicial organ of the United Nations (although the Court deals only with cases among states, and not between a state and individuals). Where we have regional charters or declarations of rights, legal institutions such as the Inter-American Court of Human Rights and the European Court of Human Rights have been established. It is fair to say that while there continue to be efforts at providing philosophical or theoretical justifications for human rights since the time of the UDHR, the defense of human rights has been made primarily by appeal to political and legal instruments, such as charters, constitutions, and international conventions and agreements, and, where possible, to those bodies concerned with the implementation of rights.

The concept of rights that appears in political and legal instruments has been influenced by earlier philosophical discussion of rights which has, in turn, been a product of how we understand nature and especially human nature. Have these political and legal instruments affected our understanding of rights or how we theorize rights?

In the first place, in the formulation of these charters and declarations, we note the increasing presence of "positive rights" and collective or "group" rights, so that "human rights" include language rights and the rights of minorities to act on principles inherent in, or designed to protect, their cultures. We see this also leading to the perception that people have a right to basic goods, and not just freedom from restriction in competing for them. We find a "thicker" notion of rights – as encompassing both what have traditionally been called negative, as well as positive, rights. These instruments have likely affected how people understand what their rights are.

Second, at the root of these instruments is an explicit recognition or statement of human dignity, as well as our social responsibilities and duties. As the Universal Declaration reminds us, "Everyone has duties to the community in which alone the free and full development of his personality is possible" (Article 29). Human beings are more than rational and self-interested maximizers of pleasure, but as fundamentally social beings capable of, and seeking, moral, intellectual, physical, and spiritual growth. If we look at how many people theorize rights, we find a "thicker" theory of human nature at work. The various political and legal instruments likely serve as reminders that rights must take account of the human person as a whole, and not just in his or her dimension of being a rational agent.

Third, we see not only that many national constitutions include an explicit acknowledgment of human rights, but that the introduction of notions of "rights" and "liberty," even in places where they are not native, has been successful. The Japanese constitution (3 November 1946), drafted in only five days by a "constitutional assembly" of 24 Westerners appointed by General Douglas MacArthur and headed by an American lawyer, Lt. Col. Charles Louis Kades, included a wide range of Western-style rights and liberties (see articles 11–39). This document was initially regarded as outrageous by then-Prime Minister Shigeru Yoshida.[26] Yet the concepts of liberty [*ji-yu* = to depend on oneself] and rights referred to in the document have since become an accepted part of Japanese self-understanding.

Yet critics in both the developed and the developing world take these instruments to be hopelessly naive or to have a hidden agenda. Some critics maintain that the economic and social rights of the UDHR and subsequent documents have led to an inflation of rights – there are alleged rights against not only racism and sexism but "lookism" and "classism"; there are appeals to "rights" not only to basic education, but to specialized training. The responsibilities of the recipients are rarely, if ever, referred to. Such an approach, critics continue, confuses basic human rights with human goods – that rights such as life, liberty, and association are on quite a different level than goods like "rights" to leisure, and that attempts to secure the latter are not only unrealistic (given the material resources available), but can only interfere with the former. Thus, the list of rights provided in the UDHR, and the apparent shift to an emphasis on economic and social rights, has not contributed to a better understanding of human rights or to promoting and protecting these rights.

Other critics argue that human rights instruments are ineffective and have failed to make any substantial contribution to the welfare or dignity of human beings. Human rights are only intermittently and arbitrarily enforced, and to depend on appeals to such rights for justice is at best naive. Thus, even though international bodies recognize rights, they are often unwilling or unable to enforce them. Nations such as the former Soviet Union, China, and North Korea were signatories to the UDHR and yet consistently ignored these rights – and there were little or no sanctions that any international body employed to try to change this. Moreover, the invasions of Tibet, Hungary, and Czechoslovakia, and the civil wars in Rwanda, Yugoslavia, and East Timor, are all examples which show human rights are either ineffective or non existent. Finally, different nations interpret freedom of speech in different ways. In some, it is virtually absolute, in others it is subject to "democratic limits," and in yet others it is entirely subject to the whim of the state. Many have come to be disillusioned with the whole discourse of human rights.

Some non-Western countries are particularly critical of the legal instruments of human rights, which they see as revealing human rights for what they "really are" – tools of foreign ideology and political and economic domination. In the Bangkok Declaration (March–April 1993) of ministers and representatives of Asian states preparing for the 1993 United Nations World Conference on Human Rights in Vienna, and in the series of white papers on human rights published by the Chinese State Council (in 1991 and 1995), Asian and developing nations argued that the discourse of human rights was often used as a tool of foreign policy and oppression by larger powers; that these rights cannot be applied without taking into account the distinctiveness of the cultures in which they are to play a role; that many of these abstract rights impede more fundamental concerns (for example, providing a minimum standard of health care, housing, and food, providing a basis for development, and so on); that the responsibilities of the recipients are rarely, if ever, referred to; and that many of these rights are, at the present time, luxuries rather than essential to social progress and well-being.

It is in such a charged political and legal environment that the contemporary discussion of human rights takes place. What does this experience tell us about the importance of human rights? Have political and legal instruments, like the UDHR, helped us to understand what is at stake and what might be gained in employing a discourse of rights? Are there universal human rights, and is there a place for political and legal instruments, like those of the Universal Declaration? What does the history of the past fifty years show us? And what role does philosophical theory have in the discussion of these rights?

4. Perspectives on Rights

The essays in this volume aim at addressing the preceding questions – outlining different ways of approaching what is involved in a discourse of natural or universal human rights, the advantages and disadvantages of such a discourse (in light of both world events and challenges to rights theories), the relation of this discourse to the legal and political documents that have been formulated to protect human rights and ensure a respect for persons, and the effects of this discourse and these documents in the contemporary world.

In the first five essays, the authors deal with how we have been led to our contemporary conceptions of rights. They review some of the theories and historical contexts on which the understanding of rights as "human rights" is founded, reexamine classical arguments concerning rights, and explore some of the ways in which we might make sense of the concept of human rights. In the second part, papers focus on the central and seminal place of the UDHR in the history of human rights, on the rights articulated in the UDHR, and on ways in which the UDHR has been applied in both national law and international affairs. In the final five papers, the authors discuss several challenges in applying and theorizing human rights in the years since the UDHR. Some bring classical arguments to bear on the contemporary context, some review the adequacy of current analyses of rights, and some discuss limits on the appeal to both the practice and theories of rights.

In Part 1, "Theories of Rights," the central question is whether we can give an argument for human rights or, at least, for those most basic human rights that we call "natural rights." Certainly many arguments have been advanced. Some have been rooted in "the natural law," some in "reason," some in nature as such, some in a social contact, and some in "human nature." The character of these arguments has often been strongly foundationalist – that is, rights are in some way directly deduced from natural law, or nature, or reason. But whether there can be so strong a foundation has been a matter of much debate.

To explain how we have been (he thinks, rightly) led to a discourse of human rights, Howard Kainz ("Natural Law and Natural Rights") begins with several terminological clarifications – distinguishing natural law, natural rights, and "human rights," as well as arguing that we should be able to give a foundation for believing that natural rights exist. For such a foundation, Kainz turns to one of the earliest arguments we have for natural rights – taken from the thirteenth-century texts of St. Thomas Aquinas. Kainz argues, however, against recent (non-Thomistic) natural rights theorists such as John Finnis, who attempt to replace natural law with a theory of "basic goods."

Another argument for natural rights based on natural law is found in the work of philosophers of the seventeenth and eighteenth centuries – for example, John Locke. For Locke, natural law entailed natural rights to life, liberty, and the pursuit of property. Locke's understanding of natural law, however, is quite different from that current in the thirteenth century. Not only was natural law understood simply as "the law of reason," but what people believed about human nature had also changed. Some hold that Locke's approach to natural law is the source of later arguments extending "natural rights" to women. Sarah Hutton disputes this. Hutton (in "The Ethical Background of the Rights of Women") agrees that we see in late-seventeenth- and eighteenth-century authors, such as Damaris Cudworth (Lady Masham), Catherine Macaulay, and (most famously) Mary Wollstonecraft, a gradual shift towards using the language of rights. Masham and others argue that women should have greater opportunities because they, like men, are moral and rational beings and require the means to develop this character. But Hutton argues that Masham, Macaulay, and Wollstonecraft, unlike Locke and Hume, are moral realists (believing in an eternal and immutable moral law, founded in the goodness of God) and anti-voluntarists (where what is good is defined by what is rational). The basis for their arguments for the rights of women is found in the Platonist tradition of Ralph Cudworth (Masham's father), Richard Price, and Samuel Clarke, rather than in Locke. Rights are not facts or precepts, as in Locke, but desiderata.

Understanding human nature – or, at least, what it is to be human – is commonly at the root of claims to rights, and of accounts of what rights are fundamental. But in the seventeenth century, we find several distinctive views of human beings, and corresponding views of rights. As Leslie Armour ("Economic Rights and Philosophical Anthropology") points out, we have a dualist view, commonly associated with Descartes, where minds are radically distinct from bodies, and where freedom of conscience and of thought could exist without any corresponding liberty of the body to act. We also have a Hobbesian mechanistic view of human beings as "meat in motion" – though here, the moral character of liberty disappears. Armour identifies a third view, found in philosophers associated with the French Protestant community of Saumur. The Saumur philosophers recognized the importance of religious tolerance and, given their views on salvation, were obliged to try to provide an appropriate corresponding account of the human person. They argued that human beings are creatures of infinite possibilities, but that – in a way reminiscent of Wollstonecraft – this potential cannot be expressed unless people have positive control over their lives. People must share responsibilities and resources, but they also have basic rights. We can construct an argument for human rights here, although it is not clear that these rights are "natural," or that the argument is a foundationalist one.

Eighteenth-century authors, such as T.H. Green, also held that natural rights in the Lockean sense cannot serve as the basis for civil rights. If the rights possessed by individuals are truly natural, they cannot be subject to restriction. Nevertheless, Green argued that we can still defend human (or, what he called "universal" or "general") rights. In "T.H. Green on Rights and the Common Good," Rex Martin argues that Green provides an argument for rights – one that is, moreover, suited to contemporary democratic society. For Green, there are basic rights, but they are subject to social recognition and based on a common good. Individual rights exist, but they also depend on the community or what Green calls "the state." Since there is no undue emphasis on rights, this account addresses contemporary communitarian concerns about an implicit atomic individualism of rights.

In "A Postsecular Exchange: Jacques Maritain, John Dewey, and Karl Marx," Thomas Jeannot suggests the recognition of the person as a social being, of how individual human identity is built on life in community, and of the priority of the common good in social life, is necessary to construct an adequate account of rights. Though their views are distinct in many ways, Maritain, Dewey, and Marx share a basic humanism and agree that we must go beyond classical secular liberalism (and its correlative model of negative rights). By starting with a personalism and a doctrine of the common good, we have a ground for genuinely human rights.

In Part 2, on the Universal Declaration and its place in the practice of human rights, Mostafa Faghfoury ("Human Rights: Fifty Years Later") begins with a broad picture of the circumstances that gave rise to the UDHR in 1948. Faghfoury says we generally find in thinkers one of two ways of viewing humanity – inclusively, where all of humanity is one, and exclusively, where people distinguish between "themselves" and "others" – with "themselves" usually understood as somehow superior. Both approaches have had their articulate defenders. But the latter approach, Faghfoury notes, has consistently led to war. The UDHR attempts to promote the former model and, despite the resistance to it in the decades since the Declaration, Faghfoury believes that the moral appeal of the UDHR has the best prospect of succeeding.

How, concretely, has the UDHR been helpful? In "The Universal Declaration of Human Rights, Maritain, and the Universality of Human Rights," Bradley Munro examines the views of one of the principal architects of the UDHR, Jacques Maritain, and argues that Maritain's theoretical justification for human rights is of little help in determining what people and countries should do to defend and protect human rights. Nevertheless, Munro allows that Maritain's arguments – and more broadly, the UN – succeed at a practical level. Maritain's recognition of the fundamental features of human life and his emphasis on dialogue as a means of achieving peaceful resolution of conflicts provide a practical foundation for, and enable appeals to be made to, the rights articulated in the UDHR and subsequent covenants and protocols. The UDHR has been of practical moral help.

How far has the UDHR made a practical contribution to the defence of human rights at the national and international levels? While the UDHR has contributed to education about human rights, disagreement exists whether it has had a concrete effect on the respect of rights. Jack Iwanicki ("The Universal Declaration of Human Rights in the Supreme Court of Canada") asks whether it has promoted the recognition and respect of human rights within national law. Certainly the UDHR has influenced the text of constitutions and bills of rights – Canada is a specific example of this. But after examining a number of cases argued before the Supreme Court of Canada, Iwanicki suggests that the Court often does not give much weight to international materials. He concludes that if the UDHR is to have an influence, it will have to be through legislators, not the courts.

In "Human Rights and the Survival Imperative: Rwanda's Troubled Legacy," Philip Lancaster argues that the UDHR has been of little or no help in settling the most egregious cases of violations of human rights, such as the genocidal massacre of Tutsis by Hutus in Rwanda, or in dealing with the fallout after the events. Lancaster claims that the UDHR fails to compel allegiance – that it lacks the compulsion of law, is based on a poorly formed (what he calls "Kantian") normative foundation, and does not take sufficient account of differences in power and the existence of radical evil. Lancaster doubts that the notion of universal human rights can have any concrete effect, given what we know of human persons.

In Part 3, the authors raise the question of how philosophers have theorized and applied rights in the years since the UDHR. One of the criticisms raised against the existence of social, economic, and "collective" rights – particularly those found the UDHR – is that this has led to an inflation in rights. This has been a key issue in the contemporary exchange between liberals and communitarians. Liberals allegedly not only defend an account of individual rights but, its critics claim, elevate the interests of the atomic individual over the collective good. Communitarians not only emphasize community and the common good over individual rights, but its critics charge, leave insufficient room for individual autonomy and the pursuit of happiness. Is there a way of resolving the tension between "individual" rights and collective goods?

One response to this is discussed by Paul Groarke and Jason West ("Reconciling Individual Rights and the Common Good: Aquinas and Contemporary Canadian Law"). Given the classical principle *lex iniusta non est lex* – that an unjust law is not a law – Groarke and West follow Aquinas's natural law theory in arguing that authorities can place burdens on individuals only to the extent that they are proportionate to the good to be achieved through them. Individual rights exist because they reflect natural features of the human person, but they are dependent on the social context in which they are held. This Thomistic view, they claim, avoids the Scylla and Charbides of liberalism and communitarianism. Groarke and West also argue that Thomism can provide a constitutional theory to guide interpretation of political and legal instruments, such as the Canadian Charter of Rights and Freedoms.

In "Moderating the Philosophy of Rights," Ralph Nelson agrees that respect for persons requires a discourse of human rights, but it should be "moderated" in a way consistent with a common good. One solution, proposed by Jacques Maritain, is to "graft" natural rights onto a more fundamental natural law. Thus, we need accounts both of the common good (which grounds rights in duties) and of the process of how to ascribe rights to individuals. Understanding the common good "distributively" and "instrumentally" (as in most liberal thinkers), rather than collectively (as in St. Thomas), leads to an inflation of rights. Nelson argues specifically that the attempts of John Finnis and Alan Gewirth fail in finding a place for both the collective and distributive senses of the common good. For a more complete account of the common good that avoids an inflation of rights, Nelson recommends the writings of Maritain's student and friend, Yves Simon.

Another response to the tension between individual rights and collective goods is offered by Alan Gewirth, who holds that he can provide a deductive argument for individual and collective rights – and use these rights as a basis for a moral theory. Gewirth's defence has been challenged by "communitarians," such as Alasdair MacIntyre, for being just another example of an antiquated foundationalist approach that is unproved and unprovable. But in "MacIntyre or Gewirth? Virtue, Rights, and the Problem of Moral Indeterminacy," Gregory Walters maintains that MacIntyre's arguments fail, and that Gewirth's arguments can avoid the communitarian critique. Walters adds that MacIntyre's own virtue ethics does not provide a determinate concept of what goods people ought to pursue. Theoretical foundations for human rights – and for liberalism in a broad sense – are possible after all.

Are collective rights natural rights? How far do collective rights – specifically, the rights of communities, such as linguistic, cultural, and aboriginal rights – extend? David Lea ("Universal Human Rights, Concepts of Ownership, and Aboriginal Land Claims") considers what is involved in talking about natural rights, and whether we can extend the notion of "natural rights" to apply to aboriginal rights to land. Lea reminds us of the origins of the concept of property, arguing that in early Christian thought and also in Locke, property rights are not "full blown" but usufructuary. The former justifies "control ownership," the latter simply rights to the benefits of property – that is, "income ownership." Thus, while aboriginal property rights may be natural, it is still an open question what specific entitlements follow from them.

In light of the different approaches to human rights since the UDHR, some have challenged whether "rights talk" is necessary or useful. Richard Rorty, for example, has argued that there is no need for an appeal to rights or human nature to justify a call to be in solidarity with others, and that theories of human rights are unnecessary. But William Sweet replies, in "Solidarity and Human Rights," that a discourse of human rights is not only defensible, but provides a useful means of justifying and promoting the moral call to solidarity. Rights talk and rights theories remain valuable.

The papers in this volume, then, focus on our understanding of human rights and particularly with the contribution of the UDHR and its successor political and legal documents. What drives many of the authors is the question whether the concept and the discourse of human rights have been successful, or whether they are outdated. The papers are largely optimistic. Most, if not all, hold out hope for a discourse of rights, although they recognize several important questions raised by those who challenge it. This is as it should be. If a discourse of human rights is to be viable, it must respond to those who claim that not only the theories but the political and legal instruments of human rights have failed.

5. Assessment

Over fifty years after the UDHR, the discourse of human rights still has moral force; it continues to play an important role in declaring the "inherent dignity ... of all members of the human family" and in showing humanity's recognition of this value. So while rights talk, declarations, and legal and political instruments have been criticized, we should first determine what is meant or presupposed by these criticisms. We should ask: "What is the function of a discourse – and of declarations – of human rights?," "What should we reasonably expect of such a discourse and such instruments?," and "What would suffice to show that this discourse or these instruments have been successful?" But this is only a first step. In the past fifty years, what we have learned (or, better, what we have been reminded of) is that we must be attentive to the nature of the human person – both to its dignity and to its social responsibilities and duties. A discourse of rights is a useful way of recognizing certain values, such as the dignity and duties of individuals. Thus, the papers that follow are also called on to discuss what is necessary for rights and defences of them to be coherent and effective.

For a discourse of rights to be and remain viable, it has to have a clear conception of the human person – of its nature, of its dignity and autonomy, and of its moral and social responsibilities. This could be a "foundation" for human rights and for the project that underlies the various legal and political instruments. We may not need to employ a classical foundationalist approach, where rights are derived from an axiom or a set of axioms (such as a human *telos*), even though such an approach may be more successful than has sometimes been suggested.

More importantly, for such a discourse to be and remain viable, we must have a "thick" theory of human rights. A "thick" theory can provide a middle road between libertarianism and statism. Against statism, it recognizes individual dignity, autonomy, and the value of self-realization, without making individual wishes and wants absolute. Against libertarianism it recognizes the importance of our relations to others as part of our individuality and, therefore, the necessity of social responsibilities and duties. If individual human beings have basic rights, they also have basic duties, and these rights cannot be separated from a good that is common to all humanity. These features were recognized from the very beginning, when rights were tied to natural or divine law. The recognition of the importance of duties and of a common good make the corresponding human rights no less rights and no less individual. And this may remind us that a recognition that human rights are not the "property" of just one liberal tradition.

Finally, if political and legal instruments like the UDHR are to be viable, we have to be clear on what its function is, and on what we can reasonably expect it to achieve. Its importance need not be that it is administratively effective; the United Nations does not have – and never had – the power to guarantee its respect. Still, the UDHR can be important pedagogically, practically, and politically. It can be important pedagogically, so far as it serves as a moral indication of what we have learned about humanity – of the recognized value of human dignity – and also as an indication of where those nations who are signatories to it profess to stand. It can be important practically, because these rights provide an indication of how, concretely, individuals can be just, moral, and show solidarity, but also how, concretely, these nations are called to be just in their dealings both with their own citizens and with the citizens of other countries. Finally, the UDHR can be important politically, because it provides an indication of the moral limits on what states and nations can do, without requiring that there be any prior theoretical agreement.

The essays in this volume attest that a discourse of rights and the corresponding legal and political instruments have a place in contemporary social and political philosophy. The UDHR and its protocols and conventions enumerate a lengthy list of rights and values that many take to be central to ensuring human dignity. Philosophical theory may help to provide a basic or a conceptual framework for these rights. It may also serve by raising the question whether, for a notion of human rights to be effective, we must distinguish the notion of human rights from some dominant traditions of liberalism. And it may remind us of certain "metaphysical facts" – for example, that human beings are social beings – or suggest different ways we can argue for human rights, such as appeals to history, to consensus, or even to natural law or characteristics of the individual person as a being with a *telos*.

The history of the more than fifty years since the UDHR has not been pretty, but we may still be in the process of determining how we can live up to the ideals on which theories, declarations, and charters of rights are founded.

Notes

1. *Man and the State* (Chicago: University of Chicago Press, 1951).
2. Ibid., p. 77.
3. Ibid., p. 103.
4. Ibid., p. 77.
5. Ibid., p. 84.
6. Ibid., p. 79.

7. See *Natural Law: Reflections on Theory and Practice by Jacques Maritain*, ed. William Sweet (South Bend, IN: St. Augustine's Press, 2001), p. 34.

8. *Man and the State*, p. 76.

9. Ibid., p. 104.

10. Jeremy Waldron, *Nonsense upon Stilts: Bentham, Burke and Marx on the Rights of Man* (London: Methuen, 1987).

11. Report of the Panel to Review the Canadian Human Rights Act, June 2000; reported in *The National Post* (22 June 2000).

12. See Arthur P. Monahan, *From Personal Duties Towards Personal Rights: Late Medieval and Early Modern Political Thought* (Montreal: McGill-Queen's University Press, 1994).

14. *Summa Theologiae*, I–II, question 96, article 4.

15. "Speech on Fox's India Bill (1 December 1783)," in *Edmund Burke on Revolution*, ed. Robert A. Smith (New York: Harper & Row, 1968), p. 106.

15. *Reflections on the Revolution in France*, in *The Writings and Speeches of Edmund Burke*, 12 vols. (Boston: Little Brown and Co., 1901), Vol. III, pp. 240–1.

16. Ibid., p. 418.

17. Ibid.

18. Burke, "An Appeal from the New to the Old Whigs," *Writings and Speeches of Edmund Burke*, Vol. IV, pp. 151–185; p. 188.

19. Jeremy Bentham, *Anarchical Fallacies*, in his *Works*, ed. J. Bowring, (London, 1838–43), Vol. II, pp. 489–534.

20. Karl Marx, "Critique of the Gotha Program (1875)," in *Selected Writings*, ed. David McLellan (Oxford: Oxford University Press, 1977), pp. 564–570; see Karl Marx and Friedrich Engels, *Marx/Engels Selected Works in One Volume* (London: Lawrence and Wishart, 1973), pp. 320–321.

21. See Margaret MacDonald, "Natural Rights," *Proceedings of the Aristotelian Society*, XLVII (1946–47), pp. 225–250; Richard Rorty, "Human Rights, Rationality, and Sentimentality," in *On Human Rights, The Oxford Amnesty Lectures*, eds. Stephen Shute and Susan Hurley (New York: Basic Books, 1993), pp.111–134; Alasdair MacIntyre, *After Virtue* (Notre Dame, IN: University of Notre Dame Press, 1981), pp. 66–71; Raymond Aron, *Essai sur les libertés* (Paris: Calmann-Levy, 1965) and "Is Multinational Citizenship Possible?," *Social Research*, XLI (1974), pp. 638–656.

22. See Bernard Bosanquet, *The Philosophical Theory of the State and Related Essays*, ed. Gerald F. Gaus and William Sweet (South Bend, IN: St Augustine's Press, 2001).

23. See Donnelly, "The Social Construction of International Human Rights," in *Human Rights in Global Politics*, ed. Tim Dunne and Nicholas J. Wheeler (Cambridge: Cambridge University Press, 1999), pp. 71–102, pp. 77–78.

24. Ibid., pp. 99–100.

25. Published by the International Law Institute in its plenary session in New York in 1929. See A.N. Mandelstam, "'La déclaration des droits internationaux de l'homme adoptée par l'Institut de Droit international," *Revue de Droit International*, No. 1 (1930); *Les droits internationaux de l'homme*, ed. Paul Gramain (Paris: Editions internationales, 1933).

26. Tadashi Aruga, "The Declaration of Independence in Japan: Translation and Transplantation, 1854–1997," *Journal of American History*, 85 (1999), pp. 1413–14.

Part I

Theories of Rights

One

NATURAL LAW AND NATURAL RIGHTS

Howard P. Kainz

First, I want to discuss some terms. "Natural rights" and "human rights" are closely related but not synonyms. Natural rights are connected with natural law theory and encompass human rights. If something is considered a natural right, it is also a human right. Not every proponent of human rights subscribes to natural law theory, however. From this perspective, it is false to say that if something is a human right, it is also a natural right. Although we expect a broad convergence of rights agreed on from both perspectives, divergences may occur.

Also, "natural rights" should be distinguished from "natural law." The confusions between them are traditional and long-standing. *Ius* in Latin can mean either "right" or "law." This ambiguity led the medieval jurists to make a distinction between objective *ius* and subjective *ius* (law and right).[1] Perhaps the same ambiguity helped transform the historical emphasis from law to rights, without the change being noticeable. In German, *das Recht* has a similar double meaning, leading to hesitation among translators as to whether Hegel's *Philosophie des Rechts* should be translated as *Philosophy of Right* or *Philosophy of Law*. The case is similar to *le droit* in French, *el derecho* in Spanish, and *lo diritto* in Italian. So we are faced with at least one situation where Anglophones might claim that their language is more precise philosophically than other languages!

But the ambiguities are not just semantic, they are also conceptual. Many philosophers associate "natural law" with "state of nature" theories, which are primarily concerned with the elucidation of basic rights. However, we should remember that even classical theorists like Hobbes and Locke discuss natural law as well as natural right.

Natural law addresses fundamental moral duties, natural right (and rights) concern fundamental moral claims or entitlements. John Finnis in *Natural Law and Natural Rights* develops a precise legal definition:

> We may safely speak of rights wherever a basic principle or requirement of practical reasonableness, or a rule derived therefrom, gives to A, and to each and every other member of a class to which A belongs, the benefit of (i) a positive or negative requirement (obligation) imposed upon B (including, *inter alia*, any requirement not to interfere with A's activity or with A's enjoyment of some other form of good) or of (ii) the ability to bring it about that B is subject to such a requirement, or of (iii) the immunity from being himself subjected by B to any such requirement.[2]

Natural law and natural right are correlative; neither can exist without the other. In social relationships, the existence of a right implies a corresponding duty, and a strict duty in a social context implies that someone has a right. In philosophy, natural rights are connected with individuality and personhood. Natural law, however, is associated with sociality and communality – the proper relationship between individuals, possibly in a top-down configuration, sometimes horizontally.

Natural rights are implicit in a natural law theory, but explicit attention to natural rights has evolved slowly. One hears of dubious and strained ascriptions of natural rights theory to Plato and Aristotle, but we should focus on the Stoics for definite statements about natural rights. The Stoic philosopher Epictetus writes, "Even the slave is deserving our esteem and able to claim from us his rights"[3] – a far-reaching insight coming from the second century A.D. Aquinas, however, does not present a theory of rights in the modern sense. *Ius* for Aquinas is Aristotelian justice, the virtuous maintenance of equitable relationships concerning property among individuals. He says nothing about the right to political liberty or equality, or even to life or happiness.

The modern notion of natural/human rights came into the limelight with the French *Declaration of the Rights of Man and the Citizen* (1789), which asserted that liberty, property, security, and resistance to oppression were the "imprescriptible natural rights" of all human beings. They are "imprescriptible" because no political power or legislature could grant them or take them away. Earlier, American founders like Jefferson, working in the context of Lockean natural law theory, grappled with the problem of coordinating natural law with the rights of subjectivity. Spelling out these rights, the American *Declaration of Independence* (1776), thirteen years before the French *Declaration*, opens by emphasizing the basic rights of "life, liberty, and the pursuit of happiness."

For us in the twenty-first century, the major impetus to a revival of interest in both natural law and natural rights was the Nuremberg trials in the aftermath of World War II and the Holocaust in Nazi Germany. These trials brought to the fore the question of whether there is any higher law to which we can appeal when statist laws are corrupt or evil. (How can we even judge statist laws as evil, except in terms of some higher standard of law?) Subsequently, a remarkable international consensus on basic human rights was achieved in the Universal Declaration of Human Rights, promulgated by the United Nations, which gave member nations the hope of preventing any recurrence of a holocaust. The rights listed in the 1948 Declaration included rights to life, liberty, and security of person; equality before the law; privacy; marriage and protection of family life; the ownership of property; freedom of thought, conscience, and religion; work; education; protection against unemployment; enjoyment of the arts; and many other rights in the legal, political, and cultural spheres.

As we examine this extremely extensive list, the question naturally emerges as to whether consensus, even broad consensus, is enough to provide a justification for these rights. If someone asks, "What are the grounds for the supposed right to freedom of thought?" we should be able to offer a satisfactory philosophical grounding for this alleged right. And do not some rights exist, say, the rights of women and children, which, even in lieu of a broad consensus, can be and should be justified and defended?

When asked about the foundation of natural rights, our first response might be, "Well, of course, the basis for natural rights must be in human nature itself." But this response will soon encounter the objection, "What do you mean by human nature?" Even if you could answer that objection satisfactorily, you would inevitably encounter the next objection, "You are guilty of the value/fact or 'ought'/'is' fallacy." Natural rights are obviously values, and we cannot derive a value from a fact; but is not human nature something factual? The interdiction of this fallacy is supposedly traceable to Hume, although a number of works take issue with this widespread interpretation of Hume.[4] But if, in our strenuous efforts to avoid all fallacies, we resolutely try to avoid deriving any moral values from human nature, we almost inevitably end up trying to excogitate basic values on the basis of pure reason, something that Hume, who traced moral values back to "sentiments" grounded in human nature, roundly criticized.

Hume writes:

The Ultimate ends of human actions can never, in any case, be accounted for by *reason*, but recommend themselves entirely to the sentiments and affections of mankind without any dependence on the intellectual faculties ... Reason, being cool and disengaged, is no motive to action, and directs only the impulse received from appetite or inclination by showing us the means of attaining happiness or avoiding misery ... The standard of [reason], being founded on the nature of things, is eternal and inflexible, even by the will of the Supreme Being; the standard of [the sentiments], arising from the internal frame and constitution of animals, is ultimately derived from that Supreme Will which bestowed on each being its peculiar nature and arranged the several classes and orders of existence.[5]

The major contemporary theoretician of natural law and natural rights John Finnis, following the lead of the Thomist Germain Grisez, makes a clean break with Thomistic attempts — or what seem like Thomistic attempts – to derive natural law from human nature. His non-derivation is based on a set of seven self-evident basic values – knowledge, life (preservation of life, possibly also the procreation of life), play, aesthetic experience, sociability (friendship), practical reasonableness (applying one's intelligence to problems and situations), and religion and pursuit of ultimate questions about the cosmos and life – analyzed in the light of "practical reasonableness."[6] Ironically, Finnis, whose main purpose is to develop a natural law theory adhering strictly to Humean requirements, ends up ignoring the "natural sentiments" that Hume emphasized and relying on the sort of pure rational analysis that Hume criticized. Finnis's analytical "baptism" of Aquinas's arguments has led to an ongoing dispute between traditional Thomists like Henry Veatch and Ralph McInerny.[7] More recently, Anthony Lisska tried to mediate between the two camps by discerning analogues to human nature in the concept of "natural kinds," often used in contemporary analytic philosophy.[8]

Natural rights that are not based on nature would be equivocal. Finnis indicated this in a fall 1997 colloquium in the Marquette University Law School. When asked who would be excluded as a natural law ethicist, he was unwilling to exclude any person who held a non-relativistic ethical theory. On further questioning, he included both Bentham and Kant as "natural law theorists"! He then admitted that only on the urging of his mentor, H.L.A. Hart, did he title his book *Natural Law and Natural Rights*. He refused to answer questions about his preferred title for the book. We may surmise that Finnis, Grisez, and others share the search for objective, non-relativistic ethical principles with traditional natural law theorists.

A key problem for some natural law theorists is the *Summa theologiae*, I–II.94.2, where Aquinas seems to derive natural laws from the tripartite aspects of human nature. He writes:

The order of the precepts of the natural law exists according to the order of natural inclinations. Because in man there is first of all an inclination to good in accordance with the nature which he has in common with all substances: inasmuch as every substance seeks the preservation of its own being, according to its nature: and by reason of this inclination, whatever is a means of preserving human life, and of warding off its obstacles, belongs to the natural law. Secondly, there is in man an inclination to things that pertain to him more specially. According to that nature which he has in common with other animals: and in virtue of this inclination. those things are said to belong to the natural law, which nature has taught to all animals, such as sexual intercourse, education of offspring and so forth. Thirdly, there is in man an inclination to good, according to the nature of his reason, which nature is proper to him: thus man has a natural inclination to know the truth about God, and to live in society: and in this respect, whatever pertains to this inclination belongs to the natural law; for instance, to shun ignorance, to avoid offending those among whom one has to live. and other such things regarding the above inclination.[9]

Thus, Aquinas makes the distinction between three aspects of "nature" in human beings and the fundamental inclinations consequent upon each aspect. First, he argues that humans are beings and, like all natural beings, are inclined to preserve themselves, to stay in being. Second, he says they are animals inclined to reproduce and rear their young. Third, their essence is distinctively and uniquely rational, so that they are naturally inclined to knowledge and social order. From these premises, Aquinas derives the fundamental natural laws of self-preservation, sexual responsibility and the duty to educate the young, and the duties to strive for knowledge of God and maintain amicable relationships with fellow human beings.

Finnis characterizes these passages as simply a "meditation" on the relationship of human life to three metaphysical levels – inorganic, organic, and mental.[10] Finnis argues that this could not be a deduction of values, since values must be derived independently of facts, on the basis of their intrinsic self-evidence.

I am suspicious that Finnis spends fourteen pages in *Natural Law and Natural Rights* arguing for the "self-evidence" of knowledge, the first of the seven "basic values," and twelve pages discussing the other six values. His long drawn-out and multifaceted arguments for the value of knowledge are offered as a template for the rules of self-evidence, which can be applied to the other values. But after reading these arguments, we think of the scholastic distinction between things that are self-evident *in se* and things that are self-evident *quoad nos*. Surely the moral value of the third basic value, "play," is something that for trained philosophers is not self-evident *quoad nos*, but at most self-evident *in se*.

I suggest we take a second look at Aquinas's triple division discussed above. On closer examination of the controversial Question 94 of the *Summa*, we may find Aquinas's analysis is not really guilty of deriving values from facts, and is not only the clearest exposition of basic natural "laws," but also of basic natural "rights."

First it may be a little difficult to understand how an inclination to "self-preservation" can be predicated for beings that have no "self." Also, the Aristotelian theory that natural "appetites" are intrinsic to all beings – sticks and stones, as well as plants and animals – may seem overly anthropomorphic. However, leaving some unstable elements of physics aside, we can generalize that natural kinds tend to stay in existence. It is almost self-evident that living beings, with all their built-in mechanisms for preserving themselves, tend to stay in being, even if we are anxious to avoid Aristotelian presuppositions about teleology. This tendency toward self-preservation is both a factual drive and a value. Natural beings are constituted to preserve themselves, and this is intrinsically good and valuable. Regarding the second natural aspect, sexuality, we may experience culture-shock, living in an era full of symbols of a contraceptive mentality. However, even the contraceptive mentality underlines our acute awareness of the connection between sexuality and reproduction and our understanding that rearing human children is much more arduous and time-consuming than rearing animal offspring. The birth of a human being does not just take place nine months after conception, but involves prolonged gestation by the family and the community, and immense amounts of education to supply for the comparative lack of instincts in humans. Again, we are faced with the drive to raise our offspring and the responsibility, spanning many years after birth, to further the material, intellectual, and spiritual welfare of our children. With the third natural aspect, rationality, we might balk at Aquinas's extrapolation of rationality to the quest for knowledge of God, but we can have no doubt that the human desire for knowledge has no built-in limits. Aquinas also associates rationality with sociality. This tendency of dealing rationally with fellow human beings might be characterized as the basis for the *jus naturale*, but the "facts" connected with rationality are not "just" facts. They converge with the values of expanding knowledge and increasing communality. The convergence is so close and clear in this case that discussion of the "derivation" of the values from the facts misses the point, as if some neutral hiatus exists between facts and values.

Second, in common parlance, we hear about the "law of self-preservation," so existence of such a "law" is a truism. But the self-preservation of the individual is both a duty and a right, the right to life. Self-preservation implies, for example, the duty and right to maintain health and security, the duty and right to avoid euthanasia and assisted suicide; some people even speak of a duty and a right toward things like the primary or secondary inhalation of cigarette smoke. The dutiful implications of sexual reproduction are for us more problematic than the duties of self-preservation. As the global population reaches six billion, some people speak conversely about a solemn duty "not" to reproduce. If we examine this position more closely, we find the real concern is that "poor" people stop reproducing. They cannot assure us that if poor people have fewer children, the ratio of poor people to rich people in the world will change for the better. We ask ourselves if the biblical injunction to "increase and multiply, and fill the earth" (*Genesis* 1:28) has any meaning at this time. Have we not filled the earth? Not really. The world has plenty of room for everyone. One political scientist has calculated that if the population of the world lived in Texas, there would be a little over 1,300 square feet for each individual. If an "over-population" problem exists, it is not because of too little space. What we call "overpopulation" has to do with politics and the problems of distributing the world's resources. The natural "right" of the poor and the rich to reproduce must be recognized, with the understanding that the duty of having offspring is limited, and, as Aquinas observed in regard to the status of celibates, it is not a duty for everyone. However, we should not concentrate solely on the physical procreation of human beings, for whom the "gestation period" goes well beyond nine months. Corollary with reproductive rights and duties are the right and the duty of working for a living wage to support our offspring. The most important rights and duties are to nurture and educate them, once we bring them into the world, a task many parents are unwilling to entrust completely to the state or to a third party. Finally, in the third natural aspect, we see the clearest convergence of right and duty. Our development of rational capacities and the pursuit of knowledge and social concord are not only inalienable rights that we must constantly defend, but they are irrevocable duties that cannot be shirked without a loss of our humanity.

You will note that many of the rights listed in the Universal Declaration of Human Rights – the rights to life, security of person, marriage and protection of family life, the ownership of property, work, education, protection against unemployment – are connected with the rights we have just discussed. But what about freedom? The Universal Declaration also mentions liberty, freedom of thought, conscience, and religion. For the modern consciousness, these rights have a certain precedence and preeminence. Is there such a thing as a natural law or a natural right of pursuing freedom? We should be aware that freedom in the modern sense does not appear in ancient and medieval philosophy. Explicit discussion of freedom in our sense is not found in the writings of classical natural law theorists. Yet freedom and the right to freedom is implicit in Aquinas. While he does not explicitly mention an inclination to freedom, in the Thomistic Aristotelian context, where the will is the "appetite" of the rational/intellectual faculty, an impetus toward freedom is implied. If the development of rationality is a right and a duty, then the acknowledgment and exercise of freedom is indispensable to rational living. This falls short of Jean-Paul Sartre's attempt to base all values on freedom and of the emphasis on freedom in the Western world and in modernity in general. Here the issue of the hierarchy of values becomes relevant. Reflection on the Thomistic hierarchy, which begins with the law/right of self-preservation, may be particularly timely for us. In our era of nuclear armament, as warheads are multiplied, as great nations like India and Pakistan force their way into the "nuclear club," and as potentially terrorist groups are enthusiastically acquiring "backpack" and "suitcase" atomic bombs, we could argue the "law of self-preservation" has become the chief and the most relevant natural law. The world now is faced with the pressing obligation of either eliminating its nuclear arsenals or facing imminent destruction from an accidental or intentional triggering of World War III. But this obligation of self-preservation is at the same time a right that must be claimed by the citizens of the world, despite government reluctance to change the "status quo" of "Mutually Assured Destruction." If a hierarchy of values exists, life and survival may be even more important than freedom, since they are the *sine qua non* for the existence of freedom. John Finnis's mentor, the legal positivist, H.L.A. Hart, although no proponent of natural law, suggested that survival is "the central indisputable element which gives empirical good sense to the terminology of Natural Law."[11] This is an interesting convergence of legal positivism and natural law theory.

Notes

1. A.P. d'Entreves, *Natural Law: Introduction to Legal Philosophy* (London: Hutchinson University Library, 1951), ch. 3.

2. John Finnis, ed. *Natural Law and Natural Rights* (Oxford: Clarendon Press, 1980), p. 205.

3. C.H.S. Davis, ed., *Greek and Roman Stoicism and Some of Its Disciples* (Boston: Herbert B. Turner, 1903), p. 142.

4. For example, see James Q. Wilson, *The Moral Sense* (New York: Free Press, 1993).

5. David Hume, *Inquiry Concerning the Principles of Morals*, Appendix 1.

6. Finnis, *Natural Law and Natural Rights*, p. 102.

7. Henry Veatch, "Natural Law and the 'Is' - 'Ought' Question," in *Natural Law*, ed. John Finnis (New York: New York University Press, 1991), vol. 1; Ralph McInerny, "The Principles of Natural Law," *Natural Law and Theology*, ed. C. Curran (Mawah, NJ: Paulist

Press, 1991), p. 148.
   8. Anthony Lisska, *Aquinas's Theory of Natural Law* (Oxford: Clarendon Press, 1996), ch. 8.
   9. Aquinas, *Summa theologiae*, I–II.94.2.
   10. Finnis, *Natural Law and Natural Rights*, p. 94.
   11. Lisska, *Aquinas's Theory*, p. 24.

Two

THE ETHICAL BACKGROUND OF
THE RIGHTS OF WOMEN

Sarah Hutton

1. Human Rights and the Modern World

Dictionary definitions are often historically revealing. The term "right" as used in the expression "human rights" is usually understood as some kind of entitlement or "privilege." The term has both legal and ethical connotations. According to the *Oxford English Dictionary*, a right is a "justifiable claim, on legal or moral grounds, to have or obtain something, or to act in a certain way" or "a legal, equitable or moral title or claim to the possession of property or authority."[1] What is right is also just. The legality and moral value of rights is implied in the definition of "right" as "just or equitable treatment; fairness in decision; justice." My paper is concerned with the moral component of this elision of meanings.

2. Human Rights and History

The importance of the eighteenth century in the history of human rights is almost a commonplace. While the terminology of rights has a strong legal component with a history reaching further back than the eighteenth century, the century of the American and French Revolutions, the political vocabulary of the eighteenth century takes over the terminology of rights. Arguments for the basis of rights in this period were naturalistic rather than conventional. Eighteenth-century discussion of such rights invoked not convention, but nature, a fact still registered in the *OED* definition of "right" as both "that which is morally just or due" and that which is "consonant with equity or the law of nature."

Also, as with the rights of man, the eighteenth century is significant in the history of women's rights. In the eighteenth century, women began to use the language of rights in political discussion. The most famous book in English to employ this language is Mary Wollstonecraft's *ur*-text of modern feminism, *A Vindication of the Rights of Woman* (1792). The title aligns Wollstonecraft's discussion of rights firmly with Thomas Paine's *Rights of Men* (1791) as well as her own *A Vindication of the Rights of Man* (1790).

Prior to Wollstonecraft, politically conscious women did not use the term "rights," never mind "women's rights." Yet their writings sound a number of common themes: women's education, marriage, and equality of the sexes. These go hand in hand with women's clear sense of their position as women and their dissatisfaction with their social position. A question, therefore, for the historian is why the shift toward the language of rights. An ancillary question for researchers of women's history is whether the common themes reveal consciousness of a school of thought, either in the sense that the authors were aware of one another, or in the sense that parallels occur in the arguments they use. The last part of this question presents areas of philosophical interest. To explore these questions, I will discuss the writings of three women of the English Enlightenment: Damaris Cudworth Masham (1658–1708), Catherine Macaulay (1731–91), and Mary Wollstonecraft (1759–97). The interconnection of these women thinkers on which I focus is less personal than philosophical. As far as I know, neither Macaulay nor Wollstonecraft knew Lady Masham's writings, although Wollstonecraft was an admirer of Macaulay. I will argue that the ethical positions of Masham, Macaulay, and Wollstonecraft have much in common. Further, the only one of the three to discuss women's rights as such, Mary Wollstonecraft, founded her argument on ethics.

3. Damaris Masham (1658–1708)

The daughter of the Cambridge Platonist Ralph Cudworth and an intimate friend of John Locke, Lady Masham wrote two small books, *A Discourse Concerning the Love of God* (1696) and *Occasional Thoughts in Reference to the Christian Life* (1700), both published anonymously.[2] The Lockean tenets of these publications show that she was one of the first writers to adopt the philosophical principles of Locke's *Essay Concerning Human Understanding*. In *Occasional Thoughts*, Lady Masham makes a case for the education of women, based on woman's role as mother, and consequently the first educator of the family. Masham links women's education closely to morality, but not in the sense that women need instruction in the precepts of moral conduct. Quite the contrary. Learning by rote, she argues, is no education and no foundation for moral conduct. True morality requires rational understanding of right and wrong. Women need to be educated so they can understand the principles of virtuous conduct by which they ought to live and instill the principles of virtue in their children. Women are rational beings who need to improve their reason both to conduct themselves as rational creatures and to educate their children. Virtue, Lady Masham argues, is not identical with innocence, nor does it consist in performance of a few laudable actions, "a partial Practice of Actions praiseworthy,"[3] but is a predisposition to obey the law of God. Virtue is not reducible to a number of precepts and it presupposes freedom to act. "Its extent is equal to our liberty of Action; and its Principle the most Active one of the Mind."[4] To act morally, then, entails knowing how we should behave. Virtue requires "Antecedent Knowledge in those design'd to be instructed."[5] For Lady Masham, the truly moral person is a virtuous, rational theist, whose guiding principle is the law of being, namely, "adherence to the Law of Right Reason, not arbitrary but founded in Relations, and Connexions, which are as immutable as that determinate constitution of Things, which makes everything what it is."[6]

Lady Masham's ethical position is founded on a liberal theological position that entails an optimistic view of the deity and stresses the freedom of the human will. As an anti-voluntarist, she places emphasis on God's wisdom and goodness, rather than his power and will. God is

> the Creator of All Things, who is an invisible Being only knowable to us in, and by, the exemplifications of his Attributes: The infinite Perfection, and the inseparable Harmony of which (discernible in the Frame and Government of the Universe) plainly tells us That the Divine Will [is] ... one steady, uniform, unchangeable result of infinite Wisdom and Benevolence, extending to, and included in All his Works.[7]

God's wisdom and goodness ensure his commands are just and the order of nature is rational. The law of nature is the law of reason; the "Law of Reason, or Nature" (as she puts it) is accessible to reason ("discoverable by our natural faculties"), and consists in "those dictates which are the result of the determinate and unchangeable constitution of things." To disobey God is therefore to act irrationally.

> Sin, or disobedience to our Maker, is manifestly the greatest Nonsense, Folly and contradiction conceivable, with regard to the natural immutable Perfection of the Divine Nature; and to the natural constitution of things, independently upon any positive command of God to us, or his irresistible power over us.[8]

Lady Masham's anti-voluntarism and her founding of her ethics in the goodness and wisdom of God sets her closer to the moral and theological position of her father, Ralph Cudworth, than to that of Locke. Although understated in her two short treatises, the Cudworthian concept of ethics as "eternal and immutable morality" is implicit in her ethical thinking.

4. Catherine Macaulay (1731–91)

Catherine Macaulay is known as an historian, because of her *History of England from the Accession of James I to the Present* (1763–91), a book which earned her fame both in England and France. She was also the author of a number of political polemics. She earned a reputation as a feminist through *Letters on Education* (1790). In this, she argues for equality of the sexes and for equality in the education of boys and girls. The second half of the book extends to philosophical and theological topics, summarizing much of an earlier book, *A Treatise on the Immutability of Moral Truth* (1783). In both works, Macaulay demonstrates she was widely read in philosophy and conversant with contemporary political, theological, and moral debates. Her career is, by itself, a feminist testament *avant la lettre*. As her biographer, Bridget Hill, put it, "As an historian, apologetic polemicist, a 'learned lady' with scholarly pretensions, an independent and fearless critic of all she thought wrong, Catherine Macaulay broke every rule in the eighteenth-century book on how a woman should conduct herself and the role she should occupy."[9] Macaulay's profile is one which combines political radicalism (republicanism), a commitment to female equality with men, and a strong interest in the issue of female education with a clear theological and ethical position, opposed to voluntarism and moral relativism. In her *Letters*, as in her *Treatise*, she argues for the existence of moral absolutes as "a necessary and essential difference of things, a fitness and immutability of right and wrong, necessarily independent of the will of every being created or uncreated."[10] She insists we cannot construct such a system of morals except on a Christian foundation. Instead we must build

> on those principles which are consonant to the enlightened reason of man, and which form the principles of the Christian religion, viz. an abstract fitness of things, and unlimited power, wisdom and goodness of God, and a future state of rewards and punishments.[11]

Far more explicitly than Lady Masham, Macaulay links just political systems and female equality to an ethics rooted in the divine law of nature. A system of ethics founded not in reason but in sense, Macaulay argues, amounts to nothing more than "a moral taste ... intimately connected with natural disposition," and subject to the arbitrary impulses of "the passions, and affections ... from a variety of impressions to which the creature man is exposed."[12] Moral relativism will result, "for what one of the species asserts to be a moral action, will be disputed by another ... [and] every man will think he has a right to determine for himself on points of interest or happiness."[13] The political implications of this are in effect Hobbist: the seizure of power by a few, who will dictate the laws of right and wrong. In her critique of Henry Saint John, Viscount Bolingbroke, she makes a link between feminism, religion, and ethics, founded in a right understanding of natural law. Here she turns Bolingbroke's vaunted empiricism back on him to expose the anti-feminism inherent in his appeal to the law of nature. Bolingbroke's example of a political system founded in nature is the Chinese system of government. Macaulay points out that the society he so much admires is one where the lot of women is "as grievous a servitude as is in the power of imagination to form."[14] Shortly afterwards, in reference to Jewish laws of inheritance, Macaulay attacks Bolingbroke for arguing the advantage of abrogating religious laws to override religious injunctions forbidding intermarriage, in order to conserve property with a particular family group. Macaulay argues that this expedient disadvantages the women concerned.

His lordship, not content with sacrificing the liberty of this more helpless part of the species [i.e., women] to the capricious lusts of the lords and masters of the creation, seems to admire that part of the Jewish law which deprives women of property for the sake of preserving the opulence of families in the male species ... [approving the amendment which requires] female children ... to take husbands of their own race. Now this amendment, which denied to women the right of choice in their domestic tyranny, his lordship observes that if in many cases it be agreeable to the law of nature to extend the bonds of society by a prohibition of marriages between persons too near a-kin, it is, in many cases, at least, as agreeable to their law to preserve the possessions and wealth in the families to which they belong, and not to suffer them to be carried away by any female caprice.[15]

Bolingbroke's failure, Macaulay notes, is a failure to understand the law of nature in anything but human terms. And that is a failure of his religious understanding.

It is thus that Lord Bolingbroke reads the law of nature, and on this reading forms his religion and his ethics. Nor is it any wonder that justice, in its more abstract or general sense, should be little considered, or little understood, by those who can believe that it is agreeable to the wisdom and goodness of an all-perfect Being to form two species of creatures of equal intelligence and similar feelings, and consequently capable of an equal degree of suffering under injuries, and should consign one of these species [i.e., women] as a kind of property to a different species of their fellow creatures [i.e., men], not endowed with any qualities of mind sufficient to prevent the enormous abuse of such a power.[16]

This passage is important for understanding the link between arguments for women's rights and a theologically sound understanding of the law of nature. A key phrase here is the reference to God as "the wisdom and goodness of an all-perfect Being." Macaulay found a link between ethics and theology, and was clearly an anti-voluntarist in theology.

5. Mary Wollstonecraft (1759–97)

Although she spoke up for female liberty and sexual equality, Mary Wollstonecraft's book on the rights of women is, in some respects, baffling to modern feminists. It has been called a book on manners rather than a book on rights.[17] In it, Wollstonecraft champions reason and apparently denigrates female sexuality.[18] In an otherwise illuminating introduction, her most recent editor, Sylvana Tomaselli, interprets Wollstonecraft's stress on reason as evidence that she wanted "the transformation of women into their opposite."[19] Wollstonecraft's piety is another aspect of her feminism that today's readers find hard to deal with.[20] In sum, much of *A Vindication of the Rights of Woman* offends the character of modern feminism, which is as politically activist as it is articulate, often takes a stridently anti-rational stance, and is largely secular in its values. Especially troubling to her modern readers is that Wollstonecraft is highly critical of contemporary women. Much of *A Vindication of the Rights of Woman* is given over to a damning critique of the social role and the behavior either expected of them or actually performed by them. That Wollstonecraft's religious position and her rationality are integral to her feminist position, can, I think be seen when we compare her to Masham and Macaulay. Wollstonecraft's *Vindication of the Rights of Woman* contains the same combination of topics noted in Masham and Macaulay, arguments for women's education accompanied by an emphasis on virtue and a discussion of morality. Wollstonecraft's theological views feed directly into her arguments for women's rights.[21]

What Wollstonecraft criticizes in *A Vindication of the Rights of Woman* is not so much women, but their conduct. In her analysis, this conduct is inevitable in a society where women are subordinate to men, and have power neither to improve their minds nor control their own lives. Such a society is one where men too are subordinated one to another by the political and social system. Thus, the subordination of women is the product of a tyrannical political system affecting both men and women. It follows, therefore, that female liberty and equality belong to political radicalism.

In many ways, Wollstonecraft's conception of *rights* belongs alongside other Enlightenment champions of the same. I have already said that the titles *A Vindication of the Rights of Woman* and *A Vindication of the Rights of Men* echo Thomas Paine. Wollstonecraft uses Enlightenment terminology, echoing Locke. She writes, for example, that the "rights of men" entail "such a degree of liberty, civil and religious, as is compatible with the liberty of every other individual with whom he is united in a social compact, and the continued existence of that compact."[22] Liberty is to be regulated only by controls that preserve it by ensuring the liberty of one individual does not encroach on the liberty of another. She regards hierarchical and autocratic systems of government as the enemies of liberty. In this respect, her understanding of rights must be seen as politically radical. Even so, what Wollstonecraft provides is not list of specific rights, but a general account of rights as human liberties. Even when she writes about the rights of woman, she does not list them as precepts. However, she regards as desiderata things like equal freedom to men, education, economic independence, and control of childbirth, all topics which are now enshrined as women's rights.

The key word of Wollstonecraft's political writing is not "right" but "virtue," and "virtue" is firmly linked to reason. Although her concept of virtue is linked to her conception of God, she does not understand "virtue" as a particular religious principle or as actions sanctioned by religious belief. Instead, she has in mind a standard of conduct that is necessary for right living and includes good citizenship and justice. Virtue, she tells us at the beginning of *Rights of Woman,* "exalts one being above another," in the same way reason gives human beings "pre-eminence over the brute creation."[23]

According to Wollstonecraft, human happiness and the improvement of the human condition depend on the exercise of reason and virtue, for which knowledge is required and on which human society depends. As she states in the opening chapter,

> the perfection of our nature and capability of happiness, must be estimated by the degree of reason, virtue and knowledge, that distinguish the individual, and direct the laws which bind society: and that from the exercise of reason, knowledge and virtue naturally flow, is equally undeniable, if mankind be viewed collectively.[24]

We should note that Wollstonecraft's use of "birthright" is synonymous with "right." In the passage from *Rights of Men,* from which I quoted earlier, "birthright" refers to "disputed right" of "liberty civil and religious." The birthright she has in mind is something we are born with, not something we are born to. It is a right not conferred by human society, as hereditary titles are, but exists in our very nature, every bit as much as the power of reason that distinguishes human beings from brutes. Wollstonecraft denies that the liberty of man has ever been established by human law. It is, she writes, "a fair idea that has never yet received a form in the various governments that have been established on our beauteous globe."[25] The radical political implication of this statement is that existing forms of government are wrong. Wollstonecraft touches on the tyrannical consequences of the obverse view at this point. Liberty, she argues, is not bestowed by human convention, but has an ontological foundation, antecedent to the laws of man and the institutions of human society. Thus far, this is a standard natural law position. As Richard Cumberland wrote:

> By Laws of Nature, we understand some Propositions of unchangeable Truth and Certainty, which are to direct and govern the voluntary Motions of rational free Agents in the Election of Good, and in the avoiding of Evil: Which Laws lay Obligations upon all outward Acts of Behaviour, even in a Study of Nature, prior and antecedent to all Laws of human Imposition whatsoever: And are clearly distinct from every Consideration of all such Compacts and Agreements as constitute civil Government.[26]

But Wollstonecraft appeals further than the law of nature, to the founder of that law, God. A few pages later, she re-iterates that the foundation of rights in the divine order of nature takes us beyond human institutions to an original foundation of which there can be no greater authority:

It is necessary emphatically to repeat, that there are rights which men inherit at their birth, as rational creatures, who were raised above the brute creation by their improvable faculties; and that, in receiving these, not from their forefathers but, from God, prescription can never undermine natural rights.[27]

Wollstonecraft's appeal is not simply to a law of nature antecedent to human institution, but to a moral epistemology of divine origin. These divine attributes are the creators and guarantors of human reason and human liberty. The rights of men are, she claims, "the sacred rights of men." Liberty, she asserts,

> results from the eternal foundation of right – from immutable truth – who will presume to deny, that pretends to rationality – if reason has led them to build their morality and religion on an everlasting foundation – the attributes of God.[28]

It is precisely this investiture of rights with apparently sacral connotations that Wollstonecraft's secular successors have no use for. But to dismiss it as merely the idiom of a non-secular age is to miss the point. Nor can it be explained as merely strategy to disarm the pious pretensions of her adversaries. Instead, what Wollstonecraft is signaling here is the theological and ethical grounding of her concept of rights.

6. God and Mary Wollstonecraft

In *A Vindication of the Rights of Woman,* Wollstonecraft refers to God as "the fountain of wisdom, goodness and power." Although she correctly stressed the unity of God's attributes, this sequence indicates her anti-voluntarist stance, placing divine wisdom and goodness before divine power among the divine attributes. Echoing her claim in *A Vindication of the Rights of Man* (see note 29) that "the eternal foundation of right" is "immutable truth" and morality derives from "the attributes of God," she argues that the foundation of morality derives from the divine attributes, namely His justice, wisdom, and omnipotence:

> The only foundation for morality appears to be the character of the supreme Being; the harmony of which arises from a balance of attributes; – and, so to speak with reverence, one attribute seems to imply the *necessity* of another. He must be just, because he is wise, he must be good, because he is omnipotent.[29]

Wollstonecraft's conception of the human as rational enables her to found her argument for the equality of the sexes not on parity with males, but in the general category of the human, which embraces both male and female. Hers is an argument not for liberty, equality, and fraternity, but for liberty, equality, and humanity. Human nature is part of nature itself. So too are the moral principles that govern the conduct of both men and women. With a basis in divinity, the laws of human conduct are not merely antecedent to positive law of human institution – not merely natural – but part of the divine order, part of being and truth. They are therefore invested with the unassailable authority of the divine, than which there could be no greater obligation to obey. Since God is God of wisdom, not merely of power, His laws may be understood by reason. And indeed reason, Wollstonecraft insists in Platonic vein, is "an emanation of divinity, the tie that connects the creature with the Creator."[30] The obverse of Wollstonecraft's intellectualist conception of God is the voluntarist God of power, incompatible with human reason and morality. To emphasize God's omnipotence is to distort the character of God and produce a tyrant model of the deity:

He bends to power; he adores a dark cloud, which may open a bright prospect to him, or burst in angry lawless fury, on his devoted head – he knows not why. And, supposing that the Deity acts from the vague impulse of an undirected will, man must also follow his own, or act according to rule, deduced from principles which he disclaims as irreverent.[31]

Politics and theology go together. The voluntarist understanding of God, according to which "His omnipotence is made to swallow up or preside over his other attributes," is the inevitable result of the mental conditioning wrought by the experience of a despotic political regimen, where man is "accustomed to bow down to power in his savage state."[32] The obverse of this position is that the "just conception of the character of God" of liberal theology goes together with libertarian politics.

7. Platonism and the Rights of Women

Wollstonecraft's adoption of the vocabulary of rights to argue for political, social, and pedagogical equality of women with men can, and to some degree must, be explained in terms of her adoption of the political vocabulary of a revolutionary age. After all, both her *Vindications* were deeply connected to contemporary debates on the French Revolution. *A Vindication of the Rights of Men* written in defense of her friend, the radical preacher Richard Price, against the attack on his *Discourse on the Love of Our Country* (1789), was first delivered as a sermon to the London Revolution Society. The attack was made by Edmund Burke in his *Reflections on the Revolution in France* (1790), a book which prompted Paine to write *The Rights of Man*. It also prompted Catherine Macaulay's *Observations on the Reflections of the Right Honourable Edmund Burke* (1790). We should not forget that Macaulay took Burke to task in 1770 with her *Observations on a Pamphlet entitled Thoughts on the Cause of the Present Discontents*. Price's view in his *Discourse on the Love of Our Country* echoes this pamphlet. Wollstonecraft's two *Vindications* belong historically with the opposition to Burke and supporters of the revolution in France. The link between Wollstonecraft and Macaulay and Price is acknowledged by Wollstonecraft scholars.[33] But their importance for her intellectual formation has not been fully drawn out. It is often pointed out that the figures of Locke and, more ambiguously, Rousseau stand behind Wollstonecraft's *Rights of Women*. Locke was an influential figure for both Lady Masham and Catherine Macaulay. However, we cannot account for the ethical position of Masham, Macaulay, and Wollstonecraft through Locke. Their moral realism and anti-voluntarism sets them apart from him. These features of their thinking ally them with what has been called the ethical rationalists, but might also be termed an English Platonic tradition. A key figure in eighteenth-century ethics was the aforementioned Richard Price.

8. Richard Price (1723–91)

Political historians know Price as I have already introduced him: a dissenting minister of radical views who defended both the American and French revolutions and was the principle instigator of Burke's *Reflections*. Philosophers tend to treat that aspect of Price's career as incidental to his authorship of an original statement of rationalist ethics, *A Review of the Principal Questions in Morals*, first published in London in 1758. The heir of Cudworth, Locke, and Clarke in epistemology, Price was, according to D.D. Raphael, innovatory. Raphael argues that Price's approach, "typically 'deontological' or 'Kantian' approach, the insistence that duty often conflicts with private interest and sometimes with public; the distinction between 'absolute' and 'practical' virtue, the realization that what is imputable to man is his obligation to do what he thinks right; and the perception that obligations may conflict," distinguishes Price from his predecessors.[34] For present purposes, I simply note that Price was an anti-voluntarist in theology, who held that moral principles were absolutes belonging to the nature of things.

> That morality is *eternal and immutable*. Right and wrong ... denote what actions *are*. Now, whatever a thing *is*, that it is, not by will, or decree, or power, but by *nature and necessity*.[35]

Virtue is therefore inscribed in being itself, independent of and prior to the dictates of mere human order. Virtue entails the idea of duty: "Virtue, *as such*, has a real obligatory power antecedently to all positive laws, and independently of all will; for obligation, we see, is involved in the very nature of it."[36] The foundations of virtue are the moral attributes of the deity, goodness, justice, and truth, subsumed within "absolute and eternal rectitude."[37] For Price, God is "*the necessary exemplar and original of all* perfection,"[38] the original of virtue. "The principal design" of his book is to prove that

Virtue is of intrinsic value and good desert, and of indispensable obligation; not the *creature of will*, but *necessary* and *immutable*; not *local* or *temporary*, but of equal *extent* and *antiquity* with the DIVINE MIND; not a *mode of* SENSATION, but everlasting TRUTH; not *dependent on* power, but the *guide of all power*.[39]

9. Samuel Clarke and Ralph Cudworth

Price was much admired by Wollstonecraft. His philosophy was the culmination of a strand of political and ethical thought that may be traced back to Samuel Clarke (1675–1729),[40] whose influential Boyle lectures propound an anti-voluntarist view of God as "a being of infinite goodness, justice and truth."[41] Moral obligation, Clarke argues, is antecedent to the will and command of God who always acts "according to the strictest rules of infinite goodness, justice, and truth."[42]

A neglected figure in the history of philosophy who lies behind both Price and Clarke is the Cambridge Platonist Ralph Cudworth (1617–88). The motif of eternal and immutable morality discernible in the three women discussed above and in Price and Clarke is the ethical trademark of Cudworth. In his *Treatise Concerning Eternal and Immutable Morality*, Cudworth argues that "Wisdom, knowledge and understanding ... are eternal and self-subsistent things," so much so that they are not only the same in all times and places, but are capable of existence even in the absence of thinking minds and of the universe:

> These rationes and verities had a real and actual entity before [Euclid, Pythagoras, Archimedes, etc.], and would continue still, though all the geometricians in the world were quite extinct, and no man knew them or thought of them. Nay, though all the material world were quite swept away, and also all particular created minds annihilated together with it, yet there is no doubt but the intelligible natures or essences of all geometrical figures, and the necessary verities belonging to them, would notwithstanding remain safe and sound. Wherefore these things had a being also before the material world and all particular intellects were created.[43]

A Treatise Concerning Eternal and Immutable Morality was undoubtedly more influential after his death than in his lifetime, since it was not published until 1730. It gives Cudworth a posthumous "life" as an eighteenth-century philosopher. The philosopher who shows its influence more than any other is Richard Price. Price's *Review of Morals* is a major conduit of Cudworth's philosophy. As custodian of his papers, Lady Masham had access to his unpublished writings, including the manuscript of this book. Scholars find no direct evidence of Macaulay or Wollstonecraft having any direct knowledge of Cudworth. However, the title of Macaulay's most philosophical book, *A Treatise on the Immutability of Moral*

Truth, echoes the title of Cudworth's text. Evidence reveals also that Price helped shape Wollstonecraft's thinking, especially the more metaphysical dimensions of it. Macaulay too would have been aware of Price's writings.

The metaphysical theological Platonism of mid-seventeenth-century Cambridge has little in common with the engaged political arguments of the 1790s. The three women I have discussed drew on a number of philosophical strands. Among these, the rationalist ethics common to all three is underpinned by a theological liberalism that is traceable to the theological Platonism of the seventeenth century. The key exemplar here is the Cambridge Platonist Cudworth, who was not just a distant ancestor of eighteenth-century ethical theory, but, through the posthumous publication of his *Treatise,* a presence in eighteenth-century debates.

In light of this connection, note that *A Vindication of the Rights of Woman* contains more than a tinge of Platonism, and Catherine Macaulay acknowledges a Platonic foundation to her moral realism. "Immutable right and wrong" she writes, are

> explained by the philosophy Platonism under the form of everlasting intellectual ideas, or moral entities, coeval with eternity, and residing in the divine mind: from whence, by irradiating rays ... they enlighten the understanding of all those intellectual beings, who, disregarding the objects of sense, give themselves up to the contemplation of the Deity.[44]

Damaris Masham, Catherine Macaulay, and Mary Wollstonecraft all contributed to the development of the concept of women's rights, and they did so in terms of applied ethics. The ethics which they formulated drew directly or indirectly on the heritage of English liberal theology that may be traced back to Platonizing divines of the previous century. They were not card-carrying Platonists, they rarely cited Plato, but they drew on a version of the theological, rational Platonism of the early Latitudinarians, otherwise known as the Cambridge Platonists.

Notes

1. Cf. *The Cambridge Dictionary of Philosophy* (Cambridge: Cambridge University Press, 1995), pp. 695–696.

2. On Lady Masham, see Sarah Hutton, "Between Platonism and Enlightenment: Damaris Cudworth, Lady Masham," *British Journal for the History of Philosophy,* 1 (1993), pp. 29–54. Also, Patricia Springborg, "Astell, Masham, and Locke: Religion and Politics," ed. Hilda Smith, *Women Writers and the Early Modern British Political Tradition* (Cambridge: Cambridge University Press, 1998).

3. Lady Masham, *Occasional Thoughts in Reference to the Christian Life* (London: A. & J. Churchil, 1700), p. 11.

4. Ibid.

5. Ibid., p. 16.

6. Ibid., p. 106.

7. Ibid.

8. Ibid., p. 69.

9. Bridget Hill, *The Republican Virago: The Life and Times of Catharine Macaulay, Historian* (Oxford: Clarendon Press, 1992), p. 130; on Macaulay, see also, Wendy Gunther-Canada, "The Politics of Sense and Sensibility, Women's Rights, and Patriarchal Power," ed. Smith, *Women Writers*, pp. 128–147.

10. Catherine Macaulay, *A Treatise on the Immutability of Moral Truth* (London, 1783), p. 31.

11. Ibid., p. 325.

12. Ibid., p. 135.

13. Ibid., p. 144.

14. Ibid., p. 155.

15. Ibid., p. 158

16. Ibid., p. 156

17. Emma Rees-Mogg and Janet Todd, eds., "Introduction," *Mary Wollstonecraft, Political Writings* (London: Pickering, 1993).

18. Mary Poovey, *The Proper Lady and the Woman Writer: Ideology and Style in the Works of Mary Wollstonecraft, Mary Shelley, and Jane Austen* (Chicago: University of Chicago Press, 1984), pp. 79–81; Cora Kaplan, "Wild Nights," *Sea Changes: Culture and Feminism* (London: Verso, 1986), pp. 31–56.

19. Mary Wollstonecraft, *A Vindication of the Rights of Men; with, A Vindication of the Rights of Woman, and Hints*, ed. Sylvana Tomaselli (Cambridge: Cambridge University Press, 1997), p. xxxvi.

20. Anne Snitow, "A Gender Diary," ed. M. Hirsch and E. Fox Keller, *Conflicts in Feminism* (London: Routledge, 1990), p. 29.

21. See Trudy Govier, "Wollstonecraft: The Oak that Braved the Storm," *Socrates' Children* (Peterborough, Ont.: Broadview Press, 1977).

22. Wollstonecraft, *A Vindication of the Rights of Men; with, A Vindication of the Rights of Woman*, ed. Tomaselli, p. 7.

23. Ibid., p. 79.

24. Ibid.

25. Ibid., p. 7.

26. Cf. Richard Cumberland, *Treatise of the Laws of Nature*, tr. John Maxwell (London: R. Phillips, 1727), pp. 2–3, originally published as *De legibus naturae*, 1672.

27. Wollstonecraft, *A Vindication of the Rights of Men; with, A Vindication of the Rights of Woman*, ed. Tomaselli, p. 13.

28. Ibid., p. 7.

29. Ibid., p. 118.

30. Ibid., p. 127.

31. Ibid., p. 118.

32. Ibid.

33. See, for example, Kate Lindemann, "Mary Wollstonecraft," *A History of Women Philosophers*, ed. M.S. Waithe (Dordrecht: Kluwer, 1991), vol. 3, pp. 153–170, and Govier, *Socrates' Children*.

34. Richard Price, *A Review of the Principal Questions in Morals*, ed. D.D. Raphael (Oxford: Clarendon Press, 1974), based on the 1787 edition.

35. J.B. Schneewind, ed., "A Review," *Moral Philosophy from Montaigne to Kant* (Cambridge: Cambridge University Press, 1990), vol. 2, p. 592.

36. Ibid., p. 598.

37. Ibid., pp. 248–250.

38. Ibid., p. 243.

39. Price, *A Review,* p. 266.

40. See Peter N. Miller, *Defining the Common Good: Empire, Religion, and Philosophy in Eighteenth-Century Britain* (Cambridge: Cambridge University Press, 1994).

41. Samuel Clarke, *A Demonstration of the Being and Attributes of God ... wherein the Notion of Liberty is Stated, and the Possibility and Certainty of it Proved, in Opposition to Necessity and Fate* (London, 1705), ed. E. Vitali as *A Demonstration of the Being and Attributes of God* (Cambridge: Cambridge University Press, 1998), p. 83. This edition also prints the second sermon by Clarke, *A Discourse Concerning the Unchangeable Obligations of Natural and Revealed Religion and the Truth and Certainty of the Christian Revelation* (London, 1706).

42. Clarke, *A Demonstration of the Being and Attributes of God,* p. 84.

43. Ralph Cudworth, *A Treatise Concerning Eternal and Immutable Morality,* ed. Sarah Hutton (Cambridge: Cambridge University Press, 1996), p. 127.

44. Catherine Macaulay, *A Treatise on the Immutability of Moral Truth,* p. 31.

Three

ECONOMIC RIGHTS AND PHILOSOPHICAL ANTHROPOLOGY

Leslie Armour

1. Two Sets of Rights; Two Views of the Human Being

When the Universal Declaration of Human Rights was put forth a little over fifty years ago, there was a rough division of the world in two – and a rough division of the proclaimed rights into two groups. Traditional personal rights and liberties fell into one group and what came to be known as economic rights fell into the other. But in between were what might be called "social rights," and blurring these perhaps permitted both sides to feel that they had done rough justice to the ideas of the other.

Though both groups were able to agree on the Declaration, despite its mixture of personal, social, and economic rights, each side tacitly agreed to bury a number of clauses. In the West, personal and social rights associated with political activity were deeply entrenched, and the signatories had every intention of maintaining them. The relations between government and the press might differ a good deal as one traveled from Paris to London and on to New York, but (though Jean-Paul Sartre is supposed to have said, wryly, that he was not a Maoist because he was too old to run from the police) freedom of speech was broadly recognized. In the American south it was still difficult for a black man or woman to vote and, in Québec, Maurice Duplessis was making life hard for Jehovah's Witnesses, but political and religious freedoms were well established over large areas. Economic rights, the right to a job and the right to health care and adequate unemployment insurance, varied widely. Nearly a half-century later, William Clinton could win an election by promising universal health insurance, but he could not produce it.

In 1948, in what was oddly called the "Eastern Bloc," unemployment was a rarity; health care was universal, even if its quality was sometimes questionable; and higher education was generally available without fees. But the right to form a political party or advocate for an alternative economic system was non existent, and religious freedom was more difficult to obtain in Moscow than in Montréal. Some economic rights held only sporadically. Universities were free, but applicants whom the authorities thought politically unreliable were often denied entrance.

Differences between East and West reflected differences in widely held philosophical anthropologies. They also represented, on both sides, a license to inflict or permit a good deal of misery, and many millions of lives were devoted to hopeless drudgery within both. The thesis that we can have political freedom without the ability to act in the physical world – the notion that negative political freedom, freedom that is simply the absence of interference by others, is possible without its positive counterpart – was roundly attacked in the last quarter of the nineteenth century by Thomas Hill Green[1] and a host of those who followed him. In the last half of the twentieth century, however, a philosopher as reasonable as Isaiah Berlin could view Green's doctrine as foreshadowing tyranny – as a step on the road to a world in which society forces one's choice of incommensurable goods.[2] The belief that negative freedom, effectively guaranteed, would bring about positive freedom was often held – more often by the rich and powerful than by the poor and helpless. The corresponding belief, vaguely enunciated by Marx, that economic control of institutions by the people brings about negative freedom was also widely held, though probably not by people in the gulags.

2. A Free Mind in a Bound Body?

The thesis that negative freedom can exist without positive freedom reflects a mind-matter dualism that became deeply entrenched during the major economic and political reorientation which characterized the period from the end of the thirteenth century to the development of the great empires of the nineteenth century. It was supported in its middle years by arguments poorly drawn from the philosophies of Descartes and Locke.

This dualism, which (although it had ancient origins) took shape in the seventeenth and eighteenth centuries, held that the human mind somehow exists in isolation or independently from the human body in a way that enables our minds to be free even though our bodies are enslaved. Bodies were widely supposed to be controlled mechanically in two different senses, while the mind was not. Bodies obeyed the laws of physics and chemistry, but were controlled by inheritance. Curiously, people thought therefore that black persons could not behave like white persons, or women like men. But in some sense it was thought that a black man or a white woman could be "free" in the sense of not being a slave. The obfuscation caused by such combinations of doctrines led to debates about whether persons who were neither white nor male could really do philosophy or reach the dazzling intellectual heights that white males were imagined to achieve with ease. Examples were, and sometimes still are, debated hotly.

The idea of negative freedom, however, was also a doctrine that associated human existence with freedom from the community. In this way social rights, which are associated with a place in a community that functions well enough to permit the full development of our humanity, were often little explored. When people spoke about rights the most central idea was that thought is independent and that what chiefly needs to be protected is freedom of thought and the associated freedoms of expression. Even now, attacks on free speech and freedom of the press are the easiest assaults on human rights to defend against in England and America.

On this theory, it was supposed that, given freedom of thought and expression, men and women would generate and circulate whatever ideas are necessary to change their social and economic circumstances. What chiefly tells against all such theories – apart from the metaphysical difficulties, arising when you try to establish intelligible relations between distinct entities – are the facts of history and culture. The ideas, which develop in a place at a given time invariably, have deeply rooted histories. The individualism which made Western capitalism possible developed slowly out of a long critique of the relations between people and God and between people and the state. The great medieval syntheses of the thirteenth century, especially those of St. Thomas Aquinas and Duns Scotus, implied a strong notion of community. Some of the systems that were supposed to usher in the Reformation for instance, both Wyclif's and that of his great opponent Reginald Peacock, also supported strong notions of community.[3] But the breakdown of religious hegemony and in the face of the notion that men and women are related to one another through God and have no need of an intervening religious community, these systems failed to keep their hold on the public. The change was not sudden, resulting from some individual's free choice, but slow, resulting from a breakdown of central institutions, the fragmentation of European politics and religion, and a shift away from the association of land and wealth. Religion and powerful landlords alike made it relatively easy to hold communities together.

A different example of how ideas change with consequent shifts in power can be found in the growth of science. Western science emerged out of many factors. Some of these were associated with the critique of existing philosophical and religious ideas, and others developed from the culture of the time. The art of the Florentine Renaissance generated an interest in the physics of optics, and the politics of the Renaissance city stimulated the intellect and provided a measure of breathing space for thought.

The pattern of developing ideas must be considered, but there seem to be constant factors in the appearance of efficacious ideas. Cracks gradually appear in the existing view of things, and political and social circumstances permit a measure of freedom to exploit them. There is surely no real freedom without a culture to support it.

3. Economics and the Embodied Mind

The Marxist counter-position, developed out of Hegelianism in an ongoing critique of what Jacques Maritain dubbed Cartesian "angelism,"[4] was called "materialism." It was not, however, the reductionist materialism of the physicalists, linguistic behaviorists, and socio-biologists of our time. It was the doctrine that social circumstances, especially economic ones, are apt to fix a person's mindset in a number of ways. It arose as a response to a Hegelian position, which was a critique of the individualism of the seventeenth and eighteenth centuries. Hegel was demanding social rights, but he was not unaware that economic rights were necessary to obtain the kind of community that can provide social rights.

Hegel was not alone, and the issue is not so much about the technical details of his philosophy as about the circumstances of his time. The French Revolution changed the world and made many human dreams capable of realization. But it also destroyed a well-entrenched dream. The belief that people, once freed of political tyranny, would emerge as full-fledged, upright, decent-minded liberal democrats, proved false. Given political chaos, people turned out to be willing to lop off one another's heads in the scramble for power, and the chaos of revolution only bred a demand for the greater tyranny of Napoleon and his friends. No violent revolution since has escaped this tendency. Revolutionary disorder breeds demands for order that result in a new tyranny. The earlier American Revolution was an exception, but it was essentially a demand by colonists for rights they believed to be their existing natural heritage, and no generation of Americans has escaped the fear that the ever-growing power of the central administration will end in tyranny.

Hegel and others supposed rightly that one cannot simply extract people from their social and psychological circumstances by bringing society crashing down around them. The difference between Hegel and his Marxist critics was that Hegel tended to see human entrenchment as cultural, as bound by ideas. Some Hegelians thought, and this is a non sequitur, that ideas should therefore be changeable by other ideas. This has never been that easy, and Hegel always vacillated on the edge of a kind of historical determinism. Marx saw the issues only slightly differently, in a way that created a tangled perspective now difficult to sort out. In Marx's view, not ideas, but social circumstances, above all technological circumstances, mire human beings.

Both Hegel and Marx were devotees of Aristotle in one way or another. They attributed to Aristotle the thesis that people are not like bees whose work is predetermined and repetitious. Marx also mentions how consciousness differentiates human beings from sheep.[5] People innovate but, in the process of innovation, create works that shape them. Marx's economic determinism was really a theory about technology and human nature, and it only became "deterministic" because he shared much of the passion of the time for ironclad laws. His thesis was that we have to learn to take charge of these technological processes collectively in order to be free. The theory developed into a monster largely because the notion that a select few "class-conscious" people must effect the necessary change was developed by Lenin into the theory of the Vanguard Party, and circumstances conspired to permit its instantiation.

4. The Puzzle of the French Revolution

These reflections and searches were provoked by what seemed to be the disaster of the French Revolution. Time would show that the French could turn disaster into the society that we know as modern France. Few people now hope for the return of the kings or even for the magnificence of Cardinal Richelieu. French society is imperfect as all human enterprises tend to be, but it has become something that has added stature to the human race.

At the time the French Revolution seemed to be a disaster. This disaster was generally put down to four causes: people behaved badly because they were badly educated; because they were poorly integrated into a social order; because the socio-economic system in which they lived provoked or demanded violence; or because, as Hobbes thought, they were simply nasty and destructive. The last proposed cause is a materialist variant on the ancient doctrine of original sin, but original sin could be added to the mixture in any one of these cases. People desperately needed education because they had lost contact with their natural, but divine, source of wisdom, they were poorly socialized because post-lapsarian man was a creature with a good deal of natural malice, and their social orders were destructive for the same reason.

Let us look at these causes one by one, for they correlate with philosophical anthropologies that illuminate the debates about human rights. Though we may argue about them and though one of them, the educational explanation, is a favorite of people who also favor negative freedom and deny economic rights, they all suggest that any decent society requires more than negative rights.

a. The Right to Know

First, people may behave badly because they lack understanding and need education. It is probably fair to say that in France and the United States this was – and remains – the most popular explanation and from it arises the most popular solution: Education, widely enough distributed, will civilize the masses and perhaps even the upper classes.

In England this has always been taken with a grain of salt. My old tutor, C.E.M. Joad, once remarked dryly, "We taught them to read, and they read the *Daily Mirror*." Now they read *The Sun,* and *The Mirror* is regarded as an intellectual newspaper, chiefly because the young women it portrays usually keep their clothes on, but the point remains. You may notice Joad's "we." Education is conceived of as a set of ideas and mental skills, which pass from one mind to another. It always has a central cluster of received doctrines and a set of recipients. Joad was a life-long socialist, but Oxford gave him the accents of those who own and control things and he became one of the "we" who teach "them." Unlike the theoretical Marxists, he thought of the "working class" as a group of people who need to be taught a different way of life and not as a repository of a kind of natural wisdom which would emerge when the restraints were off. In practice, Lenin's followers also adopted the bourgeois view of education, but they saw it as a device for inculcating their own special brand of Marxist doctrine. They too wanted to change the working class, but they lacked Joad's conviction that the way to do it was by the inculcation of a wide variety of liberating ideas. Education is also odd. Roughly half the professional philosophers in the world live in the United States, but of all the philosophers who have lived and worked there, perhaps only John Dewey is clearly known to have had a major influence on public and private life. To what extent thousands of little-known philosophers have civilized their charges over the past couple of centuries, no one knows.

The educational theory about the failure of what we might call "enlightenment man" – that being who brought about the French Revolution and, more arguably, the American Revolution – goes generally with the thesis that minds are free and independent and can be addressed directly. Education is unlikely to set one free unless it takes place within a culture in which independent thinking is actually possible. Our own educational processes in the industrialized nations of the twenty-first century are largely vocational in orientation. In a sense they always were. Roger Bacon complained not long after the founding of Oxford that the faculty of civil law was overflowing with young men learning how to make money, and that the university had little interest in supporting original research. A couple of hundred years later, Thomas Bradwardine, the founder of mathematical physics, found it convenient to become the Archbishop of Canterbury rather than stay at Oxford, though he quickly died of the plague. Then as now, education was aimed at fulfilling a public need – in those days for officials educated enough to handle the public business and for clergymen to keep the church running. In our day businessmen, doctors, lawyers, computer experts, and, for that matter, practitioners of mortuary science are demanded by society. There is a difference nevertheless. A thirteenth-century clergyman with a university education, by no means the commonest case among the clergy, was expected to have a general grasp of the affairs of the universe, whereas it may now be enough for a university graduate to have a full grasp of the principles of reinforced concrete and a good understanding of rusting metals or the marketing of coffins. Roger Bacon's university had not yet set itself the task of providing the training which entrepreneurs might be expected to provide for themselves.

The truth, St. Paul averred, shall make you free. But not just any truth will make you free, and "the" truth is hard to come by.

b. The Right to a Dignified Place in the System

This brings us to the second explanation for human bad behavior: People behave badly because they are poorly integrated into the social order. Thinkers like Hegel argued that individuality is not some simple property with which everyone is born into the world – a property conferring rights and duties quite independently of any circumstance. Instead, people become individuals in a social context, and their ability to make decisions, even their ability of reason, is based on those circumstances. The educational liberators generally continue to ignore, forget, or even deny this premise. In most Western democracies, entry into university is not overly difficult to achieve, though recent changes in fee structures in many countries and the new imposition of tuition fees in British universities suddenly makes it more difficult. Nevertheless, even in the easiest times and places, disproportionate numbers of the middle-class young end up in universities and, as one proceeds towards what are regarded as the "best" universities, the disproportion grows. The reason is probably not that intelligence is inheritable, but simply that social expectations and conditioning determine to a large extent what we do. The expectations of others are likely to influence our successes. Institutions in fact are biased consciously or unconsciously. A prince of the line is less likely to be failed out of the Royal Naval College, Dartmouth, than is a working-class youth whose presence there may be slightly surprising. But ordinarily, people from the upper and middle social classes conform more easily to the expectations of most institutions of higher education than do people from the working classes.

If one takes a kind of Hegelian view of things, it seems obvious that all social orders are filled with tensions that produce conflicts. Civilization demands a measure of division of labor – Plato's original problem. We might all live well enough like the Semai in Malaysia, with little social structure and with the tasks of hunting and gathering spread as evenly as possible among the whole population. The Semai have no need for government and seem to have few rules.[6] However, much that we call human potential would be forever hidden – art, music, literature, philosophy, and science included. Even among the Semai only women give birth to children, though child rearing is widely shared. There are no doubt many things the very young and the very old cannot do, and which require a division of labor.

I think that few people imagine the hunting-gathering society as an ideal. Apart from some very special societies like the Semai and the !Kung San of the Kalahari, such societies have generally died out. And even the !Kung San live under a threat of elimination. Although such societies have little ability to resist aggression from their technologically oriented neighbors, individual human beings are not easily confined to such a framework.

As a consequence of development, people are divided into classes, occupations, and places of residence. Inevitably not all social positions are equally desirable. John Rawls advises us to choose the society we should prefer if we were the worst-off individuals in it, and he defines being best off in terms of fulfilling our self-interest.[7] So we should choose the society in which the worst-off person would be better off than in any other community. But this somehow misses the point. The poorest people may be a little better off in societies which permit some racial and gender injustices because the mechanisms for remedying such injustice are costly, and affirmative action tends to result in some jobs filled by marginally less productive people than those who would otherwise hold them. Rawls would have us weigh human dignity, but it is hard to say whether the indignities of great poverty are more or less bearable than the indignities of occasional racial slurs. The complications of such schemes are an endless maze. Many American cities are divided into a patchwork of small self-governing communities. Suppose that in your community the best candidate for the job of city manager is black, and so naturally you choose him. But a Rawlsian points out that in the surrounding communities many officials are racially prejudiced, so your manager will likely be forced to accept worse deals than a white manager, and this will put a strain on the poorest people in your community.

This illustrates the "missed point." What we actually want is a community without the stresses and strains that such examples presuppose. Not that we want a certain outcome for individuals, but we want a community where individuals can develop and make reasonable choices. The only society that might achieve these aims is a society in which, if not all social positions are equally desirable, then undesirable activities are shared. Luckily, some activities are highly regarded by some people and shunned by others. I would not want to be a golf pro, and few golf pros would want to be philosophers. Some people delight in fixing large truck engines and others in brain surgery. But there are activities, like underground coal mining and public toilet cleaning, which few people enjoy.

We may imagine different ways of removing the tensions that the division of labor produces. One is to eliminate undesirable work. Much of this has been done and more can be done. We can also design a society where anyone can, in principle, move from one position to another position for which he or she is competent by some known and reasonably secure means. Where there are fewer positions than competent people desire, we can strive to ensure that they are filled by the most competent people. I suppose the most important single "social right" is the right to live in a society where social mobility is effectively possible.

On this view, the cause of the failure of the enlightenment dream of a society where civility is uniformly natural is bad social design. The problems are those of political sociology, and the solutions are found in legislation governing equal opportunity, safety, and design of the working environment, and can be tackled by legislation. The rights involved are what I have called "social rights."

If we leave aside the problem of historical determination, we can regard the provision of social rights as a kind of Hegelian solution. People live and behave in the context of complex social structures. These structures determine the options open to them. When the choices are too constricted and the life too miserable, people behave badly.

c. The Right to a Decent Living

The conviction that legislated solutions rarely work and an underlying system provokes bad behavior provides a justification for the kinds of theories Marx and Engels held. The difference between Hegelian "sociological" explanations and the Marxist account of the matter is that, according to Marx, social structure is determined by how production is ordered. In feudal times wealth depended mainly on land. Land was productive only when it could be farmed in an orderly and uninterrupted way, and it secured its value from the feudal lords who protected it in return for a share of the crops. Let us imagine a simple-minded exercise. In the ancient kingdom of Oz, a large, fertile, and level plain was presided over by Lord Bountiful who, with his knights and miscellaneous followers, charged a fee and protected the land from neighboring marauders outside Oz. In exchange for a share of his takings, he arranged with the King of Oz to prevent rival lords from encroaching on his territory. One day Lord Bountiful read a philosophy book and discovered that all men and even all women are born equal. He therefore established a parliament based on universal suffrage and gave it power to govern. The first thing the parliament did was reduce Bountiful's share to 7 percent. Bountiful agreed this was right and just, but said he could not pay Oz and still have enough left to run the business. Knights and horse feed were becoming ever more expensive. He therefore retired and took his knights and horses off into the night. The next day, the territory was invaded by Lord Ready.

This is what Marx would have predicted. He would also have predicted that if an elected socialist government in our time were to seriously threaten the capitalist system, the result would be analogous. Some capitalists would flee, others would bid the currency up or down on the world markets until there was general economic disaster. The people would then elect a different government.

We must change the entrenched economic and technological features of the social structure before we can have actual freedom. To change an existing system we must act in a different way. Marx reasoned further that the tensions created by the capitalist system were ultimately destructive. Competition tends to eliminate competitors and generate monopolies, exerting downward pressure on wages until subsistence levels are reached. Marx was right. Capitalism generates McJobs. Marx also believed that capitalism tended to dehumanize people by demanding the maximum amount of work possible, in a way that depraves human nature. We must trade our subsistence for the utmost we can produce or be replaced by someone who can produce more. More than that, our work becomes a commodity integrated into a system. The worker on the Ford assembly line contributes a tiny bit to a finished product with which he cannot easily identify. In these circumstances, the system inevitably breaks down. Sometimes it does so sporadically, producing occasional crime. Sometimes the breakdown occurs on a large scale in depressions caused in part by the constant erosion of purchasing power even though production is more efficient. Wars, which increase markets, dispose of surplus production, and distract people from their miseries, become a useful part of this process.

Some of the predictions Marx made about capitalism failed in a way that suggests the Hegelian thesis is stronger than he imagined. Legislation permitted the development of the trade-union movement, somewhat inhibited the formation of monopolies, and created a banking system that kept some capitalist systems more open to innovation and concerned with consumer well-being than he expected. Consumer movements, green movements, and popular movements to control some elements of the arms industry have been, though hardly successful in their major aims, more effective in ameliorating the capitalist system than Marxists were prepared to believe. Yet other phenomena have developed – especially the increasing gap between rich and poor in the industrialized world and the ever-widening gulf between rich nations and developing countries – in ways that sustain elements of the Marxist thesis.

Desperate people have plenty of reason to behave destructively. Even this way of putting it tends to obscure the stark reality. Both Hegelians and Marxists would claim the essential problem lies in a lack of effective ways for people to co-operate. The Hegelian responds by demanding social rights, those rights associated with a place in a well-designed society. The Marxist's answer is to insist on economic rights, rights to resources that empower people.

People in contemporary liberal democracies can form political parties and find that the social structure is rich enough to provide openings for the relevant organizations. However, the realities of modern communications technology make it imperative that a US senator in a large state raise about $100,000 a day from the day he is elected until his next election if he hopes to be re-elected. He does not do this by passing the hat among people coming out of church or by going about knocking on doors in back streets in the Bronx. The necessary money is likely to belong not even to rich individuals but to large corporations, usually multi-national corporations whose aims are not exactly those of people who live on poor streets in Queens. The art of getting the money despite complex electoral laws about political financing is highly developed.

We can form trade unions. Trade unions, however, stumbled over two evident realities. First, the great industries like those of the American rust-belt were replaced in the economy by many smaller and harder-to-organize companies based on new technologies. The old discipline disappeared with the old factories. Workers have become harder to organize. Second, the trade union is an institution with a vested interest in conflict. Where workers and employers get along easily, unions are weakened. However, trade unions did not fade because workers and employers get along better, but because employers spend more money and energy evading them and because, in what Ernest Gellner called "the modular society," employers can easily dispose of existing workers and hire more.[8] As institutions with a vested interest in conflict, trade unions invited conflict. Their resources have generally been less than those of their employers, and the end of certain skilled industries spelled doom for many unions. Printers were once the best-organized workers. Suddenly they could be replaced by anyone who could type and use a photocopy machine. The old printing trade unions collapsed.

For reasons more difficult to pin down, other modes of organization also failed. In Europe and England, religion was increasingly marginalized as a social force in the twentieth century. The old Christian democratic parties remained in name on the European continent, but they were hardly radical reform groups. "Christian socialism" in England remained the concern of a tiny minority.

In the United States and Canada, the "main line" religious denominations developed strong social policies with roots going back into the nineteenth century and beyond. But their numbers shrank in recent decades while religious fundamentalists and charismatics – traditionally much more concerned with saving souls for the next world than filling stomachs and educating the young for this one – have grown considerably. Thus yet another institution in which people controlled their environment has weakened. People remain divided and the Enlightenment dream has not been realized.

On such views – Hegelian or Marxist – it would seem that there is not much we can do. The human rights we are discussing are matters of fact. They occur in certain cultures or they do not. One reading of Hegel's philosophy holds that whatever happens is the natural working of reason over time, and we cannot do anything about it. Another says that while the march of history is not absolutely fixed – the freedom that dominated the West did not shape the rest of the world – we live in a puzzling combination of the abstract and the concrete. Once the idea of freedom was unleashed in the West it worked its way through history, but no one can foresee when the twists and turns it engenders will come about. Still less can anyone properly forecast the coming to earth of the Absolute, though Hegel seems to have believed the pattern of the Prussian state foreshadowed significant parts of it. But we are blind to those parts of the future that are open. The Owl of Minerva flies only at twilight. One reading of Marx is that historical determinism is true. The leaders of Eastern Europe, who welcomed the Universal Declaration of Human Rights only to ignore large parts of it, no doubt reasoned that history would make things right if they should be made right. Another reading of Marx is more like the second reading of Hegel. Capitalism will collapse, but it may do so sooner rather than later if some effort is put into it. The creation of class-consciousness is thus a worthwhile activity, but we are blind to its results. Marx thought Russia an unlikely place for the classless society to begin, and perhaps he was right. But it seems unlikely that he thought a rational plan could easily be developed. Marxists, however, tend to take the view that, although history would have its way with us, we could speed it up or slow it down, and so it was worthwhile to invest some time and energy in revolutionary activities. Too much emphasis should not be placed on political history and prophecy. Hegelians tended to think that as we caught on to the general line of the spirit of history, we might further the affairs of the Absolute. Although Hegel saw history as the march of God in the world, many Hegelians thought the rational reform of religion and the development of philosophy would bring the human mind into closer touch with the Absolute.

There were many complications and many ways to evade the simplest attempts to falsify such theories. But we must in any case notice that the Hegelian and Marxist pictures in some sense fail. If the original Enlightenment vision of human beings as creatures who could be free in their minds, regardless of social and economic condition, fails to account for the facts of social and economic determinism, the Hegelian and Marxist visions fail to allow for certain actual and discernible elements of freedom. There are always social, cultural, and economic explanations for the emergence of new ideas. But such ideas do not appear by necessity. Ideas did not appear evenly across Europe. Italy and England are different. The more we look at specific ideas the more obvious this is.

d. Is There a Right to be Properly Conditioned?

The fourth explanation for the failure of Enlightenment expectations to materialize is the Hobbesian one: People are just nasty. They consist of matter in motion, tend to collide with one another, and will generally eliminate one another unless organized by a powerful government. No one needs on moral grounds to submit to such a government. Indeed it seems to be Hobbes's view that we are naturally entitled to do whatever we can do. Whether this is because the Hobbesian God, who figures oddly in this materialist universe, made us that way and intended us to use our powers, or whether, despite Hobbes's unpersuasive protestations, there is no God and nothing beyond us which should influence or control us, it is hard to tell.

Hobbes's natural successors are various reductionist materialists, socio-biologists, and miscellaneous social Darwinists. They argue that all life – vegetable as well as sentient – is involved in a natural competition for space and resources, and that we are programmed to maximize our opportunities to reproduce and spread our genes. This leads to a struggle for dominance. We can take the view – as David Gauthier does – that we can maximize self-interest by a series of contractual agreements that generally encourage co-operation.[9] But all such theorists agree that the reasons for co-operation, if any, are prudential and not moral, and some thinkers turn out to be supporters of unfettered capitalism. Indeed, these thinkers have played a significant role in the unraveling of the kind of social-democratic consensus that animated countries like Britain, Canada, Australia, New Zealand, Denmark, Norway, and Sweden in the years after the Second World War. On this view, no natural things may be called rights and duties, there are only negotiated settlements. Hobbes's notion of a set of absolute original rights turns out to be only a linguistic confusion. Hobbes identified what we have a right to do with what we can do, but it turns out that to say that we have a right to do something adds nothing to the claim that we can do it.

To persuade the rich and powerful to share their power and riches – or indeed to permit the development of civil rights generally – they must be persuaded it is in their interest to do so. Though David Gauthier thinks that civil rights could be promoted if the rich and the powerful were rational in the sense of being dedicated seriously to their own self-interest, such attempts have been conspicuous by their failures. For the most part it has been possible to persuade the rich and powerful that ordinary people should have certain civil rights. Economic rights impinge directly on their wealth and power and the rich have tended to resist them vigorously and, in recent years, have been successful in dismantling substantial parts of what was called the "welfare state."

A modern Hobbesian view seems to imply one new right – the right to be properly conditioned. The whole argument depends on the notion that everyone would agree a stable organized society is better than a world that is one long Wild West shootout. Nearly everyone except, perhaps, those who live in Texas would agree to this. However, no amount of force will produce this end. The American belief in armed force has produced one of the highest crime rates in the world, and even former President Suharto learned that force does not by itself produce peace.

What might produce peace if the Hobbesian theory were true would be effective psychological conditioning of the whole population. This conditioning would use all the latest techniques of behavior modification and brain washing and all the available chemicals that have already emptied most mental hospitals.

But is the Hobbesian picture correct? Ideas do change in ways that make human rights intelligible.

5. The Saumur Philosophers

Let me take one example, crucial to our concern here, which may provide a clue to how freedom comes about and ideas change, so we can learn how to avoid social disaster. If we understand the conditions for freedom and change, perhaps we can gauge the extent to which the various kinds of rights must fit together to be effective. Social, political, and economic rights all play their part, and the ability to solve some technical philosophical problems plays a role.

The idea of religious toleration has become part of the standard belief of educated people in Western liberal democracies. It is a puzzling and unlikely idea, and in many parts of the world, advocating it invites sudden death. Yet the connection between political tolerance, essential to any democracy, and religious toleration is close. In the Christian tradition, the notion that human beings are naturally free, possessed of moral consciences decisive for them and of infinite worth, is closely tied to central doctrines. The line between religion and politics is never clear. In the Soviet Union, Marxism was something like an official state religion, and the quarrels between the West and the Islamic world, which figure so largely in our day-to-day affairs, involve an uneasy fusion of politics and religion. Yet someone who possesses religious truth, on which the eternal salvation and damnation of others is known to depend, has a duty to save people from their own follies. A close and troubled connection exists between moral practice and religious enthusiasm.

The problem of religious "toleration" became pressing with the Reformation. It played a large part in sixteenth-century thinking.[10] But the rival denominations were ferociously attached to the view that there was only one truth and only one sect could be right. Only in the seventeenth century was a different notion, the possibility of a pluralism that is not simply a relativism, developed. Some argue that only with such an idea are real peace and reconciliation possible. Perhaps modern tolerance owes much to the weakening of religious belief. But ideas about religious pluralism played a part in the increase in toleration too, and the possibility that we might be tolerant in good conscience without loss of faith was and is an important one.

One place to which we owe the idea of religious tolerance as a rational and positive doctrine is a little French town in the Loire Valley, Saumur. Although now more celebrated for its good wine than its theological and political theories, it was once spoken of as another Geneva. In Saumur, a group of philosophers, especially John Cameron, a Scot who shuttled back and forth to France; Moïse Amyraut; and Isaac d'Huisseau introduced the idea into a most unlikely setting, French Calvinism. William Penn studied in Saumur where he sharpened the ideas of toleration and charity so widely associated with the Quaker movement.[11] Cameron played a part in introducing these ideas into England and Scotland. Richard Baxter read him; Coleridge studied Baxter; and the British Idealists, including John and Edward Caird, were influenced by Coleridge. Edward Caird's pupil John Watson brought them to Canada.[12] The Saumur philosophers wrote in French and Latin, but were widely translated into English. The massive collection of their writings and writings about them in Dr. Williams's Library in London illustrates the scope of their influence.

The point of the example is this: These ideas of toleration occurred first of all in a society of sufficient complexity and with sufficient diversity of institutions to permit the development of conflicting ideas. The Saumur movement occurred among a group of people, mostly prosperous, with enough resources to found their own academy and secure leisure time to debate seemingly arcane issues about nature and grace and free will. They disagreed among themselves and with others passionately, but they had enough stake in the community to want to settle their disputes peacefully. They were literate men and women, many of them passionate book readers, and the community gained not only printing presses, but citizens skilled at publishing.

Their debates forced them not only to come up with a picture of human nature, but also to examine their own circumstances. Amyraut was strongly moved by Descartes. But he felt it necessary to establish a more unified view of human nature than he thought Descartes had proposed. Ideas arise out of social circumstances and require the means to act if they are to become meaningful. Thus there is a strong implication that personal liberties must have social and economic expression.

The "Saumur phenomenon" arose in the period from 1608 to 1660. French Protestantism prospered and then foundered, mostly because of political ineptitude. Protestants numbered around 800,000 or 5 percent of the population in the early seventeenth century. They had natural allies across the Channel, and in an effort to gain political power they conspired with the English, but lost at La Rochelle when the rebellion of 1627 was put down in 1628. The French Protestants lost more of their political power, which stemmed partly from the need for the French to stay on good terms with the Dutch in order to keep the Spanish at bay, when the Dutch signed a separate peace treaty with Spain in 1648. The most hopeful avenue for French Protestantism was the pursuit of religious tolerance and the development of a rational theology to convince the French church and state that religious pluralism was an acceptable possibility. But not everyone, by any means, saw this.

In the first half of the seventeenth century, France had three leading Protestant academies, Sedan, Montauban, and Saumur. At Saumur, a new Calvinism sprang up. The others often supplied its hostile Calvinist critics. (The hostility was not uniform; Cameron taught for a time at Montauban and died there. But he was physically assaulted there in 1626 and suffered injuries from which he never fully recovered.) The Salmurians were not short of non-Calvinist critics, either. Bossuet found Isaac d'Huisseau especially alarming.[13] Huisseau argued that religious pluralism is inevitable and not undesirable. It was inevitable because humans harbor tendencies that bear upon religion, and not everyone gives each of them the same weight. It was not undesirable because we are, after all, only human and we benefit from seeing that the great mysteries cannot easily be dissolved into dogmas.

The proponents of the Salmurian theology argued that its roots were in the writings of Calvin, but few Calvinists were convinced. The views of the Salmurian thinkers seemed quite surprising. At Saumur, William Penn found some of the ideas he needed, but that was surprising too. The original English Quakers were more famous for their stubbornness than their addiction to toleration.

The origins of the Quaker notion of toleration are uncertain. Something provoked William Penn to go to Saumur. If by toleration we mean acceptance of the Cameronian doctrine that all people can be saved by a revelation embedded in their natures which enshrines the image of God, the Quakers were certainly not always tolerant. Nor were they tolerant if toleration means accepting people of other faiths as equals in the Quaker community. If one means by toleration the doctrine that religious sects should be free of political interference, the Quakers usually were tolerant, for they needed tolerance themselves. As late as 1693 *The Christian Doctrine and The People Called Quakers* asserted, "none can come to God but by Christ." The document is signed by George Whitehead and six others, "on behalf of the people aforesaid." But as early as 1663, when Penn was at Saumur, we find in *Toleration or no Toleration, A Discourse Between Conformists, Non-Conformists, Papists, Anabaptists, Quakers etc.* that the Quakers are quoted as wanting to "lift the yoke: of intolerance."[14] (The author seems to mean political intolerance of the sort experienced by the Quakers.) In 1678, Robert Barclay published his *Apology for the True Christian Divinity*. A Latin version had appeared two years earlier in Amsterdam. The English text was still circulating fifty years later in an Irish edition. In the preface, Barclay asks the King for toleration of the Quakers on the ground that they are good Christian people. In Proposition 14 of the *Apology*, he takes Locke's position that the civil magistrate has generally no business with religious beliefs that do not harm the community, though, indeed, there are restrictions. Barclay was also something of an egalitarian. Proposition 10 asserts the right of women to preach, for instance. In his *Universal Love*

Considered,[15] Barclay speaks of the heathen as capable of the "inner light." However, it seems clear, as John Norris pointed out in *Two Treatises Concerning the Divine Light*,[16] Barclay believed heathens could be saved only if the light took them to Quaker practice or something like it. Penn, nearer to Barclay perhaps, but influenced by Cameron and Amyraut to go a little further, published his *Reasonableness of Toleration* in 1687. But Penn quarreled with Lodowick Muggleton. Penn's friend George Whitehead threatened him with legal action for arguing with Penn, and Muggleton landed in jail for six months. In the nineteenth century, Quaker disputes about tolerance continued.[17] Some kinds of religious intolerance seem to have been the model in British Quakerdom, despite Penn. Walvin documents the Quaker policy of excluding all those who married out of the sect.[18] The rule was finally relaxed in 1858, but 4,000 members, almost half the membership, were lost. (In the seventeenth century, membership may have reached 80,000.) It has remained small ever since.

The modern ideal of religious pluralism – an ideal which has certainly taken firm root – seems to have its earliest full and consistent expression in the writings of Isaac d' Huisseau, who was able to distinguish between relativism and pluralism in a way that is still useful. Pluralism, which is not mere relativism, stems from three considerations. First, although only one truth exists, more than one interpretation is possible, given the nature and capacities of the human mind. Second, echoed in our time by Sir Isaiah Berlin,[19] objectively demonstrable competing values exist and we must choose between them. Relativism believes in many equal truths and acknowledges that values are not objective, but reflect something else to which they are relative, usually human desires. The third, urged by Isaac d'Huisseau, stems from the notion that religion has different features which appeal to different aspects of human nature. Huisseau argued that one kind of relativism is not incompatible with objectivism, on the ground that religion appeals to a great range of human response. No one would deny that emotion, reason, and our moral and charitable instincts all play a part. Not everyone is equally moved by all of these, and so religious life will take on many colorings. This does not mean that some of them are not responding to the objective truth.

Traditionally, the Church dealt with this phenomenon in a natural way in the development of different religious orders and different forms of the religious life. For the less complicated structures of the Reformation churches, this posed a problem. The Salmurian thinkers believed in one Christian truth that had advantages over rival claims, even though it did not undermine the natural basis of those claims. But Christianity has always embraced competing visions of the good life – marriage and celibacy for instance – and not all questions of doctrine have been settled. One pope of the Reformation period had to tell the Jesuits and Dominicans to keep their peace over free will and predestination, and ordered the Jesuits to stop calling the Dominicans Calvinists and the Calvinists to stop calling the Jesuits Pelagians.

The academy at Saumur was founded in 1599 and drew its students from Geneva, Basel, Bern, Schaffhausen, and Zurich.[20] It quickly became a center of controversy. The arguments over predestination later attracted much attention, and it is those which F. P. Van Stam has in mind when he says the controversy should be dated from September 1634.[21] This was the year of the publication of Amyraut's *Brief traité de la predestination et de ses principales dependances.*[22] However, the issues were much broader and the serious debate begins with John Cameron. Amyraut, though he was Penn's inspiration, may well have been the least original of the three philosopher-theologians. Paul Testard, the pastor of a Protestant church in Blois, said much the same things in a book published in 1633.[23] Testard wrote in Latin jargon; Amyraut in plain French.

The original seed of the idea of religious toleration was a thesis of John Cameron, first put forward orally during a visit to Heidelberg in 1608, that there are not just two "covenants" as the orthodox insisted (the Old Testament and the New). A third, the covenant of nature, is open to all men.[24]

Cameron argued that God loves us in two ways. First, he loves as a creator; second, he loves us for what we do in the world. This second is a voluntary love on both sides. Cameron adds that the "Covenant of Nature" is fundamental.[25] It declares God's justice. God's mercy is declared in the two "Covenants of Grace," essentially the doctrines of the Old Testament and the New Testament.

The covenant of nature requires perfection; the covenants of grace are for sinners. In the covenant of nature there is no mediator; in the covenants of grace there is.[26] This is Cameron's explanation of the superiority of Christianity. In Christian belief, God actually appears to the world, but the heathen are not to despair and should not be despised. The covenant of nature can also bring us to Christ.[27]

This doctrine opened the door to religious tolerance – despite Amyraut's own arguments in the *Traitté des religions contre ceux qui les estiment toutes indifferentes.*[28] Amyraut argues that Christianity is superior to the other religions. He reluctantly has to admit that God has given a natural message even to heathens. But it is a dark and obscure message. Indeed, the advantage of Christianity, as he says, is that in the New Testament the offer of God is laid out plainly. Mohammed turns out to be "so gross and mad a fool." Yet somehow, Amyraut admits, Islam does preserve certain truths, even if it has lost all claims to divine revelation. He is hardly kinder to the Jews. The "time of Moses's Law has expired."[29]

The row about predestination started with a softening of Calvin's doctrine as it was usually read, but it developed into a further argument for religious tolerance with claims – Cameron's and Amyraut's – that God intended to save everyone. If God intends to save everyone, then it seems odd that so many believers lie outside the realm of whatever particular faith is supposed to provide salvation. Predestination was never the central point. Amyraut simply argued that the problem arises because God sees the world from the perspective of eternity. When we translate his decisions into a temporal sequence, we see that some sinners repent and are saved and others do not repent and are not saved, even though God wants to save them all. From our perspective, we can say that God "always knows," but the temporal relation is not in God's mind.

I think Amyraut understood that the problem is a moral one. There is a necessary connection between being good and being saved and being an unrepentant sinner and being damned. But the necessary connection is between the moral qualities. To be damned is to be forever an unrepentant sinner. From the perspective of eternity this is one simple fact. Temporally, it is complex, since Amyraut always insists on our freedom.

In this, he follows Cameron who argued for a universal and necessary connection between the will and the understanding. The important issue, as he puts it, is always "illumination." If one knows, one acts appropriately.

6. Philosophical Anthropology and the Change of Ideas

In the ideas developed at Saumur, we see how the people involved in this change came to think about philosophical anthropology, and how they slowly worked out an account of the human being that would do justice to their ideas. It turns out that the picture they felt driven to was neither that of the "angelists," who believed that free-floating minds could feed on negative freedom, nor that of those who find the human animal mired in social conditioning and brutish nature.

Both Cameron and Amyraut insisted on attacking the "faculty psychology" of the time. Though Amyraut talks about the distinction of mind and body, he argues that there is in the end only "one subject."

In *Discours sur l'estat des fidèles après la mort*, Amyraut explores these issues.[30] He presents himself as a qualified dualist. But his dualism is not quite what we expect. Even though soul and body are "very different substances," they "make one subject."[31] "The soul cannot reason without a well-tempered and well-disposed body."[32] But this is true only so long as the soul is lodged there.

The fact that we can do metaphysics makes the case for independence. Amyraut's progress is from sensible things to natural philosophy to metaphysics. He associates us with a kind of infinity.[33]

On his view, the soul and the body are not really functional without each other, but the soul could function after death with a different arrangement of some kind. He thinks we are different from horses chiefly because of the way in which the intellect works in us.

What is crucial to his argument and to the argument leading up to the human rights issue is his notion of intellect. He speaks of the human being as "infinitely above all other creatures" – *emporté infiniment*.[34]

Brian Gary Armstrong says that Amyraut followed Cameron in developing a more "existential" – and a more unified – concept of man than most thinkers of his time.[35] Amyraut believed in a "perfect correspondence between the two rational faculties in man, the understanding and the will."[36] The "understanding is the 'absolute governor.'"[37]

We can see how these ideas lead to the idea of religious tolerance and to a view of human rights that includes both personal and economic rights. Amyraut knew his particular defense of Christianity demanded people act in the world and rejected the abstract notion of the human being as wholly divorced from the material world.

We can see that in this case the introduction of new ideas has a complex explanation. Protestantism is not easy to explain, especially in France. Weber's thesis that it was closely tied to the rise of capitalism and the upsurge of bourgeois individualism and its related "work ethic" has been questioned severely.[38] Nor does Protestantism's growth in France seem to have been religiously necessary.

The period in which the Saumur thinkers flourished was the height of the Catholic Counter Reformation movement, a movement which included – or was at least contemporaneous with – Jansenism, a flood of monastic reforms, and a wave of nationalism in the French Church. It included close parallels within the Catholic Church to nearly all of the Protestant movements, so the survival of Protestantism in the time of Cameron, Amyraut, and Huisseau cannot be explained by demands for Church reform. Richelieu and Bérulle associated it with politics, and certainly its downfall was spurred by an unfortunate attempt to rouse political support from across the Channel.

Whatever the cause and effect relationship, the Protestant insistence on direct one-to-one relationships with God attracted the same people whose business and other interests made them individualists. Also, the various elements in the French Counter Reformation are largely attempts to meet Protestantism head-on and confront it on its own terms. Jansenists drank from the same wells as Calvinists and Lutherans.

Protestantism was more, not less, dogmatic than the official Catholic Church. It lived by the promulgation of specific doctrines, while the official Church, with its host of distinct religious orders, its array of religious practices, and its much older doctrines – all of which had been subjected historically to many distinct interpretations – could never manage anything like such a dogmatic front. Just this point was made by the Protestant Cameron, who hoped that one day everyone would be united in a genuinely "broad church."

How then do we explain the rise of new doctrines of tolerance and the attendant notions of human rights? Partly, they come from the ideas themselves. Calvinism was widely criticized for its narrow exclusiveness and accused of denying the universal promise of Christianity. The Saumur philosophers wanted to answer this charge. To do so, they had to hold that God had made an offer to all human beings and had done so as generously as possible. This is the basis of Cameron's covenant of nature. But this supposes that human beings can understand complex issues, can understand nature in itself, and then act in the world so as to give their choices efficaciously. This requires philosophical anthropology, which the Saumur philosophers slowly developed. Secondly, there was a gulf to be filled. People were aware of the great differences of opinion not just between Protestants and Catholics, but between different Protestant groups and different Catholic factions. They wanted to know how this could be so, and many of them wanted some way of coming to terms with their neighbors, business associates, and political allies who had different religious views. The public unity of the community had been fractured in a way that must, especially in towns like Saumur, have been troubling to many people on a daily basis. Finally, practical considerations made it necessary to be as tolerant as possible. The French Protestants were in a politically weak position, though not all of them seem to have been aware of it. If we are tempted to think, however, that these practical considerations are what turned the day alone, just look at the religious fanatics in politically doubtful positions who simply dig their heels in. Militant Islamic groups in Egypt are an excellent example.

Human beings are capable of making the choices the Saumur philosophers exemplify, but this requires a concatenation of events, forces, and possibilities.

The Saumur story provides a good and clear example of how ideas can change and societies can be restructured, and how human rights must be considered if they are to be effective. What moved the Saumur philosophers and others like William Penn was a certain vision of the human being as a creature of infinite capacities. Amyraut's and Huisseau's thesis asserts that the real possibilities for human beings can never be confined within any fixed set of concepts, but that relativism is an equally dangerous doctrine. The belief that human beings have an infinity of possibilities and are therefore entitled to something like Descartes's ethics of generosity makes us insist on open societies.[39] But the association of that infinite richness, which transcends by definition the physical world, gives us the authority to insist on human rights.

This example also shows that we require a measure of positive control over our lives and our societies – that we are not creatures who are angelic abstractions. This unification can be explicated in the philosophical anthropology of Jacques Maritain and even more clearly in that of his mentor, Thomas Aquinas. I will try to explain this and then I will address the central question of the scope and application of the two kinds of rights.

7. Developing a Philosophical Anthropology for Understanding Rights

We cannot accept a vision of the human being that suggests people are somehow minds in bodies so arranged that the mind can be free while the body is in bondage. Nor should we hold that the human being is simply a mechanical device whose needs can be met by responding adequately to the biological demands of the animal. Genuine novelties are found in human affairs, as the Saumur example suggests, and they are of such a kind that biological explanations verge on the absurd.

But equally separate minds and mechanical bodies do not fit together in a way that suggests that a classical mind-matter dualism will work. Any real example, like the one we just examined, suggests a seamless interplay of mind, social reality, and physical reality. It helped that the bourgeois Protestant reformers at Saumur were rich enough to eat, and had a community to which to react. One cannot easily imagine that men and women scrabbling for their next meal in a hunter-gatherer society would have much time for the subtleties of debates about predestination. More importantly, they would not have the means to store the kind of history that makes such debates intelligible. A society that rests on oral traditions is likely to be good at connected narrative, story telling, and myth making, but less skilled at sustained logical analysis. We cannot even do complicated arithmetic if we cannot write down our data and operations.

To think of the Saumur philosophers as possessing independent minds interacting with their environment seems odd. As we saw, Amyraut was at pains to insist that the human being was a single subject.[40] His problems were those of an embodied man. He was provoked to think about the ultimate nature of the human being by the death of his daughter and the grief of his wife.

Is there an alternative to dualism and materialism? The situation is this: If we think of the human being as merely a socialized body bound in space and time we cannot understand how genuine novelty comes about. Everything, then, is reducible to our glands, our digestion, and our genes. In the realm of physics everything must be analyzable into its immediately preceding states. Nothing can appear *ex nihilo*, even if, as in quantum theory, some things can appear in unexpected places or seem to have incomplete descriptions. If we think of the human mind as something quite apart from the phenomena in the world, then we cannot explain how such a thing could be efficacious in the world or how understanding its workings should so obviously demand an understanding of the workings of the world.

We must accept, therefore, that the mind is not exhausted by the states of the world, but can only be understood as something that expresses itself in and through the world. The mind is, as the scholastics maintained, in one sense unlimited. It can know whatever there is to be known, and so St. Thomas Aquinas insists on the human being as a knowing creature. The human intellect is infinite, and therefore capable of novelty. I cannot here go into all the philosophical issues concerned with the idea of genuine freedom. We should notice, though, that if we are capable of real novelty, if human actions are unique and innovation is truly possible, we must be able to reach beyond the confines of any fixed system. Yet our actions must not be random. They must always be expressible through an orderly world.

This unlimitedness that we possess as knowing creatures is both obvious and of a special kind. We cannot imagine a geographer who could know and understand the geography of Australia, but not that of South America. We may not know anything about South America, but if we can know the facts about Australia we are also capable of knowing the facts about South America. In principle the number of facts about either is infinite. Whoever can know any of them can know all of them, because there is nothing in principle about the facts which would make one set of them knowable and another set unknowable. A mathematician who can know the first ten integers can know any and all of the infinite set – though we cannot be aware of all of them simultaneously. Understanding integers brings us face to face with the idea of infinity. The ability to grasp the infinite sets us beyond the limits of the mere finite, as philosophers and mathematicians from Descartes to Cantor have maintained. With the ability to reach beyond any finite set, we attain freedom. No doubt only a god, understood in a traditional way, could be perfectly free to range over all the infinite simultaneously. However, each of us has enough power to reach beyond the finite to attain some measure of freedom.

Yet this power can only be expressed in and through a world where things can be individuated. This is certainly so for us, and I would argue it must be so for God as well, though the question of whether or not God must seek such an expression is different. Human beings must seek such an expression or lapse into emptiness.

One reason Jacques Maritain was concerned with questions of economic rights was because his philosophical anthropology demanded it. He insisted that we are linked to spirit by personality, and to matter by individuality.

In his recent *Christianity and Liberal Society*,[41] Robert Song calls attention to the relation between Maritain's metaphysics and his political philosophy, where the insistence on human beings as embedded in a community is balanced with the claim that they have an aspect that transcends all human communities. This aspect, however, must be expressed through those communities. In her perceptive study, Norah Michener[42] argues that the theory of the intellect is the key to Maritain's philosophical anthropology. "Man can through his intellect know – and hence intentionally become – all things."[43] This dramatic reach gives the human being his or her dimension of infinity. But this reach has to be expressed – at least in this life – through the individuality, which comes from the space-time world of mortals. The dualism is not one of mind and matter – the human mind is rooted in the processes of sensation – but one of an infinity of possibilities which must be expressed through a finite frame.

"What does this amount to?" I would put it this way: The human potential cannot be realized, humanity cannot be achieved, except in a society that provides the necessary support for life, learning, security for reflection, and the ability to act freely. Yet the community does not exhaust the human being. The possibility of freedom is necessarily the freedom to stand outside the community, to criticize it, to claim a place for ends and activities which at any given time the community may not recognize. There is an aspect of infinity about the human being, but in expressing it, the human being is still tied to the world and the community.

This theme is expounded by James H. Robb, who derives it from St. Thomas Aquinas. He says, "there seems to be something even contradictory in speaking about spirit as finite."[44] Robb associates the agent intellect whose "role" is "to make species actually intelligible" with the infinite. "Intelligible being which is the object of any intellect and the infinite is not merely the sum of finite elements."[45] Robb admits that in many texts, Aquinas, whom he is expounding in this passage, speaks of the human being as finite. The human being, though it draws on infinity, is always a finite expression of that infinity. The infinite itself can never be fully expressed, for our lives are bounded by the finite world.

The best explanation is given by Aquinas in Question 54 of Part I of the *Summa Theologica* in which he says both knowing and willing partake of infinity, for their objects are the true and the good. But the object to which they are ultimately directed is beyond us.

We are not the angels whose habits are discussed in that question and so the problem of economic rights arises for us. Let us look for a minute exactly at what the economic rights proposed in the Universal Declaration amount to.

8. The "Economic Rights" Clauses

Nine articles in the original declaration are crucial. Articles 17, 22–26 and 29–30 insist everyone has a right to property, social security, secure work, participation in trade unions, equal pay for equal work, and a decent education, as well as a right to live in a society where normal human potential can be developed. The subsequent protocols present some of these rights in more detail. For citizens lucky enough to live in countries that ratified the protocols, they provide a chance to have their condition reviewed, but the most essential matters remain unchanged.

Article 17
(1) Everyone has the right to own property alone as well as in association with others.
(2) No one shall be arbitrarily deprived of his property.

Article 22
Everyone, as a member of society, has the right to social security and is entitled to realization, through national effort and international co-operation and in accordance with the organization and resources of each state, of the economic, social and cultural rights indispensable for his dignity and the free development of his personality.

Article 23
(1) Everyone has the right to work, to free choice of employment, to just and favorable conditions of work and to protection against unemployment.
(2) Everyone, without any discrimination, has the right to equal pay for equal work.
(3) Everyone who works has the right to just and favorable remuneration ensuring for himself and his family an existence worthy of human dignity, and supplemented, if necessary, by other means of social protection.
(4) Everyone has the right to form and to join trade unions for the protection of his interests.

Article 24
Everyone has the right to rest and leisure, including reasonable limitation of working hours and periodic holidays with pay.

Article 25
(1) Everyone has the right to a standard of living adequate for the health and well-being of himself and of his family, including food, clothing, housing and medical care and necessary social services, and the right to security in the event of unemployment, sickness, disability, widowhood, old age or other lack of livelihood in circumstances beyond his control.
(2) Motherhood and childhood are entitled to special care and assistance. All children, whether born in or out of wedlock, shall enjoy the same social protection.

Article 26
(1) Everyone has the right to education. Education shall be free, at least in the elementary and fundamental stages. Elementary education shall be compulsory. Technical and professional education shall be made generally available and higher education shall be equally accessible to all on the basis of merit.
(2) Education shall be directed to the full development of the human personality and to the strengthening of respect for human rights and fundamental freedoms. It shall promote understanding, tolerance and friendship among all nations, racial or religious groups, and shall further the activities of the United Nations for the maintenance of peace.
(3) Parents have a prior right to choose the kind of education that shall be given to their children.

Article 29
(1) Everyone has duties to the community in which alone the free and full development of his personality is possible.
(2) In the exercise of his rights and freedoms, everyone shall be subject only to such limitations as are determined by law solely for the purpose of securing due recognition and respect for the rights and freedoms of others and of meeting the just requirements of morality, public order and the general welfare in a democratic society.
(3) These rights and freedoms may in no case be exercised contrary to the purposes and principles of the United Nations.

Article 30
Nothing in this declaration may be interpreted as implying for any State, group or person any right to engage in any activity or to perform any act aimed at the destruction of any of the rights and freedoms set forth herein.

These rights are also affirmed in nine articles of the European Social Charter passed on 30 October 1989. These rights provide for freedom of movement through the professions and throughout the community, "equitable" wages, a commitment to the improvement of living and working conditions, "sufficient resources" for people outside the labor market, freedom of association and collective bargaining, vocational training, gender equality, consultation when businesses or industries are restructured or moved, healthy and safe working environments, the outlawing of child labor, retirement resources, and resources for the retired and the disabled.

9. Working Out the Metaphysical Implications

Two interesting questions arise: Suppose we take the view of the human being I suggested, we are beings with infinite capacities that must express these capacities in a finite world. I think we are driven to this view if we are to understand how rights are exercised. Our ideas of individual freedom are not separable from our ideas of the social and political order. And none of these ideas is intelligible without an account of how they can be expressed.

But, then, are the economic rights in this list essential? And if they are, in exactly what sense are they rights, and how do we cope with the problem of how to provide them? Economic rights have costs of a different order from those of individual, moral, and political rights. Moral and political rights are not free. The state needs no resources to grant them, but such rights must be proclaimed and publicized, disputes about them must be adjudicated, violators of them must be constrained, and all the apparatus of political life must be provided. Yet they do not pose the problems that public health care poses. A health system could use up all the resources available if the best possible care was provided for everyone in the world and if everyone's life was prolonged as much as possible. In a different vein, many economists think full employment is not possible because, if everyone has a job, the economy would be frozen and competition for labor would create massive inflation. Some countries cannot ensure that all their children are adequately fed, schooled, and housed.

The creation of personal and political rights makes everyone responsible for the well-being of society. Everyone is responsible, even when rights are not granted. Legal systems are not possible unless only small minorities take to crime and subversion. If no one returned a library book, or if everyone walked out of pubs with a glass in hand, libraries and pubs would have to grin and face it. The jails of the world – as the Americans are finding – will not hold everyone. Drivers who choose the wrong side of the road are prosecuted, but only because they are a small minority. If everyone in England decided to follow the rest of Europe and drive on the right, driving on the right would become the only possibility.

No one can carry out citizenly duties without the necessary support. The theory that we can choose widely and freely on an empty stomach is empty. Sick men and women are a problem to society as much as to themselves.

The situation is worse than it appears. A whole social complex is necessary for civil rights to be organized. My argument is that economic rights are the correlative of duties, but are also necessary conditions for the expression of humanity in the world. Without them people must live pinched lives, something less than the full humanity of which they are capable. They may surmount the barriers, and many do, but they are marked and scarred by the process.

How are we to cope with the apparent contradiction? People may be entitled to rights that no society can provide. The answer seems obvious – what there is has to be shared. We can at least accept the logic of this situation. Because people will not be able to carry out their citizenly duties, moral and political rights of individuals are apt to be a sham. We cannot think of a society that possesses effective political rights and yet denies economic rights. India struggles and does remarkably well, but no one believes that individual rights are as readily exercisable there as they are in Denmark. And India lives under the constant shadow of parties of religious fanatics who may at any time extinguish much of the country's growing democracy. India adopted an instructive solution, to establish the basis of a social democracy where resources are shared. Although a long way from achievement, it is the only answer.

We can imagine a society based on shared resources and responsibilities, a negotiated society where individuals and groups determine what they want and what they are willing to do to get it, and in which negotiations go on until there is a general measure of agreement. In the past, it has been impossible to collect enough information or to conduct negotiations on such a vast scale. Computers and electronic communications have changed all that.

Notes

1. See A.C. Bradley, ed. *Prolegomena to Ethics* (Oxford: Clarendon Press, 1883); for the best account in recent years, see Geoffrey Thomas, *The Moral Philosophy of T. H. Green* (Oxford: Clarendon Press, 1987); for a discussion of the issues of the relationship of Green's moral and political theory to his metaphysics and his theory of knowledge, as they originally appeared, see D.G. Ritchie, *The Principles of State Interference* (London: Sonnenschein, 1890).

2. Isaiah Berlin, "My Intellectual Path," *The New York Review of Books,* 15:8 (14 May 1998), pp. 53–60; see also John Gray, *Berlin* (London: Fontana Harper Collins, 1995), pp. 15–21.

3. See Lowrie John Daly, *The Political Theory of John Wyclif* (Chicago: Loyola University Press, 1962); John Wyclif, *Tractatus de Officio Regis* (London: Wyclif Society, 1887); for Peacock, see Vivian Herbert Green, *Reginald Peacock* (Cambridge: Cambridge University Press, 1941); Reginald Peacock, *The Repressor of Over Much Blaming of the*

Clergy, ed. Churchill Babbington, 2 vols. (London: Rerum Britannicarum Medii Aevi Scriptores, Longman, Green, Longman, Roberts for the Public Records Office, 1860).

4. See Maritain, "Descartes," *Trois réformateurs* (Paris: Plon, 1925), ch. 2.

5. *The German Ideology, The Collected Works of Marx and Engels* (London: Lawrence and Wishart; New York: International Publishers, 1976), vol. 5, pp. 31 and 44. See Aristotle, *Politics,* 1253a.

6. See Robert Knox Dentan, *The Semai, a Nonviolent People of Malaysia* (New York: Holt, Rinehart, and Winston, 1979).

7. John Rawls, *A Theory of Justice* (Cambridge, MA: Belknap Press of Harvard University Press, 1971).

8. Ernest Gellner, *Conditions of Liberty, Civil Society and Its Rivals* (London: Hamish Hamilton, 1994).

9. See David Gauthier, *Morals by Agreement* (Oxford: Clarendon Press, 1986); and David Gauthier, *Moral Dealing, Contract Ethics, and Reason* (Ithaca: Cornell University Press, 1993).

10. See Joseph Lecler, *Histoire de la tolérance au siècle de la Réforme* (Paris: Editions Montaigne and Desclée de Brouwer, 1955; Paris: Albin Michel, 1994).

11. Catherine Owens Peare, *William Penn* (Philadelphia: Lippincott, 1957), pp. 39–42.

12. See William Ian P. Hazlett, ed., *Traditions of Theology in Glasgow, 1450–1990* (Edinburgh: Scottish Academic Press, 1993), *passim* and pp. 12–13, 22–23, 43–56; Robert Leighton, *Works*, ed. G. Jerment (London: Nicholson, 1808); J.D. Douglas, *Dictionary of the Scottish Church*, ed. Nigel Cameron (Edinburgh: T. & T. Clark, 1993), pp. 478–479; for John Watson, see especially *Christianity and Idealism* (Glasgow: Maclehose, 1897); Samuel Taylor Coleridge, *Aids to Reflection* (London: Taylor & Hessey, 1825); Coleridge's *Collected Works,* Vol. 9, ed. John Beer (Princeton, N.J.: University Press, 1993); Coleridge annotated Richard Baxter's *Reliquiae Baxterianae* (copy in the British Library, 1505/305); material from Coleridge's notebooks on Baxter is found in *Literary Remains of Samuel Taylor Coleridge*, 4 vols., ed. Henry Nelson Coleridge, (London: William Pickering, 1836–1839), vol. 4, pp. 76–156.

13. See Isaac d'Huisseau's *La réunion du Christianisme: La manière de rejoindre tous les Chrestiens sous une seule confession de foy* (Saumur: René Pean, 1670?); trans. as *The Reuniting of Christianity or the Manner How to Rejoin All Christians Under One Sole Confession of Faith* (London: John Winter, 1673); and Boussuet, *L'antiquité éclaircie sur l'immutabilité de l'être divin sur l'égalité des trois personnes: Sixième et dernier avertissement contre Monsieur Jurieu (1691),* see Michaud, *Biographie Universelle,* vol. 14, pp. 580-581; see also Eugène and Émile Haag, *La France protestante* (Paris: Joel Cherbuliez, 1855), vol. 6, p.10; and Richard Stauffer, *L'affaire Huisseau, une controverse protestante au sujet de la réunion des chrétiens, 1670–1672* (Paris: Presses Universitaires de France, 1969); and J. Meyer, *Bossuet,* (Paris: Plon, 1993), p. 154.

14. I.V.C.O. *Toleration or no Toleration, A Discourse Between Conformists, Non-Conformists, Papists, Anabaptists, Quakers etc.* (1663), p. 37.

15. Robert Barclay, *Universal Love Considered* (London, N.P., 1677).

16. John Norris, *Two Treatises Concerning the Divine Light* (London: S. Manship, 1692).

17. See Wemyss.

18. James Walvin, *The Quakers: Money and Morals* (London: John Murray, 1997), pp. 133–135.

19. See Steven Lukes, "Berlin's Dilemma," *The Times Literary Supplement* (27 March 1998), pp. 8–10.

20. See F.P. van Stam, *The Controversy over the Theology of Saumur, 1635–1650,* (Amsterdam and Maarssen: APA Academic Publishers, 1988).

21. Ibid., p. 22.

22. (Saumur: Lesnier et Desbordes, 1634).

23. Paul Testard, Ειρηνιχου *seu Synopsis doctrinae de natura et gratia* (Blaesis: M. Huyssens, 1633).

24. John Cameron, "De Triplici Dei cum Homine" trans. Samuel Bolton as *The trve bovnds of Christian freedome. Or a treatise wherein the rights of the law are vindicated, the liberties of grace maintained ... Whereunto is annexed a discourse of ... John Camerons, touching the three-fold covenant of God with man* (London: Philemon Stephens, Golden Lion, in St. Paul's Churchyard, 1645); originally published as a tract, "De Triplici Dei cum Homine" (Heidelberg: 1608); see *Johannis Cameronis, Opera,* ed. Samuel Boucherellus, Moïse Amyraut, and Louis Cappel (Frankfurt: C. Schleichij, 1642), pp. 544–551. For all Cameron's work, see Axel Hilmar Swinne, *John Cameron, Philosoph und Theologe (1579–1625),Bibliographisch-kritische* (Marburg: Elward, 1968).

25. Cameron, *Opera*, p. 544; Bolton, p. 356.

26. Cameron, *Opera*, p. 544; Bolton, pp. 356–357.

27. Cameron, *Opera*, p. 549; Bolton, p. 385.

28. In some editions, *Traitté* (Saumur: Girarde and de Lerpinière, 1631, second edition, corrected, Saumur: Jean Lesnier, 1652).

29. See Amyraut, *Traitté,* ch. 4, chapter heading as translated in the English translation (*A treatise concerning religions, in refutation of the opinion which accounts all indifferent: wherein is also evinc'd the necessity of a particular revelation, and the verity and preeminence of the Christian religion above the pagan, Mahometan, and Jewish rationally demonstrated* [London: M. Simons, W. Nealand, Cambridge, 1660]).

30. Moise Amyraut, *Discours de l'estat des fidèles après la mort* (Saumur: Jean Lesnier, 1646).

31. Ibid., p. 9.

32. Ibid., p. 11.

33. Ibid., p. 19.

34. Ibid., p. 144.

35. *Calvinism and the Amyraut Heresy* (Madison: University of Wisconsin Press, 1969), pp. 242–243.

36. Amyraut, *La Morale chrestienne,* 6 vols. (Saumur: Isaac Desbordes, 1652–1660), vol. 1, p. 55.

37. Amyraut, *Sermons sur divers textes* (Saumur: Isaac Desbordes, 1653), p. 269.

38. Richard F. Hamilton, *The Social Misconstruction of Reality* (New Haven: Yale University Press, 1996), pp. 32–106.

39. See my "Descartes and the ethics of generosity," *The Bases of Ethics,* ed. William Sweet (Milwaukee: Marquette University Press, 2000), pp. 79–102.

40. Amyraut, *L'estat des fidèles,* p. 9.

41. Robert Song, *Christianity and Liberal Society* (Oxford: Clarendon Press, 1997), ch. 5, pp. 128–175.

42. Norah Willis Michener, *Maritain on the Nature of Man* (Hull: L'Éclair, 1955), p. 52.

43. Ibid., p. 53.

44. *Man as Infinite Spirit*, (The Aquinas Lecture) (Milwaukee: Marquette University Press, 1974), p. 4.

45. *Ibid.*, p. 15, Thomas Aquinas, *Summa Contra Gentiles* II, 98, and *Summa Theologica* I, 54, 2.

Four

T.H. GREEN ON RIGHTS
AND THE COMMON GOOD

Rex Martin

T.H. Green's posthumously published *Lectures on the Principles of Political Obligation* (1886) is one of the finest books in the philosophy of rights to date. In it, Green emphasized two distinct elements of rights: the requirement of social recognition and the idea of a common good. But this leads to a tension in his theory. Either of the two principal elements could plausibly be said to exist in the absence of the other. Where this happens, or could happen, does the element that stands alone lose all claim to the status of a right? An attempted resolution of this potential source of confusion in Green's theory is one of the concerns of this chapter.

It is not, however, my first order of business. Instead, I want to first consider Green's idea of social recognition – a difficult and controversial idea – necessary to any right properly understood. Green writes, "The right to the possession of them, if properly so called, would not be a mere power, but a power recognized by a society as one which should exist. The recognition of a power, in some way or another, as that which should be, is always necessary to render it a right."[1] This emphasis on the role of social recognition lies behind Green's notorious remark that "rights are made by recognition. There is no right but thinking makes it so."[2]

Green's notion of social recognition was developed dialectically out of his careful attention to the theory of natural rights, where such rights were understood as powers that held good in a state of nature. Against Hobbes and Spinoza, Green argued that rights were not mere natural powers, but had normative force (especially as involving duties and other kinds of normative direction of second parties).[3] Against Locke, one of the first philosophers to make the preceding point about the normative force of rights, Green argued that the relevant duties necessarily implied some sort of awareness or recognition by the duty holders. Thus, by what amounted to an internal critique of the natural rights tradition, he could reach his own distinctive idea that all rights, including natural rights, involve social recognition. Social recognition belongs to the definition of rights, to the concept of rights.

The notion of the common good or of a mutual and general good belongs, however, to the dimension of justifying something as a right. Or at least, it belongs to the justification of the most important kind of right, the universal right (the right of each and all).

Green divides general or universal rights into two categories: the natural and the civil. In some sense each is a universal right. Natural rights, as normally understood, are rights of all persons. Active civil rights, for Green, are political rights universal within a given society.[4] They are ways of acting or being treated that are specifically recognized, affirmed, and actively promoted in law, and apply to each and all citizens or, in the limiting case, to all individual persons.

Thus, both natural rights and civil rights are special cases of what Green called general rights. They are rights of all people or all citizens and, in some important cases (for example, the right to life) they constrain generally all other people or all other citizens, either directly or through the mediation of public law.

All universal civil or political rights are important rights and all reflect a high level of social commitment. But not all can be justified as natural rights, what we today call human rights. Still, all can be justified in a distinctive way – in accordance with one and the same pattern.

The background supposition is that all rights, both natural rights and civil rights, are in some way, beneficial to the right-holder. Thus, all civil rights (all political rights universal within a given society) should identify specific ways of acting or of being treated that are of benefit to each and all of the citizens or to each and all of the persons there. For these claimed ways of acting or being treated are, arguably, part of the "good" of each person or instrumental to it.

Where this requirement of mutual and general benefit is upheld, a legal civil right becomes a way of acting or being treated that is correctly understood to be in everybody's interest, or would be so understood, upon reflection, and given time and experience. All active civil rights could be regarded as justified if they identify and sustain ways of acting or ways of being acted toward that satisfy the criterion of mutual perceived benefit.

Even where a degree of official or social recognition exists in a body politic, there can be no such thing as a fully "justified" universal political right without the element of a mutual and general good, that is, without the identifiable and reflectively available interest of each and everyone within a given society that certain identical ways of acting (or of being treated) will be acknowledged and maintained.

Green's principal idea is that civil rights are justified by being of mutual perceived benefit, and that such benefit refers to interests each citizen has in the establishment, within the society, of certain ways of acting or of being treated, ways that are identically the same for all.[5] The essential sense of what Green capaciously calls "common good" is captured, for purposes of the justification of civil rights, by what I have been describing as mutual perceived benefit.

Green sometimes uses other senses of "common good," especially in discussing individual human perfection or the moral perfection of society.[6] And there are, for Green, links of common good with metaphysical principles such as the eternal consciousness[7] or with corporate entities such as organized society. But affirmation of these other senses or links goes beyond what is required for the justification of rights.

With the justification of rights, we need only consider mutual perceived benefit. Here each individual understands his or her interests and knows what ways of acting or being treated might contribute to those interests for everyone.

As Green points out, this awareness of interests and ways of acting or being treated depends, further, on an ideal of the (not yet realized) self. If we move our focus to this particular dimension, a mutual good can be said to exist where each individual conceives himself or herself and others as having (some) identical traits of character, at the point of full self-realization, or as requiring identical means to those traits. Since Green typically talks of rights as establishing "conditions" for such self-realization, his emphasis, when discussing rights and their justification in this context, is on an identity of such means and not of the ends per se (as given in the notion of the traits of a fully realized self).[8] That is, his emphasis is on justified rights as established ways of acting or being treated, identical for each and all and, secondarily, on establishing the conditions for such ways to be exercised. Thus, my discussion of common good in this essay will be restricted to the notion of identical ways of acting or being treated – as giving the one, necessary rights-justifying conception of mutual perceived benefit in Green's theory.

Thomas Hurka takes exception to my use of mutual perceived benefit as the principal justifying ground for civil rights and, by implication, takes exception to it as a helpful way of explicating Green's notion of common good.[9] Hurka's point is to distinguish a "parallel" sense of mutual benefit (where person A has a right R that benefits person A, and person B has the same right R that benefits person B) and a "reciprocal" or "shared" sense (where person A's right R benefits person A and all other persons, and person B has the same right R that benefits both person B and all other persons). He claims that what I call mutual perceived benefit is a case of "parallel" benefit, but that only "shared" benefit can justify civil rights. I accept Hurka's location of mutual perceived benefit with the notion of "parallel" benefits, but I think that mutual perceived benefit so conceived can ground an adequate justification of civil rights. And I do think it affords an adequate and proper interpretation of Green's notion of common good in the envisioned context, that of justifying rights.

Let me briefly elaborate my claim that mutual perceived benefit, understood as "parallel" benefits, can justify civil rights. Here the parallel benefit in question is that the same way of acting or the same way of being treated is beneficial for each and every one of the right-holders (that is, all citizens or all persons within a given body politic), beneficial in that this way is a means to, or a part of, some good, some interest of the holders.[10] Here, person A's having a right R benefits person A, and person B's having that same right R benefits person B, and so on.

The claim is not that these persons benefit on every single occasion the right is exercised (by themselves or by someone else), or benefit in precisely the same way, or benefit equally (as regards the result of so acting or so being treated). Nor is the claim made that everyone or anyone benefits maximally by being in a situation where identical ways of acting or of being treated are established in law.

Though we might grant all this, these legally established ways of acting or being treated (identical for all) are regarded by everyone as beneficial. People see these ways of acting as a means to or a part of things they regard as valuable, and they would rather have these ways available than not. Indeed, each person would rather have these ways available than not, even on the condition that this same way is available to others – in fact, to everyone.

Here everyone's having the same right R benefits (in the manner just described) everyone, person A and person B and so on, down the line. It must be this way for those civil rights that have been justified by the relevant standard, by satisfying the test of mutual and general benefit.

The test here is not the same as Hurka's idea of "shared" benefit, where person A's having a right R benefits both person A and all other persons. For nothing like this would follow, as to mutual and general benefit, simply from A's having a right that benefits A, or from B's having a similar right. Instead, it is from the fact that "everyone" has the same right(s) that this mutual and general benefit arises. Legally established ways of acting or being treated, identically the same for everyone, are justified when they actually are beneficial (in parallel fashion) for each and all.[11]

Hurka's version ("shared" benefit) is too strong a notion to be typically found in the real world. It is unlikely we'll find that, in being beneficial for person A, a given way of acting or being treated is also beneficial for all others. This will likely be so only if that same way of acting or being treated is extended to everyone. Hurka's understanding of "shared" benefit carries a whiff of the claim that the good of each person harbors the good of all others (or is non-competitive with the good of others or is the same good for everyone), that critics of Green have seized on time and again.[12]

There is, however, an account of reciprocity appropriate to Green's theory. We start with the obvious point that sometimes a way of acting or being treated – the same way in each case – can be beneficial for most people. Then it would be likely (where this was so) that when someone perceived it was a good for him or her, she or he would also perceive it was a good for others as well. Now, such ways of being treated have to be sustained in practice; they do not just happen. They have to be accomplished and maintained through some sort of effort and choice. Typically, they are sustained through joint effort.

The citizens or lifelong members of a system of civil rights pool their efforts to achieve a common set of values or norms for conduct in their society, as in the civil rights laws that constitute or are among the main rules of this particular system of rights. The texture of any body politic is revealed not only in the list of civil rights that all enjoy, but also in the normative directives imposed on every person by those rights. Thus, citizens or lifelong members of that society are right-holders and make their contribution to society and its system of rights when they act as typical citizens, conforming to law. This makes it "their" system. Its flourishing is their work and that of others like them. A system of rights so understood is always the work of its citizens or lifelong members, who are both its primary beneficiaries and its progenitors.

Some features of that particular system may be unique. The citizens have accorded a sort of preference to achievement of this precise set of rights. They emphasize the achievement of legally secured ways of acting or being treated, in the interest of each and all. They have established a priority of determinate universal rights in that society over other options. (The priority I have in view here is a priority of basic rights over (i) any common good that serves the social or corporate good but not necessarily the good of each individually [for example, national defense] and over (ii) majority decisions that serve the good of some individuals but not all, and may even be injurious to some [for example, a particular tax code as regards allowable credits, deductions, exemptions, and so on].[13]) In these ways, a kind of reciprocity and a "social" sense of common good – an active concern for the good of each as connected with the good of all – comes to characterize the conduct and ultimately the attitudes of typical citizens in a particular system of civil rights.

Green's theory – unlumbered with the baggage of atomistic individualism, non-cooperative bargaining strategies, and maximization of rational self-interest – appeals to the idea that some ways of acting or being treated are mutually beneficial, if engaged in by everyone. Green deepens this account, in the ways I have indicated, by showing that reciprocity is required to make that idea work. Recognition of this fact in turn generates an abiding and reflective commitment, presumably a widespread one, existing on many sides, to a sense of each person's own good as a "social" good, fully realizable only in a certain kind of society.

I want to continue the line of thought suggested in this last point. Green argues that though rights can and do arise and are sustained in social relations, a certain overarching political arrangement is also required. Green calls this arrangement "the state." The state exists to formulate, maintain, and harmonize legal rights, especially universal civil rights in a given society.[14]

The question arises as to what particular institutional processes, if any, are apt in the formulation, maintenance, and harmonization of civil rights. However, Green did not put that question directly to himself or his auditors. Failure to ask and to attempt to answer this question is the most central failure of Green's theory of rights.

An answer could be suggested that is not uncongenial to Green's overall view, however. Active civil rights require an agency to formulate, maintain, and harmonize them. They require an agency to identify and establish ways of acting or being treated that we can reasonably suppose to be in everyone's interest. Democratic institutions – universal franchise, contested voting, and majority rule – can effectively perform this job and provide the setting required by civil rights. Democratic procedures are a stable and relatively reliable way of identifying, and then implementing, laws and policies that serve interests common to the voters, or at least to a majority of them.

An argument would be required to show that democratic institutions have a special affinity for civil rights and would accord them the sort of priority mentioned earlier in the discussion of reciprocity. But such an argument could, I think, be set out. The upshot, then, would be that the setting required by civil rights can be provided by democratic majority-rule government. Democracy needs a suitable justification that is best provided by giving preference to policies that serve the interests of each and all and by avoiding policies that override these interests. Such a preference would include universal political (or civil) rights.

Thus, what were initially two quite independent elements – civil rights and democratic procedures – have been systematically brought together and connected to one another by the line of argument just sketched. Our two key notions (accredited civil rights of individual persons and justified democratic government) are mutually supportive, and can serve to undergird a political system in which civil rights have priority. This priority does not arise from universal rights, but from democratic institutions, as suitably justified.[15]

Green believed the operation of democratic institutions afforded authority to the laws produced. He was an enthusiastic supporter of the tendency toward democracy reflected in the governmental institutions of the USA and Britain, and supported the extension of the franchise in the direction of one person/one vote. The turn to democratic institutions, then, would not be uncongenial to Green.[16] But Green did not suggest that democracy bore any special relationship to civil rights, such that bringing these two ideas together could provide any sort of closure to his idea of a sustainable system of civil rights. What conclusions can we draw from this?

Green's theory of a system of civil rights, grounded in democratic institutions and norms and embedded in the practices and attitudes of reciprocity, stakes out a middle ground. It provides a middle ground between devil-take-the-hindmost atomistic individualism and the celebration of community as an overarching value in and of itself (without undue concern for the question of what goods the community invests in and for what people). Green's vision of the good society can avail itself of the resources of a robust sense of the common good.[17] This is possible because the theory of rights is not individualistic in the unattractive way deplored by communitarianism and because it is democratic, depends on reciprocity, and engenders allegiance to an appropriate kind of body politic (and, within that kind, to particular ongoing societies). For Green, notion of community must be emphasized in any sound theory of rights.[18]

In the notion of an institutionally justified right for everyone – a "democratically" justified right in a system of rights that require reciprocity – we find Green's basis for reconciling the two main elements in his own account of rights – the elements of social recognition and common good. That notion provides the basis for Green's conception of individual rights, certainly of basic civil rights, as compatible with the common good.

Basic rights are those civil rights, such as the right of habeas corpus, identified and established by democratic decision, that exhibit a high level of social consensus, have survived the self-correcting processes of the democratic institutions, and now enjoy explicit endorsement by different checking devices (such as judicial review).

I suspect that a lingering hankering for old-style natural rights, or something like them, is the single greatest obstacle that my Greenian account of basic civil rights must overcome. Why should we prefer, as a way of understanding fundamental rights, Greenian basic civil rights over traditional natural rights? Consider an example from American history. In the eighteenth-century United States, the usual sources combed for basic civil rights were the constitutions of the individual states (former colonies of Great Britain) and common law (judge-made law that relied on previous judicial decisions and dominated Britain and America's civil and criminal law at the time). Some of these rights, presumably the most important of them, were thought to be grounded in natural rights.

If we stayed with the rhetoric and patterns of thought of these eighteenth-century forebearers, a plausible definition of basic civil or constitutional rights is "rights that are endorsed as basic by natural rights."

Natural rights (except for a brief mention) play almost no role in the present essay. Instead, basic civil or constitutional rights are certified by some combination of the standard of mutual perceived benefit with a democratically exhibited willingness (on the part of citizens and the governmental agencies) to accord priority to universal rights, over other considerations.

What is wrong with natural rights? Why have they been shunted aside? The main problem, as I see it, is that natural rights cannot form a coherent set and are ineligible to serve as grounds of basic civil or constitutional rights. Whatever natural rights are, they are non-institutional in character. (In one famous formulation, they are the rights that we would have in a state of nature.) Green argued, however, that the scope of rights must be authoritatively set (to preserve their central content); without such setting and adjustment of scope, rights will conflict internally, with one another, and with other (non-rights) considerations. Since such conflict is only resolved or prevented by the action of agencies that formulate and harmonize rights (through scope adjustment, competitive weightings, and so on), rights that lacked such agencies would necessarily conflict, and the set of them could not be coherent. Natural rights, which are non-institutional in character, lack such agencies in principle. Natural rights, as traditionally understood, cannot provide a plausible alternative, or even a useful addition, to the account of basic rights I have here attributed to Green.

The most likely way to save natural rights theory from this crucial disability is to relocate its main thrust. We could re-describe such rights as moral norms (reached by sound inferences from the accredited principles of a critical morality).

Such norms, which are allowed for in Green's account, provide reasons or grounds for saying certain ways of acting or being treated ought to be civil rights, ought to be formulated in law and maintained for all people in a given body politic.[19]

Such norms, when authoritatively acknowledged as they were in the American Declaration of Independence (1776) as the rights to "life, liberty, and the pursuit of happiness," are proto-rights – "manifesto rights" as Feinberg called them.[20] These norms or proto-rights or manifesto rights in order to be active civil rights – and, hence, active constitutional or basic rights – require specification of content, scope setting and scope adjustment, competitive weighting, and institutional devices for the on-site resolution of conflicts. Otherwise, such norms will conflict with one another and collapse into an incoherent set. They require promotion and maintenance or they will be nominal rights and not active functioning basic civil rights.

Natural rights (conceived as norms of critical morality that can underwrite some civil rights) have a place in a Greenian account. But we cannot think adequately about such natural rights (where they are thought to be true rights, as distinct from mere norms) by dispensing with the institutional features – scope adjustment, competitive weighting, promotion, and maintenance. These features are necessary to make such norms into basic civil rights, disqualifying them as natural rights, understood in the old eighteenth-century way.

Let me conclude these remarks by applying Green's analysis to the case of human rights as understood today (as exhibited, for example, by those rights found in the United Nations Universal Declaration of Human Rights, 1948, and the European Convention on Human Rights, 1954). We have three background considerations. First, authoritative recognition (if sometimes only in effect) and promotion and maintenance (usually on a wide variety of occasions) are internal to the notion of an active right. Second, a univocal sense of "rights" is desirable: one capable of capturing both civil rights (as a special case of legal rights) and human (and other moral) rights under a single generic heading. Third, all active moral rights must be construed as involving appropriate social practices of recognition and maintenance. Since human rights, as a special case of moral rights, are thought to be addressed to governments in particular (though not exclusively), we must regard practices of government recognition and promotion as an appropriate and essential form that the recognition and maintenance of rights must take.

In this analysis, full human rights are tied to the existence of bodies politic or states, as Green called them. Thus, if a nation has active, full-bodied human rights, then these rights must be morally well-grounded civil rights, recognized and maintained within such bodies.

Green's focus is not on the "manifesto rights" element of the United Nations Declaration, but on the embodiment of those norms as active civil rights within states, where such rights could be and were authoritatively recognized, harmonized, and maintained.

But Green's understanding of rights is not limited to "nation-states." I think a Greenian account allows for the notion of basic rights in an emerging "super-state" or, better, a confederation of states (like the nascent European Union).

The plausibility of this claim about a confederation of states is recognizable in Canada's recent and Britain's current parallel attempts to incorporate basic rights into domestic law. In Canada, this was accomplished through the creation of a written constitution that included a Charter of Rights. In Britain, it will probably be done by making the European Convention of Human Rights part of British domestic law. Perhaps not all of the European Convention would be adopted, but much of it would be. This adoption would be by act of Parliament.

In both cases, the rights in question would be constitutional or basic civil rights, concurring with Green's two main guidelines – social recognition by democratic institutions and common good. As basic civil rights, these rights would be guidelines for parliamentary law, enforceable in courts of law.

However, under the philosophy of the current Labour government, British courts lack the power of American judicial review. Instead, they would take on an advisory stance toward Parliament, respecting a law thought to be defective by the standard of those incorporated basic civil rights, rights derived originally from the European Convention. Thus, the famous sovereignty of parliament of the Westminster system would be preserved.

So far, we have examined one hard case (that of a confederation of states) and determined that rights originally formulated by such a confederation, in "manifesto" fashion, could become full basic civil rights if certain concrete steps were taken. Britain's proposed way of incorporating and maintaining the European Convention rights (as fundamental rights of British citizens) is an example of such steps. In this manner, Britain's way is different from Canada's way of identifying fundamental rights for Canadian citizens (in its constitutional system) and for maintaining those rights. But both ways conform or can conform, despite these differences, to Green's standards for a viable scheme of basic civil rights.

Whether a Greenian theory could countenance a special International Criminal Court of Justice (concerned, for example, with the direct trial and punishment of suspected war criminals, as was proposed at an international conference in Rome, in July 1998) is not so clear. At a minimum, such a court would require the continuing support and cooperation of a wide variety of states. It must be an agreed-upon international agency for dispensing justice in a certain range of cases (concerning, for example, suspected war criminals, of the sort being dealt with in the present Bosnian trials) within a system of independent nation states. Can existing domestic legal systems be integrated with such a court? Can the norms of common good and democratic decision making effectively underwrite the rights charter of an international criminal court and superintend the development of that charter and the workings of that court over time? These are the questions of moment. At this point, we do not have enough information to pass competent judgment; we might do well, then, to set this thorny and speculative matter aside, for further reflection and await further developments.

We have, however, made some progress on our project of linking Green's theory with human rights as currently understood. We can see how human rights are becoming clearer and more coherent in the domestic law of Britain and Canada and the United States. This way of understanding rights has a major place in the world today, and Green's theory can be helpful, in both articulating and justifying it.[21]

Notes

1. T.H. Green, *Lectures on the Principles of Political Obligation* in *Lectures on the Principles of Political Obligation and Other Writers*, ed. Paul Harris and John Morrow (Cambridge: Cambridge University Press, 1986), vol. 2, sec. 3, p. 45.

2. Ibid., sec. 136, p. 106; see also sec. 41, p. 38; see also secs. 23–26, 31, 99, 103, 113, 116, 121, 139, 142, 144–145, 148, and 208.

3. For details, see Rex Martin, "Green on natural rights in Hobbes, Spinoza and Locke," *The Philosophy of T.H. Green*, ed. Andrew Vincent (Aldershot, UK: Gower, 1986), pp. 104–126; Rex Martin, *System of Rights* (Oxford: Clarendon Press, 1993).

4. Green, *Political Obligation*, sec. 24.

5. Green, *Political Obligation*, secs. 29, 217, and 25–27, 30, 38-39, 41, 99, 114, 121, 143–144, 151, 206, 208, 216.

6. Ibid., secs. 6–7, 19, 21, 23, 186; and Peter Nicholson, *Political Philosophy of the British Idealists: Selected Studies* (Cambridge: Cambridge University Press, 1990), ch. 2.

7. Green, *Political Obligation*, sec. 131; T.H. Green, *Prolegomena to Ethics* (1883), bk. 1; *Collected Works of T.H. Green*, ed. Peter Nicholson (Bristol: Thoemmes Press, 1997), vol. 4, pp. 12–89; Geoffrey Thomas, *The Moral Philosophy of T.H. Green* (Oxford: Oxford University Press, 1987), ch. 3, pp. 14, 141–145, 148.

8. Green, *Political Obligation*, secs. 20–21, 23, 25, 29.

9. Thomas Hurka, "Review of Rex Martin's *System of Rights*," *Mind* 104 (1995), pp. 178–182.

10. Martin, *System of Rights*, ch. 5, sec. 3, pp. 104–109.

11. Ibid., pp. 103; 182; 203–205; and Appendix, pp. 413–415.

12. John Horton, *Political Obligation* (Atlantic Highlands, NJ: Humanities Press, 1992), ch. 3, pp. 70–79, 177; Peter Nicholson, *Political Philosophy of the British Idealists*, ch. 2, secs. 2–4.

13. Martin, *System of Rights*, chs. 7, 12, and Appendix.

14. Green, *Political Obligation*, secs. 134, 138, 141, 142, 143.

15. Rex Martin, *System of Rights*, chs. 6, 7; Rex Martin, "Basic Rights," *Rechtstheorie* Beiheft, 15 (1993), pp. 191–201.

16. Green, "Political Obligation," sec. 100; Sandra M. den Otter, *British Idealism and Social Explanation: A Study in Late Victoria Thought* (Oxford: Clarendon Press, 1996), pp. 164–165; and Nicholson, "Introduction," *Collected Works of T.H. Green*, Vol. 1, pp. xxiv–xxv.

17. Stephen Mulhall and Adam Swift, eds., *Liberals and Communitarians* (Oxford: Blackwell, 2nd ed. 1996).

18. Green, "Political Obligation," sec. 39. I am indebted to Will Sweet for drawing this section to my attention.

19. Green, "Political Obligation," sec. 9.

20. Joel Feinberg, *Social Philosophy*, [Foundations of Philosophy] (Englewood Cliffs, NJ: Prentice-Hall, 1973), pp. 63–64, 66–67, 94–95.

21. In the writing of the present chapter I have drawn at points, sometimes verbatim, on my book *System of Rights* (Oxford: Clarendon Press, 1993) and on earlier papers, particularly a longer and different version of the present essay, "T.H. Green on individual rights and the common good," *The New Liberalism: Reconciling Liberty and Community*, eds. David Weinstein and Avital Simhony (Cambridge: Cambridge University Press, 2001), pp. 49–68. I wish to thank the editors and publishers for allowing me to draw on this material here.

Five

A POST-SECULAR EXCHANGE: JACQUES MARITAIN, JOHN DEWEY, AND KARL MARX

Thomas M. Jeannot

Suppose a conversation among three humanists from the recent modern past could be staged: namely, Jacques Maritain (1882–1973), a principal figure in the twentieth-century revival of Thomism and a leading Catholic philosopher; John Dewey (1859–1952), the American pragmatist and ambivalent apologist for liberalism; and Karl Marx (1818–83), founder of modern communism and the most trenchant critic of the capitalist mode of production. What might it contribute to the way we understand our contemporary situation? A successful conversation does not require complete agreement as its outcome, but it can lead to what Hans-Georg Gadamer called a "fusion of horizons," the occupation of common ground. Still, why pick these three? I begin, I hope not too idiosyncratically, with my own circumstances.

First, I was born in the United States. Even though it is the center of capitalist development, and even though its history has been the history of economic imperialism, drenched in blood, I want to believe in its possibilities for atonement. I want to believe this probably for theological reasons, and especially because the capitalist mode of production is an impersonal, abstract system of domination that knows no loyalties or community allegiances, whereas people in the United States, like people anywhere, are basically more good than evil, mainly trying to make it by from day to day.[1] The non-national communism that lies on the distant eschatological horizon will certainly be multicultural, and wé should count on the continued existence of regional and national cultures and identities. I imagine Canadians will still speak English and French and play more hockey than soccer, while Brazilians will still speak Portuguese and play more soccer than hockey. Meanwhile, if a social and political philosophy is to be practical – whether in Maritain's, Dewey's, or Marx's sense – then it is incumbent on us to achieve one rooted in the concrete experiences of the people for whom it is practical, and among whom it must be practiced if it is to be practiced at all. I am drawn to Dewey because his social and political philosophy, a radicalized liberalism, is cut from the grain of an American experience capable of addressing the dominant culture to which I belong.

Second, the family resemblances between Dewey and Marx make conversation between them congenial, although I cannot develop those resemblances here. For instance, they both cut their teeth on Hegelianism, they retained prominent aspects of Hegelian philosophy in their own thinking, and their respective critiques of Hegelian idealism led each to achieve a naturalistic and experimentalist reconstruction of it (for Marx, historical materialism; for Dewey, pragmatism). Each insists on the unity of theory with practice and on the priority of practice, regarding not only the theory of knowledge, but its point as well. Moreover, each can be read, in our contemporary idiom, as a communitarian, just as Aristotle's "political animal" is fundamental to their respective philosophical anthropologies. But this also means that each can be read as a humanist and as philosopher of liberation, once the appropriate meaning of our moral freedom (positive freedom, autonomy) has been grasped. When Dewey achieves the radicalization of his own commitment to liberalism, for example, in *The Public and Its Problems, Individualism Old and New* and *Liberalism and Social Action*, he focuses on the socialization of the means of production as the key to overcoming the failed liberalism, the bourgeois individualism, of the nineteenth century. Although the social conditions of his writing would have made it highly improbable that he ever thought of himself as a communist (not even in Sidney Hook's lower-case sense), he explicitly advances the theory of democratic socialism – not a Millian socialism of distribution, but socialized production and radical economic democracy.

Third, however, how can one expect Maritain to join in? The autobiographical fact of my Catholicism gives him a certain psychological relevance, but if I succeed in this essay, his role in the proposed conversation will have a better basis than that. At first blush, if it is plausible to conceive of a Marx/Dewey dialogue without doing too much violence to the integrity of either philosopher, they also belong to a profoundly different social and intellectual universe than the one Maritain inhabited. The largest obstacle to overcome in order to bring him into a common orbit with them is religious and theological. Marx and Dewey, as they are often interpreted, are archetypal secular humanists. However, if secularism is best understood through its affiliation with classical liberalism, and if Marx and Dewey are thinking beyond classical liberalism, then the best reading of them will interpret them as post-secular theorists.[2] Again, I cannot make a complete case for reading Marx and Dewey as post-secular theorists here, although it is crucial to the overall coherence of my argument. I will briefly explain why.

Neither Dewey nor Maritain can be blamed for their harsh indictments of canonical Marxism. Each received what had become an orthodox interpretation by the time Stalin consolidated power, organized on the basis of dialectical materialism. For Dewey, dialectical materialism was only the mirror image of the Hegelian speculative idealism he had repudiated, and he foresaw that its dogmatic presentation could only facilitate a totalitarian politics. This was bound to be the case with any theory that surreptitiously substituted its own abstractions, for example, matter, history, the proletariat, for concrete historical experiences and the concrete problematic situations that should orient social and political theorizing.

Not surprisingly, Maritain's criticisms of Marxism, for example in *Integral Humanism*, are similar to Dewey's. Maritain criticizes what he calls Marx's "radical realist immanentism," noting that "Hegel's immanentism is already, as such, a virtual materialism, and only his idealism prevents it from unveiling itself." Also, Marx's "anthropocentric monist metaphysics," as Maritain sees it, proceeds "not in the name of the human person," but "in the name of collective man," which can only denote an abstraction, an aggregate of individuals rather than a community of persons.[3] While these criticisms have merit, an emerging consensus indicates the Stalinist reading of Marx is an aberration, and the textbook presentation of dialectical materialism has no solid foundation in Marx's own text.

Once Marx achieved his own insight into the priority of practice, he lost patience with the abstractly theological criticism of religious and theological abstractions that preoccupied his Young Hegelian contemporaries. He was intent to move from "religious" to "irreligious" criticism, to advance the nascent German project of a critical theory of society from the abstract heaven of ideas to the earth of concrete, lived social experience.[4] The axis of his thought was not theology (or philosophy in the Hegelian-theological mode), whether positive or critical, but political economy. In the Paris manuscript on "Private Property and Communism," Marx evinces his impatience with cosmological and metaphysical speculation in general: "Who begot the first [human being], and nature as a whole? I can only answer you: Your question is itself a product of abstraction ... Give up your abstraction and you will also give up your question." He then proceeds to argue that atheism lies on the same abstract speculative plane as the doctrine of creation:

> the question about an *alien* being ... which implies the admission of the unreality of nature and of [humankind] ... has become impossible in practice. *Atheism*, as the denial of this unreality, has no longer any meaning, for atheism is a *negation of God*, and postulates the *existence of [humankind]* through this negation; but socialism as socialism no longer stands in any need of such a mediation.[5]

However we evaluate its merit, this argument reveals that Marx did not regard the atheistic critique of religion and theology as an integral part of his developing critical theory, the critique of political economy.

The young Marx believed the critical-theoretic fixation on theological matters that characterized his Young Hegelian contemporaries was also systematically misleading. For example, in his essay "On the Jewish Question," he relentlessly criticizes Bruno Bauer's solution of what Bauer takes to be the fundamental social problem. For Bauer, atheism and secularism "are" the key to human emancipation. An emancipated German society would be one in which the theocratic state (especially of the Prussian Hohenzollerns) became a secular state, one in which both Christians and Jews forsook their religious commitments in the body politic. Among other points, Marx notes that Bauer's proposed solution has already been implemented in the United States. However, he points out that this political emancipation from theocracy has not achieved a genuinely human emancipation: oppressive social relations still deeply persist there, and the secular society should not be mistaken for the social order of genuine human freedom.[6]

For Marx, the theological mode of theorizing is essentially an exercise in mystification. This conclusion followed inevitably for him from his critique of Hegelianism. Therefore, in his later work, and especially *Capital*, his references and allusions to theology and religion signify his position that political economy itself belongs to the theological mode. To the extent that it apologizes for the capitalist mode of production, he argues that it is really an ideological mystification of the hidden social relations upon which bourgeois society is actually founded. Thus, for example, in the famous final section of the first chapter of volume one of *Capital*, "The Fetishism of Commodities and the Secret Thereof," Marx writes that the commodity-form of the value-relation "is nothing but the definite social relation between [human beings] themselves which assumes here, for them, the fantastic form of a relation between things. In order, therefore, to find an analogy we must take flight into the misty realm of religion." Then he argues that this religious "veil is not removed from the countenance of the social life-process, i.e., the process of material production, until it becomes production by freely associated [human beings], and stands under their conscious and planned control."[7]

What Marx is really suggesting in his presentation of the commodity, money, and capital fetishes integral to the logic of capitalist production is that capitalism is objectively, even if only implicitly, a religious form. In the tellingly titled chapter on "The Trinity Formula" of profit, interest, and rent in volume three of *Capital*, Marx calls capitalism "this religion of everyday life," and in the reading I am urging, he is not writing merely metaphorically.[8] The bourgeois epoch literally, if only implicitly, worships money: the ceaseless accumulation of value on which the logic of capitalist production is predicated is its matter of ultimate concern. Its system imperatives exercise a final causality comparable to Aristotle's first unmoved mover, to which all other imperatives, whether technical, ecological, or humane, are subordinate. It will have no strange gods before it.

To the extent that the capitalist mode of production can be understood as a religious formation, which is the final import of Marx's discovery and presentation of the fetishism of commodities, the secular society of the bourgeois epoch has not really achieved the emancipation from the shackles of religion that it professed. From an anthropological point of view, can any human culture be post-religious? If the answer is no, then the religious function in experience, which Dewey identified as anthropologically ubiquitous and which led him to criticize "militant atheism," cannot be simply cast aside.[9]

Likewise, Maritain, exploring "the roots of Soviet atheism," brought out the irony and contradiction of a militantly atheist state, which, far from eradicating or eclipsing religion, only enshrined itself as a substitute: "faith in the Communist revolution really presupposes a whole universe of faith and religion in the midst of which it constructs itself ... Communism is so profoundly and substantially a religion, an earthly one, that the Communist does not know it is a religion."[10] I would only add that what is sauce for the goose is sauce for the gander. For Maritain, "liberal-bourgeois" humanism is in no better a position, "now no more than barren wheat and a starchy bread."[11] He argues, "bourgeois humanism" is logically continuous with the "socialist humanism" that follows it, predicated on the "radical atheism" already implicit in the bourgeois horizon of values. "The demand" of bourgeois humanism "was for culture to free [human beings] from the superstition of revealed religion and to open up to [their] natural goodness the perspectives of a perfect security to be attained through the spirit of riches accumulating the goods of the earth."[12]

Maritain's point is that atheism cannot be lived. "One may cite here in witness the heroic and tragic experience of Nietzsche," and also Dostoyevsky's character Kirlov in *The Possessed*, who announces to Peter Stepanovitch, "a few minutes before his suicide ...'I shall kill myself to prove my independence and my terrible new freedom.'"[13] But then if atheism, the myth of human *aseitas*, cannot be lived, the logic of capitalist accumulation is also religious. As Marx puts it, "Accumulate, accumulate! That is Moses and the Prophets!"[14]

The classical Marxist critique of religion is that it functions ideologically to legitimate class divisions, the power of the ruling class, oppression, and exploitation. Its logic is a logic of mystification. Accordingly, a Marxist can also argue that any ideology that mystifies social relations performs a religious function, as does the ideology that supports the fetishism of commodities, money, and capital. In *Capital*, Marx satirizes that ideology as "a very Eden of the innate rights of man. It is the exclusive realm of Freedom, Equality, Property and Bentham."[15] In this ideology, "freedom" is essentially the absolute right of private property, private appropriation, and private accumulation of capital, and "equality" is essentially the Hobbesian and Benthamite doctrine of bourgeois individualism, the equality of self-interests and the unrestricted right to pursue your own private advantage. This constellation of values constitutes the foundation of classical liberalism that establishes the horizons of discourse within which the mainstream debates about justice and rights in the United States still take place; consider, for example – despite their serious differences with one another – Rawls's *A Theory of Justice*, Nozick's *Anarchy, State, and Utopia*, Dworkin's *Taking Rights Seriously*, and Rorty's *Contingency, Irony, and Solidarity*.

The texts just enumerated, bread-and-butter texts of virtually every contemporary ethics course taught in the United States, are nothing if not secular. In just this connection, despite their differences, they share several positions in common. Their commonalities include a prioritization of negative rights, or rights of noninterference; a sharp distinction between private and public domains; a profound privatization of substantive conceptions of the good; and an individualism which, despite disclaimers, is deeply indebted to the Hobbesian philosophical anthropology, according to which human beings are essentially self-interested agents competing with one another for scarce resources. These are the deepest assumptions of classical liberal ideology, which, in Marx's words, "provides the 'free-trader *vulgaris*' with his views, his concepts and the standard by which he judges the society of capital and wage-labour."[16]

The universe of discourse just described is "ideological" in Marx's sense to the extent that it mystifies or veils the hidden social relationships it sustains, by imputing a moral legitimacy to them that more or less blatantly defies the social facts. As Marx states it, according to the ideology of "Freedom, Equality, Property and Bentham,"

> The only force bringing [human beings] together, and putting them into relation with each other, is the selfishness, the gain and the private interest of each. Each pays heed to himself only, and no one worries about the others. And precisely for that reason, either in accordance with the pre-established harmony of things, or under the auspices of an omniscient providence, they all work together to their mutual advantage, for the common weal, and in the common interest.[17]

According to this ideology, the just social order is one in which essentially private individuals, all pursuing their own private interests whatever they happen to be, first agree not to interfere with one another's life projects, and then enter into social and cooperative relations only on the basis of their own private choice. Here, the free market model of private property and the contract reigns supreme, extending beyond the exchange of commodities to recast all social relations on the principle of market exchange, including such otherwise capital-transcending institutions as marriage and family life, schooling, and public office.

The point of characterizing this classically liberal ideology as "secular" is first of all to link secularism with bourgeois individualism and what Maritain calls "bourgeois humanism." But both Marx and Dewey are as critical of it as Maritain himself, even if their reasoning does not ultimately coincide. Moreover, both Marx and Dewey, as we have seen, distanced themselves from atheism, whose deeper meaning Maritain discerned in *Integral Humanism* as the myth of individual aseity, crystallized by Kirlov's bitter choice (even if the militant atheism of the Soviet state was promoted in the name of the abstraction, "collective man"). If secular liberalism, in its mystification of social relationships, goes hand in glove with commodity fetishism, then it too falls within the purview of the classical Marxist critique of religion, well and rightly enough made regarding its proper object, if not regarding religion per se. Finally, whereas Marx is at least indifferent to any further cosmological and metaphysical speculation ("Give up your abstraction, and you will also give up your question"), Dewey constructively recognizes the positive role of the religious function in experience, refusing to see it only as ideological, and he rejects a totalizing secularism on this basis. These are the grounds on which Marx and Dewey can be characterized as *postsecular* theorists, and the point of achieving this characterization has been propadeutic, to clear the way for a conversation with Maritain.

Secularism, liberalism, and bourgeois individualism belong to the same horizon. Marx, Dewey, and Maritain share in common that they attempt to think beyond it. But the constellation of values coming in for critique belongs to the epoch of the capitalist mode of production. If Marx is obviously the most critical of capitalism, Dewey and Maritain's critiques of capitalism deserve to be profiled as well. Dewey's has been all too briefly indicated, and only a brief mention of Maritain's can be made here.

In the social context in which Maritain formed his basic conception, a capitalism in crisis confronted the specters of fascism on one side and Stalinism on the other. On Catholic grounds, Maritain also recognized the moral and spiritual bankruptcy of the capitalist regime, and he attempted to envision a new social order beyond it, which he christened in *Integral Humanism* the "historical ideal of a new Christendom." This new regime, neither fascist nor Stalinist (two forms of totalitarianism) would be a "personalist democracy."[18] It would "presuppose a radical change not only in the material but also in the moral structure and in the spiritual principles of the economy." However,

> In the present civilization, everything is referred to a measure which is not human, but external to [human beings as persons]: primarily to laws belonging to material production, to the technological domination of nature and to the utilization of all the forces of the modern world for the fecundity of money. In a truly humanist culture, it is to [human beings as persons] and [their] measure that the things of the world would be referred.[19]

The movement to a "personalist democracy" and "a truly human culture" therefore "presupposes," as Maritain writes, "the preliminary liquidation of modern capitalism and of the regime of the primacy of money-profit."[20] This personalist democracy would include "a collective form of ownership" and a "communal organization of production," and it would enforce "the law of *usus communis*" that mandates that "for what concerns the primary needs – material and spiritual – of the human being, it is fitting that *one have for nothing as many things as possible.*"[21]

Living in a social world "caught between Fascism and Communism," threatened by "fascist totalitarianisms" on one side and "communist totalitarianisms" on the other, but also grasping the inhumane anti-personalism and spiritual emptiness of capitalism, neither could Maritain accept the "socialism" he knew mainly from Sorel's school, and he was ambivalent about various "corporatist" and "syndicalist" proposals also in the air.[22] Even in the context of the mid-1930s, then, he found it difficult to align his vision of a "new Christendom" with any of the prevailing political trends. He was part of a Catholic generation, including Mounier and Berdyaev as members of his own salon, searching for a "third way."[23] When he wrote *The Rights of Man and Natural Law* in 1943 as the Second World War was raging, he hoped that a successful outcome of the war would mean a new opportunity to refashion the economic and political order, "the 'new Democracy' which is in preparation at the core of the present death-struggle." However,

> It would be easy to show that all [the] characteristics of a sane political society are denied or disregarded, from different points of view, both by the old bourgeois individualism and by the totalitarianisms of today, whose worst form is Nazi racism. Surely it will be something new that [human beings] must build up after this war, in the midst of the ruins, if intelligence, good will and creative energy prevail.[24]

Although Maritain would not have thought of himself as a radical, even though he knew he was attempting to envision something genuinely revolutionary, his hopes for building up the "new Democracy" after the war, beyond the horizons of "the old bourgeois liberalism," have been dashed.

The latter half of the twentieth century was dominated by the cold war, during which economic imperialism instrumentalized American foreign policy, under the banner of "leader of the free world," to install and nurture authoritarian regimes and brutal dictatorships throughout the world. Yet the successes of the Reagan-Thatcher revolution in political discourse accomplished in the 1980s and the implosion of the Soviet Union by 1991 have ushered in a new period of capitalist triumphalism and a recuperated "old bourgeois liberalism." This was a period proclaimed by United States President George Bush, in the context of the U.S. war against Iraq, to be a "New World Order." The historical moment unfolding before us now is the global integration of a single world capitalist economy. We are at least as far away today from Maritain's "new Christendom" and "personalist democracy" as we ever were when he first envisioned them. In fact, the political project of the hour is the dismantling of the welfare state domestically and the ruthless imposition abroad of free trade agreements, IMF-mandated austerity measures, and economic sanctions on uncooperative states. Even the term "liberal" has become an epithet, and in a period when a Robert Nozick is in ascendancy, so to speak, even a John Rawls begins to look as if he were a utopian dreamer. Maritain searched not for a utopia, but for a historically realizable ideal, not the City of God, but a realizable measure of justice in the temporal city. In our present context, how can we think of him as anything less than a radical?

The radicalism of Maritain's social and political philosophy, then, brings him within the orbit of Marx and Dewey. They converge in their respective critiques of secular liberalism, bourgeois individualism, the capitalist mode of production, and the inhospitability of capitalism to genuine democracy. However, the postsecular character of the thought of Marx and Dewey creates a new opening for dialogue with a religious thinker such as Maritain. On Maritain's part, the religious inspiration that infuses his social and political thought can hardly be interpreted as an ideological legitimation of the prevailing social order. In this respect, his Christianity lies across the universe from that simulacrum of biblical fundamentalism and televangelism promulgated by such near fascists as Pat Robertson, Jerry Falwell, Jimmy Swaggart, and the Christian Coalition, who otherwise prove Marx's point and deserve his critical opprobrium. Marx should be interpreted as more indifferent than hostile to religion per se, except in the way that he exposes the implicitly religious function of secular ideology and the degraded religious form of fetishism he assigns to the deep logic of capitalist enterprise.

Nor finally is Dewey hostile to the constructive place and role of the religious attitude in the body politic. Steven C. Rockefeller's magisterial study *John Dewey: Religious Faith and Democratic Humanism*,[25] showing how Dewey's was a genuinely *religious* and not a secular humanism, should prevent Dewey's readers from reading him as a secular humanist again. In *A Common Faith*, Dewey wrote the following:

> The transfer of idealizing imagination, thought and emotion to natural human relations would not signify the destruction of the churches that now exist. It would rather offer the means for a recovery of vitality. The fund of human values that are prized and that need to be cherished, values that are satisfied and rectified by *all* human concerns and arrangements, could be celebrated and reinforced, in differing ways and with differing symbols, by the churches. In that way the churches would indeed become catholic.[26]

If Dewey extends this olive branch to Maritain, for example, then we can reasonably surmise that Maritain graciously accepts it.

Maritain can accept the olive branch based on at least two distinctions that belong to his larger philosophical conception, and that permit him to be a pluralist, rather than an ultramontanist as some might fear. The first bears on his conception of the relationship between the individual and society. To the bourgeois individualist, the individual is not a part of society; to the collectivist, the individual is only a part of society. But Maritain's Thomism allows him to distinguish between "individuals" and "persons," and further, to distinguish within persons between their transcendent relation to God and an eternal order, and their immanent relation to other persons in the temporal order. The fundamental dignity of the person derives from the former relation, although Maritain is willing to concede that "strangers to Christian philosophy can have a profound and authentic feeling for the human person and [her] dignity" as well.[27] Accordingly, "Society is a whole whose parts are themselves wholes."[28] Hence, neither the individualist nor the collectivist has it right. Persons have an inviolate dignity and autonomy, which is the basis of both individual and group rights within the body politic; but also, following Aristotle and Aquinas, people can realize their proper humanity only as "political animals," whose social relationships are therefore integral rather than accidental to their personality. It follows for Maritain that Christians have a dual vocation, religious and political, that these vocations are related by virtue of what personhood requires as he conceives it, but that they are also distinct, as the eternal and temporal orders are distinct. Owing to this distinction, the body politic, even if and when it becomes the "new Christendom," can still be "lay" rather than "sacral" in Maritain's idiom, permitting full religious liberty and being pluralist.

Second, Maritain follows Aristotle and Aquinas in distinguishing between the theoretical and the practical. Therefore, replying to John Dewey's student, Sidney Hook, in *The Nation*, he writes,

> [people] possessing quite different, even opposite, metaphysical or religious outlooks, can converge, not by virtue of any identity of doctrine, but by virtue of an analogical similitude in practical principles, toward the same practical conclusions, and can share in the same practical democratic faith, provided that they similarly revere, perhaps for quite diverse reasons, truth and intelligence, human dignity, freedom, brotherly [and I presume sisterly – TJ] love, and the absolute value of moral good.[29]

The classical distinction between theoretical and practical sciences, though neither Marx nor Dewey would share it in the way it was classically developed, is nevertheless sufficient to bring Maritain into conversation with them. A Marxist can perhaps remain indifferent to Maritain's metaphysics and theology; a Deweyan pragmatist might be courteously receptive to them, particularly as sources of nurture for the "common faith" of democracy; and Maritain, for his part, can develop a pluralism that does not degenerate into liberal agnosticism regarding anything other than market values, civic privatism, and Rorty's "liberal irony."

This last point will bring me into the neighborhood of a conclusion. Maritain's pluralism, so relevant to the contemporary debates in social and political philosophy, justified by both his personalism and his theory of practical convergence, is post secular, post-liberal, and anti-capitalist. Although he did not directly enter into a dialogue with Dewey on these issues, he came close enough to Dewey's world to respond to Hook. What evoked his response was Hook's criticism of T. S. Eliot's High Church politics, concerning which Maritain is "sincerely pleased" to find himself "this once in agreement ... with Sidney Hook."[30] Hook had taken Dewey's expression, "a common faith," to characterize their commitment to democracy. Maritain shares this commitment with them, which they alike affirm as a common and substantive good. Marx can be read as a theorist of radical economic democracy; Dewey, as a theorist of participatory democracy; Maritain, as a theorist of personalist democracy. Democracy itself is the common good that enlists their common faith.

A disenchanted liberalism that has no doctrine of the common good and its priority in social and political life will go, however, in one of two directions. Either it will privatize all substantive values, including religious ones, or it will recast them in the image of the commodity form, understanding and interpreting them as objects of consumer choice, acknowledging no higher public good than this. In his agreeable response to Hook, Maritain presciently writes,

> the error [of individualist optimism] lay in conceiving of free society as a perfectly *neutral* boxing-ring in which all possible ideas about society and the bases of social life meet and battle it out, without the Body Politic's being concerned with the maintenance of any common conditions and inspiration. Thus democratic society, in its concrete behavior, had no *concept* of itself, and freedom, disarmed and paralyzed, lay exposed to the undertakings of those who hated it, and who tried by all means to foster in [human beings] a vicious desire to become free from freedom.[31]

The immediate referent of "those who hated" freedom is the totalitarian forms of fascism and communism or Stalinism, but the ultimate scope of this passage clearly reaches even further.

Maritain develops a fuller version of his argument in *Man and the State*, from which I quote at some length:

> a society of free [people] implies basic tenets which are at the core of its very existence. A genuine democracy implies a fundamental agreement between minds and wills on the bases of life in common; it is aware of itself and of its principles, and it must be capable of defending and promoting its own conception of social and political life; it must bear within itself a common human creed, the creed of freedom. The mistake of "bourgeois" liberalism has been to conceive democratic society to be a kind of lists or arena in which all the conceptions of the bases of common life, even those most destructive to freedom and law, meet with no more than the pure and simple indifference of the body politic, while they compete before public opinion in a kind of free market of the mother-ideas, healthy or poisoned, of political life. Nineteenth-century "bourgeois" democracy was *neutral* even with regard to freedom. Just as it had no real *common good*, it had no real *common thought* – no brains of its own, but a neutral, empty skull clad with mirrors: ... it had become a society without any idea of itself and without faith in itself, without any *common faith* which could enable it to resist disintegration.[32]

This passage, which deserves more commentary than I can offer here, seems to me just as much to characterize bourgeois democracy at the close of the twentieth century – the new laissez-faire of the New World Order, the renewed reign of Marx's "free-trader *vulgaris*" – as it ever did in Maritain's nineteenth century (except that today it is exponentially larger, faster, and more all-encompassing than it ever was then). This is the form of "democracy" that Marx, Dewey, and Maritain alike reject on behalf of an authentic conception. In the light of the contemporary communitarian critique of liberalism, and from the perspective of a radical version of that critique, informed by socialist and feminist arguments concerning solidarity and difference, community and autonomy, Maritain's words might stand out more boldly now than they did in a time when it was easier to take his theses for granted.

I will close as I began on a personal note, addressing why I chose to bring Maritain into conversation with Marx and Dewey. The choice may seem inapt when we think of the enormous work carried out in political theology, feminist theology, and the theology of liberation since Maritain's day that might have offered a more contemporary Catholic conversation partner for my antecedent engagement with Marx and Dewey. However, it is just to the point to think of Maritain as a "dangerous memory," writing and thinking in a time that is lost to us now, just as the commodity form of life steadily advances. His thought can hardly be regarded as a fad in Catholic theology, drawing down the suspicion of ecclesiastical authorities. Instead, I find it both provocative and sad to think that he belonged to the mainstream of Catholic opinion in the decades in which he wrote. There is a warning here about how swiftly the church should accommodate itself to a world more capitalist than ever before, where tradition seems all too easily confused with a theme park.

Notes

1. Moishe Postone, *Time, Labor, and Social Domination: A Reinterpretation of Marx's Critical Theory* (New York: Cambridge University Press, 1993).

2. See Bill Martin, *Matrix and Line* (Albany, NY: SUNY Press, 1992); *Humanism and its Aftermath* (Atlantic Heights, NJ: Humanities Press, 1995); and *Politics in the Impasse: Explorations in postsecular social theory* (Albany, NY: SUNY Press, 1996).

3. Jacques Maritain, *Integral Humanism: Temporal and Spiritual Problems of a New Christendom*, trans. J. W. Evans (New York: Charles Scribner's Sons, 1968), pp. 46–47.

4. Karl Marx, "A Contribution to the Critique of Hegel's Philosophy of Right: Introduction (1844)," *The Marx-Engels Reader*, ed. R. Tucker (New York: Norton, 2nd ed., 1978), pp. 11–12.

5. Karl Marx, *The Economic and Philosophic Manuscripts of 1844*, trans. M. Milligan (New York: International Publishers, 1964), pp.145–146.

6. Karl Marx, "On the Jewish Question," *The Marx-Engels Reader*, ed. R. Tucker (New York: Norton, 2nd ed., 1978), pp. 26–52.

7. Karl Marx, *Capital* 1, trans. Ben Fowkes (New York: Vintage Books, 1977), pp. 165, 173.

8. Karl Marx, *Capital* 3, trans. D. Fernbach (New York: Vintage Books, 1981), p. 969.

9. John Dewey, "A Common Faith, " *John Dewey: The Later Works 9*, ed. Jo Ann Boydston (Carbondale, IL: SIU Press, 1985), p. 36.

10. Maritain, *Integral Humanism*, p. 39.

11. Ibid., p. 6.

12. Ibid., p. 31.

13. Ibid., p. 60.

14. Marx, *Capital* 1, p. 742.

15. Ibid.

16. Ibid.

17. Ibid.

18. Maritain, *Integral Humanism*, pp. 201–202.

19. Ibid., pp. 190-191.

20. Ibid., p. 190.

21. Ibid., pp. 188, 189, 192.

22. Ibid., pp. 193, 274, 275ff., 236–239.

23. Ibid., pp. 266–267, n. 4.

24. Maritain, *The Rights of Man and Natural Law* (New York: Charles Scribner's Sons, 1943), pp. 54–55.

25. *John Dewey: Religious Faith and Democratic Humanism* (New York: Columbia University Press, 1991).

26. Dewey, "A Common Faith," pp. 54–55.

27. Maritain, *The Rights of Man*, p. 4.

28. Ibid., p. 7.

29. Maritain, *The Range of Reason* (New York: Charles Scribner's Sons, 1952), p. 167.

30. Ibid., p. 171.

31. Ibid., p. 166.

32. *Man and the State*, in *The Social and Political Philosophy of Jacques Maritain*, eds. Evans & Ward (New York: Charles Scribner's Sons, 1955), pp. 136–137.

PART II

THE UNIVERSAL DECLARATION AND THE PRACTICE OF HUMAN RIGHTS

Six

HUMAN RIGHTS: FIFTY YEARS LATER

Mostafa Faghfoury

1. A Simple Distinction

There are, at least, two general ways of viewing humanity. On one account, humanity is a single entity which encompasses the whole human species: past, present, and future. On this account, whether humanity is created by God or has evolved, each person has a single origin, lives with others, forms communities, thinks and reasons, and aims for a common good.

The Persian poet Sa'di (1212–92) summarized this view of the humanity in the following verses.

> All members of each other are mankind
> Since all of one sole ore have been refined
> One member's pain of body, heart or mind
> Means that the rest no lasting peace can find.
> Thou who to share thy brother's pang declined
> Thy claim to share the name of "man" resigned.[1]

In Matthew 28:19–20, Jesus gives similar instruction, "Go ye therefore and teach all nations ... to observe all things whatever I have commanded you." The universality of the message for "all nations" is repeated in the letter to the Romans 10:12–13, "There is no distinction between Jew and Greek; for the same Lord is Lord of all." I like to call this view of humanity "inclusive."

By contrast, another approach is exclusive, viewing each human being as a particular entity belonging to a distinct nation, tribe, or country, with a specific religion or ideology, economic status and in short, anthropological distinctiveness. An example of a popular sixteenth-century saying demonstrates the exclusive approach, "Let us acknowledge God's grace in making us men, not beasts, Christians, not Moors, Spaniards not men of another nation." Another popular view among Castilians was "I swear to God I am as noble as the king and more so as he is half Flemish."[2] The notion of a people chosen by God was not limited to the Spaniards; in England, Foxe's *Book of Martyrs* propagated the same idea. The Scots had an older tradition, which the Covenanters invoked. The Swedes saw themselves as heirs of the Goths, the oldest nation of the world, and the Greeks saw themselves as the teachers of civilization. Turkish and Arabic conquest of Europe was motivated by the belief that others were not fully human, and therefore needed salvation.

By the early seventeenth century, as the boundaries of Europe were drawn, the identity of the European as a true Christian was exhibited by a similar exclusive description. Speaking of the European view, Samuel Purchas writes, "Jesus Christ is their way, their truth, their life, who hath long since given a Bill of Divorce to ingratefull Asia where he was borne, and Africa the place of his flight ... and is become almost wholly and onely European."[3]

This kind of approach was not limited to the European and Moslem conquerors. The Chinese, who defined all outsiders as barbarians, had four words for foreigners: "north barbarians," "east barbarians," "south barbarians," and "west barbarians." Even though they allowed some limited trade with the foreigners and permitted imperial princesses to marry other rulers, the Chinese still considered themselves a more advanced culture.

Small groups that wanted to remain distinct and did not want to be incorporated became the targets of onslaught from the powerful majority. The decimation of American Indians at the hands of Spanish, British, and French settlers; the treatment of Jews in many countries of Europe; and the use of Africans as slaves reveal the continuous and perpetual violence toward "others" by those who defined themselves as "us."

Michele de Cuneo, an Italian nobleman who traveled with Columbus on his second "discovery," had an encounter with a young "nameless" native Carib woman, and he describes the encounter his diary.

> While I was in the boat I captured a very beautiful Carib woman, and with whom, having taken her into my Cabin, she being naked according to their custom, I conceived desire to take pleasure. I wanted to put my desire into execution but she did not want it and treated me with her finger nails in such a manner that I wished I had never begun. But seeing that ... I took a rope and thrashed her well for which she raised unheard of screams that you would not have believed your ears. Finally we came to an agreement in such manner that I can tell you she seemed to have been brought up in a school of harlots.[4]

My intention is not to generalize about the mistreatment of powerless minorities by dominant forces in the world. My intention is to argue that our actions or relations toward "others" are shaped by the way we view one another. If we view the "other" as "us," we would probably live at least by the Golden Rule. However, if we view the other as different from us, as an inferior, we would treat him or her as a thing, not as a human person, and if we view the other as superior, we would act in submission and still not with parity. The distinction between "exclusive" and "inclusive," if it is correct, may explain two different consequences of human actions in the history of humanity. War, slavery, torture, extermination, genocide, and discrimination are manifestations of the "exclusive" view. Peace, cooperation, love, fairness, and justice among people are results of treating others like "us." Kant's thesis that there cannot be a war between democratic societies and states still holds.

At almost the same time as Michele de Cuneo, the Italian "nobleman," is raping a native girl in America, another Italian is writing a magnificent essay on the *Dignity of Man*. Pico della Mirandola, a true Renaissance scholar, believes that human beings are created in the likeness of God. This is the essence of humanism, which spread from Italy to the whole of Europe, reaching perhaps to Erasmus and Thomas More. Pico sees in humanity a dignity that is God's gift. When the spiritual and rational is ignored, humanity falls to the level of the beasts. When it is elevated, humanity becomes God-like.

The views of Pico on human dignity echo in the writings of Jacques Maritain almost five hundred years later.

> Man is an individual who holds himself in hand by his intelligence and his will ... he has spiritual superexistence through knowledge and love. He is thus in some fashion a whole, not merely a part; he is a universe unto himself, a microcosm in which the whole great universe can be encompassed through knowledge and through love he can give himself freely to beings who are, as it were, other selves to him ... It is to this mystery of our nature that religious thought points when it says that the human person is the image of God.[5]

2. Fifty Years Earlier

In 1895, Winston Churchill rushed to Cuba. The occasion was the Spanish war against the Cuban insurgency. He predicted that the war would be the last war ever in which whites would fight whites, and he had to be present. Soon into the twentieth century, however, not only did he witness two homegrown European wars that involved the whole world, he actively participated in both.

On 1 August 1914, when the German troops entered Luxembourg, the process of marking the twentieth century as the bloodiest period in human history began. The promise of a new European civilization becoming a symbol for human achievement soon started to fade. Hundreds of thousands of young soldiers were routinely killed on single mornings, soon after leaving their trenches. At Verdun on the first day of their attack, the Germans fired one million shells on the French lines. Instead of being concerned with the high casualties and reconsidering their tactics, those who were in charge became more determined in insisting on "their way" of conducting the war. Ironically, the war did not yield the intended, and most often already announced, results.

At the root of the war was nationalism. Kant's student and personal friend J.G. Herder believed that a good and civilized state should have natural borders, borders that coincided with the places occupied by its nation. The idea of the nation-state was conceived in 1785 and revisited later by Fichte, who argued that a nation's natural borders should be determined by language. Fichte provided German nationalism with its first philosophical articulation. But with the war, the nationalist experiment with men and women believing themselves to be in control of their destiny came to a speedy and disastrous conclusion. The prophecy of the *Encyclopaedia Britannica* in 1910, that "the coming nationality will be essentially a matter of education and economics," never materialized.

Instead of dealing with and attending to the causes of the war, namely tribalism and nationalism in Europe, at the end of the First World War and the treaty of Versailles, the principle of the nation-state was reconfirmed and new smaller nations were created. A recipe for disaster. The road to hell, we are told, is paved with good intentions. Woodrow Wilson became an advocate of a doctrine of national self-determination that, at least by the end of the first war, should have proven to be deeply flawed. The Wilsonian doctrine was embraced by Thomas Masaryk, a professor of philosophy in the U.S. who became the founder and the first president of Czechoslovakia.

Sir Karl Popper remarks, "The terrible effect of Wilson's attempt to apply this romantic principle to European politics should be clear by now to everybody."[6] Popper thinks the principle of national self-determination is "inapplicable on this earth, especially in Europe, where the nations (i.e., linguistic groups) are so densely packed that it is quite impossible to disentangle them."[7] He challenges the belief that the failure of the Wilsonian experiment in Europe was because it was not applied properly. He believes that such a doctrine is inapplicable in principle.

Popper's political solution to European tribalism/nationalism can be found in a footnote where he writes about Czechoslovakia,

> Masaryk's Czechoslovakia was probably one of the best and most democratic states that ever existed, but in spite of all that, it was built on the principle of national state, on a principle which in this world is inapplicable. An international federation in the Danube basin might have prevented much.[8]

The birth, life, and death of Czechoslovakia in this century is a sad tale in human history. The country was born in 1914, mainly to create a barrier against the future military expansion of the German army. It was occupied in the 1930s by the same forces it was supposed to stop, handed over to the Russians as a prize for winning the Second World War, dominated by the Red Army for more than forty years, and finally came to a sudden death in 1990. The story of Czechoslovakia in the twentieth century is the story of Europe. Suffering, war, occupation, discrimination, famine, unemployment, and political oppression are sad chapters of a book about the fifty years prior to the Universal Declaration of Human Rights.

3. Fifty Years Ago

When the German troops crossed the borders of Poland in 1937, they violated an international law, proved again the dangers of mighty neighbors, and caused the death of the League of Nations as an effective international organization committed to peace and the defense of the principle of national self-determination. They also introduced the world to a new reality, not previously experienced on such a large scale. Soon, the modern consciousness and vocabulary filled with phrases such as mass starvation, forcible confinement, systemic discrimination, concentration camps, mass exodus, torture and ill treatment, gas chamber, labor camps, and holocaust, to name just a few.

Death, which was a private and personal experience until 1914, much like sex, became an inseparable part of public life. An exaggerated example of the changed attitude about it can be found in the Spanish Fascists' slogan, "Long live Death!"

War memorials, in almost every village or city around the world, are living reminders of both the heroism of soldiers and officers and the stupidity and incompetence of politicians and generals. A British officer, in an article on Egypt, observed that the Egyptian peasant would make an admirable soldier "if he only wished to kill someone." The first fifty years of the twentieth century were dominated by two world wars, millions of deaths, indescribable destruction, and an ironic and tragic end. The use of the atomic bomb in Japan demonstrates two distinct aspects of a new humanity. First, it shows the irrationality of human actions; in order to win the war we need to risk everything including ourselves. Second, the new humanity has reached a level of technological advancement where we can destroy perhaps the only inhabited place in the universe. The new humanity has become god-like, capable of eliminating God's masterpiece, the universe and everything that goes with it.

From the ashes of two world wars, over the corpses of millions of humans in this century alone, and after witnessing the pain and suffering of survivors, on 10 December 1948 was born a simple short text that cries out "enough is enough."

The Universal Declaration of Human Rights is called very appropriately "a Magna Charta for Mankind." Unlike the American Bill of Rights (1791), whose father was Thomas Jefferson, the Universal Declaration had many parents. It came about due to the contributions of individuals from different parts of the world whose experience enriched the document. At the forefront, Mrs. Eleanor Roosevelt's commitment to the cause of human rights made her a truly universal person. Ironically perhaps, although most violations of human rights are by men, we see that a woman is a principal champion of human rights. The other members of the drafting committee were learned gentlemen: Dr. Peng-Chun Chang, a scholarly Chinese diplomat; Dr. Charles H. Malik of Lebanon, a Harvard-educated Christian humanist with an ever-ready reference to St. Thomas; and Dr. John Humphrey, a Canadian lawyer who was the UN director of the Human Rights Division. Mrs. Roosevelt's important role was to help her distinguished colleagues place their highly philosophical and legal ideas into words that the average person anywhere in the world can understand. Drafting a document that would be binding on all nations, representative of common values of every culture and religion, and simple enough to be understood by everyone seemed to be an impossible task, but it was achieved. Other notable contributors were René Cassin from France, Hernan Santa Cruz from Chile, Professor Vladimir Koretsky from the Soviet Union, and Geoffrey Wilson from the United Kingdom.[9]

The final draft of the Declaration was put to a vote at one o'clock in the morning of 6 December 1948, at the Third Committee of the UN. Although no country voted against it, there were seven abstentions. Byelorussia, Canada, Czechoslovakia, Poland, the Ukraine, the Soviet Union, and Yugoslavia. Saudi Arabia and South Africa did not participate.

Four days later, at three o'clock in the morning, the *Declaration* was before the General Assembly. Forty-eight countries in favor, none against, two absent and eight abstentions (the Soviet Union, Ukraine, Czechoslovakia, Byelorussia, Poland, Yugoslavia, South Africa, and Saudi Arabia). Canada decided to change its stance, joining the majority. Lester Pearson explained his country's earlier vote and reservation by saying that "the Declaration was often worded in vague and unprecise language."[10]

We have here an extraordinary achievement in the history of humanity. The reaction to the Declaration has generally been of two kinds: some consider the Declaration to be an international statement with no power, authority, and enforcement. Others see it as a moral manifesto of the inclusive approach to humanity. My bias lies with the latter group.

4. Opposition to the Declaration

In 1948, the major argument of "collectivists" – the Soviet Union and its East European allies – against the Declaration was that the Declaration recognized individual rights, with little or no reference to collective rights. In the words of the Polish representative, the rights in the final draft "represented a step backward if compared with the Declaration of the Rights of Man and the Citizen, which had been produced during the French Revolution; if compared with the Communist Manifesto, which had declared human rights as binding and necessary a hundred years ago; and if compared with the principles which had inspired the October Revolution."[11] Yugoslavs thought that a system of social rights needed to be widened to include the collective rights of certain communities. As Professor James Nickel has noted:

> Human rights seem to be viewed by the Soviets merely as goals and not necessarily even as high priority goals ... The Soviets tend to emphasize the duties of individuals as much as their rights, and in conflicts between the interests of individuals and the goals of the country, the Soviets seldom favour the individuals ... [However they] made good progress in providing for the material well-being of their citizens and thus in implementing economic and social rights.[12]

This opposition to the Declaration is directed more against traditional liberalism than the document itself. However in the last twenty years some notable philosophers, like Charles Taylor, have further advanced this argument.

Another argument against the Declaration came from moral relativists, who held that human rights cannot or should not be extended to all people in the world. The earliest version of this view was presented by the American Anthropological Association in 1947.[13] The Association condemned the Declaration as an example of ethnocentrism that recognizes only the cultural values prevalent in Western Europe and America. It went on to argue that since no scientific method of qualitatively evaluating cultures has been discovered, respect for cultural differences should remain.

Another popular, but inadequately examined, argument comes from some "Islamic" countries. According to this view, there are serious conflicts between human rights norms and Islamic beliefs and practices. Since the Declaration does not address the latter, the former cannot be universally imposed on the Islamic countries. During the deliberation in the Third Committee, Jamil Baroody, a Christian from Lebanon, but representing Saudi Arabia, said that Article 18 of the Declaration, which states the right of everyone to change his religion or belief, is in opposition to the rule of the Koran.[14]

The sovereignist argument against universal human rights is that since states are empowered to pass laws for their own citizens, and since even the UN's charter recognizes the principle of self-determination, any pressure on a member state to respect human rights that conflict with internal laws is deemed an interference with the domestic affairs of the country. Ambassador Vishinsky of the Soviet Union in a speech at the UN in 1948 regretted that the Declaration makes no mention of the sovereign rights of states. He forgot that "the struggle for human rights has always been and always will be a struggle against authority."[15]

Finally, we find the argument that social and economic rights in certain situations may be in conflict with some political and natural rights like political participation and dissent. On this view, human rights can be a barrier to development. In a state with ethnic conflict, a weak economy, and high illiteracy, respect for human rights may be counterproductive. This argument in a stronger version may even lead to the conclusion that severe policies aimed to stop political opposition are justifiable under certain circumstances. Countries with a one-party system may use this argument. Even some liberal philosophers have allowed for versions of this argument. Thus, J.S. Mill is prepared, on utilitarian grounds, to limit freedom of expression if it benefits the public. Even John Rawls has argued that political rights may be temporarily suspended in favor of economic and social development where such development is so low that these rights cannot be meaningfully implemented.[16]

5. Fifty Years Later

To talk about human rights is not only to talk about philosophy and history – it is to talk about real issues concerning concrete cases. Whether human rights are intrinsically or instrumentally valuable, they must also produce results. To consider the Universal Declaration of Human Rights only for its legal, political, or international applications is to miss its real force in the last fifty years. The moral appeal of the Declaration is its greatest achievement.

Critics argue that the Declaration has no enforcement mechanism. However, they always neglect to mention that legal enforcement is not that crucial with respect to moral obligations.

In some fifty years since the passage of the Declaration, the world has witnessed the good, the bad, and the ugly.

First, the good: The *Declaration* has inspired many countries, nations, and people to change their lives for the better. In writing their constitutions, many new countries have used the document as a foundation. Some countries have changed their domestic laws in order to align them with the articles in the Declaration. Daniel Paul, a Mi'kmaq Indian and former commissioner of the Nova Scotia Human Rights Commission, writes,

> An event that slowly but surely compelled Canada and Nova Scotia to repeal their written and unwritten "apartheid laws" was the signing at the U.N. of the Universal Declaration of Human Rights. The ratification of this document by Canada caused the bigots then loose on the Canadian political scene to alter their public postures. They were no longer free to make discriminatory remarks in public about race, creed, colour, religion or sex, at least not with the impunity they had enjoyed in the past ... Canada's hypocrisy caught up with it in 1956. Someone "suddenly" discovered that the country, from its birth in 1867 had denied citizenship to its First Nation peoples. What to do? Enact legislation, and make it retroactive to 1947 to make it appear that they were citizens before Canada signed the Declaration.[17]

Almost at the same time, Dr. Martin Luther King inspired blacks in the U.S. to challenge some of America's discriminatory laws. Struggles for ending the "separate but equal" principle led to the successful ending in the Brown vs. the Board of Education case before the Supreme Court.

Different regional organizations have adopted the Declaration as part of their charters. The European Convention on Human Rights (1966), the American Convention on Human Rights (1969), and the African Charter on Human and Peoples' Rights (1984) are examples of international documents inspired by the Declaration.

Many political prisoners, who may have gone unrecognized in the past, have been released from jail, and in cases like Lech Walesa, Vaclav Havel, and Nelson Mandela have become elected leaders of their respective countries, Poland, the Czech Republic, and South Africa. Although torture, racism, discrimination, and many other violations of human rights still exist, they have become moral stigmas.

Second, the bad: Although there have been many advances in the areas of human rights, in many countries, including democratic states, there are still serious violations of human rights. Capital punishment in forty states in the U.S. is a serious breach of articles 3, 5, and 6 of the Declaration. Many countries systematically employ a double standard and are hypocritical in dealing with the violators of human rights. If the occupation of Kuwait by the Iraqi government is contrary to the UN *Charter* and its Declaration of Human Rights, so is the long occupation of Palestinian land by Israelis.

Some countries are pro human rights at home and violators of them abroad. As if the moral commitment recognizes artificial borders! As the ink of the Declaration was drying, the CIA was planning to overthrow the democratically elected governments of Iran, Guatemala, and Chile.

Third, the ugly: The struggle for human rights is a journey from invisibility to recognition, from being nobody to becoming someone. The most important article in the Declaration, in my view, is Article 6, "Everyone has the right to recognition everywhere as a person before the law," when it is read in light of the first article, "All human beings are born free and equal in dignity and rights. They are endowed with reason and conscience and should act toward one another in a spirit of brotherhood." If the lessons of the past are not learned, if we do not start treating and viewing each other as equals and as equally valuable, the next thousand years on the earth will be tough and the world a difficult place in which to live. That is ugly.

Notes

1. Sultanhussein Tabandeh, *A Muslim Commentary on the Universal Declaration of Human Rights*, trans. F.J. Goulding (Guildford: F.J. Goulding, 1970), p. 16.

2. J.D. Cooper, "The Decline of Spain and the Thirty Year War (1609-48/59)," *The New Cambridge Modern History*, Vol. 4 (Cambridge, MA: Cambridge University Press, 1971), pp. 4–5.

3. Ibid., p. 5, attributed to Samuel Purchas (1625).

4. David Stannard, *The American Holocaust: The Conquest of the New World* (Oxford: Oxford University Press, 1993), p. 84.

5. Jacques Maritain, *The Rights of Man and Natural Law*, trans. Doris C. Anson (New York: Scribners, 1943), pp. 3–4.

6. Sir Karl Popper, *The Open Society and Its Enemies*, Vol. 2 (Princeton, NJ: Princeton University Press, 1971), p. 318.

7. Ibid.

8. Ibid, p. 312.

9. See John P. Humphrey, *Human Rights and the United Nations: A Great Adventure* (New York: Transnational Publishers Inc., 1984); Joseph P. Lash, *Eleanor: The Years Alone*, (New York: New American Library, 1973), pp. 46–72; Charles Malik, "The Universal Declaration of Human Rights," *Free and Equal*, ed. O. Frederick Nolde (Geneva: World Council of Churches, 1968), pp. 7–13.

10. *Summary from the United Nations Yearbook 1948 - Chapter V., Social, Humanitarian and Cultural Questions; Section A., Human Rights* (at http:// www.udhr.org/ history/yearbook.htm).

11. Ibid.

12. James W. Nickel, *Making Sense of Human Rights: Philosophical Reflections on the Universal Declaration of Human Rights* (Berkeley, CA: University of California Press, 1987), pp. 64–65.

13. "Statement on Human Rights," *American Anthropologist* 49:4 (1947), pp. 539–543; reprinted in *The Philosophy of Human Rights*, ed. Morton E. Winston (Belmont, CA: Wadsworth Publishing Company, 1989), pp. 116–120.

14. See *God and Man in Contemporary Islamic Thought*, ed. Charles Malik (Beirut: American University of Beirut, 1972); Reza Afshari, "An Essay on Islamic Cultural Relativism in the Discourse of Human Rights," *Human Rights Quarterly*, 16:2 (1994), pp. 235–276.

15. John Humphrey, *Human Rights and the United Nations*, p. 41.

16. John Rawls, *A Theory of Justice* (Cambridge, MA: Harvard University Press, 1971), p. 542.

17. Daniel Paul, *We Were Not the Savages* (Halifax, NS: Nimbus Publishing Ltd., 1993), pp. 301–302.

Seven

THE UNIVERSAL DECLARATION OF HUMAN RIGHTS, MARITAIN, AND THE UNIVERSALITY OF HUMAN RIGHTS

Bradley R. Munro

1. The Universal Declaration of Human Rights

The Universal Declaration of Human Rights (UDHR) was proclaimed by the General Assembly of the United Nations on 10 December 1948. That the Universal Declaration could be proclaimed by a body representative of most of the world's states is a remarkable achievement and worthy of celebration in this so-called post-modern world. Indeed, most of the states that since joined the General Assembly have also endorsed the UDHR. Truly remarkable about this tremendous achievement is the UDHR embracing a whole series of principles and value statements that define what constitutes human dignity. The world has an exceedingly rich array of cultures, languages, religions, and competing value systems. This broad set of differences has come together in the endorsement, by the states of the world, of the comprehensive statement/declaration of principles and values in the UDHR. The peoples of the world, as represented by their envoys to the world body, have agreed on a basic set of principles and values by which they could be judged by their peers. In contradistinction of the current philosophical tendency (post-modernism) that pervades late-twentieth-century thought and the relativism that it breeds, the UDHR is an example of a universal adoption of a set of universal principles and values.

Following the proclamation of the Universal Declaration, the United Nations set about developing what became known as the "International Bill of Rights." While the UDHR had moral force, the three instruments of the bill, the International Covenant on Economic, Social and Cultural Rights; the International Covenant on Civil and Political Rights; and its Optional Protocol were developed as legal instruments with binding force in international law. While the General Assembly adopted them on 16 December 1966, it was 1976 before they were ratified by a sufficient number of countries (35 for the Covenants and 10 for the Optional Protocol) for them to come into force. The International Covenant on Economic, Social and Cultural Rights came into force on 3 January 1976 and the International Covenant on Civil and Political Rights and its Optional Protocol came into force on 23 March 1976. The Optional Protocol permits private individuals to send communications (for example, complaints of human rights violations) for consideration by the Human Rights Committee. The Human Rights Committee is established under the International Covenant on Civil and Political Rights and consists of eighteen individuals elected by the states that have ratified the Covenant. These individuals act in their own capacity and are chosen for their high moral character and their recognized competence in the human rights field. The Human Rights Committee is charged with hearing communications (for example, complaints) from one state about another state's violations.

Generally, when a country ratifies the two Covenants, the nation intends to undertake to protect the rights of its citizens as reflected in the UDHR. In addition to the rights of individuals found in the UDHR, the Covenants added the rights of peoples to self-determination and thereby to "freely determine their political status and freely pursue their economic, social and cultural development."[1]

2. Maritain and the Universal Applicability of the Universal Declaration of Human Rights

Perhaps the most pressing issue with respect to the UDHR is the question of its applicability to all. Given the multitude of different cultures, languages, traditions, and religions, all with differing moral and value systems, how can we claim that the rights contained in the UDHR have universal application? Today there is real fear that the consensus won around the principles and values of the UDHR is beginning to unravel. Some view it as a document that reflects white Northern European and American values and not those of the peoples of the Southern Hemisphere and the Asian continent. To quote from a speech given by an economic advisor to the Malaysian government, "Developing countries particularly from the South have always been skeptical of the West's insistence that they conform to the high ideals to which even the performance of the West falls below what is expected."[2] While we could argue that the UDHR was a product of Western philosophical thought, it was not created without input by persons from other backgrounds. With this problem in mind, I was drawn to chapter four, "The Rights of Man," of Maritain's book *Man and the State*. The first division of this chapter is entitled "Men Mutually Opposed in Their Theoretical Conceptions Can Come to a Merely Practical Agreement Regarding a List of Human Rights."[3] This title reflects Maritain's conclusion that people can come to agree on a list of human rights regardless of different ideological backgrounds. So, in some sense, the question of getting peoples of differing cultures, languages, religions, and ideological backgrounds to agree on what human rights are applicable is not unique to the 1990s, but was also an issue when the UDHR was being developed.

John P. Humphrey, author of the first draft of the UDHR, the so-called Secretariat Outline, tells us in *Human Rights & the United Nations: A Great Adventure* that among others, like Mrs. Roosevelt (USA) who chaired the drafting committee, Russian Professor Vladimir Koretsky, the Chinese scholar P.C. Chang, and Hernan Santa Cruz from Chile, "had considerable influence with delegations representing the economically developing countries, whose cases he sometimes argued with great energy."[4] Of the origin of his first draft, Humphrey writes,

> I was put on the spot at the very first meeting. Colonel Hodgson wanted to know what principles the Secretariat had used in the preparation of its draft and what was the philosophy behind it. He should have known that any answer that I could give to his question would, in that ideologically divided group, get me and my draft into hot water. I therefore replied that the draft was not based on any particular philosophy; it included rights recognized by various national constitutions and also a number of suggestions that had been made for an international bill of rights. I wasn't going to tell him that insofar as it reflected the views of its author – who had in any event to remain anonymous – the draft attempted to combine humanitarian liberalism with social democracy. Essentially, my answer was true, because my draft was based on the documentation that I had before me. But I had myself decided what to put in and what to leave out, and I had made changes and additions. A more expansive reply would have been indiscreet to the point of compromising the work of the commission. Later, Colonel Hodgson took me to task over my Article 25, which said that everything not prohibited by law is permitted. That, he said, was pure nonsense. It did not deserve the scorn that Hodgson poured on it; the principle is an expression of the rule of law and, as I could have told him, was enshrined in the fifth article of the French Declaration of 1789 on the Rights of Man and the Citizen.[5]

Maritain discussed this when, as head of the delegation from France to the UNESCO's second General Conference held in Mexico City in November 1947, he was elected chairperson of the Conference. In that role he spoke to the Opening Plenary session on 6 November 1947. In chapter four of *Man and the State*, he quotes from his UNESCO speech. His remarks relate to the agreement being reached at the time on the document that was to become the Universal Declaration of Human Rights. In their preparations for the General Conference, members of the French National Commission for UNESCO expressed astonishment that persons who came from vastly differing and sometimes opposing ideological backgrounds were able to come to agreement on the list of human rights. Maritain faced the issue head on in his speech to the Opening Plenary.

> How ... is an agreement conceivable among men assembled for the purpose of jointly accomplishing a task dealing with the future of the mind, who come from the four corners of the earth and who belong not only to different cultures and civilizations, but to different spiritual families and antagonistic schools of thought? Since the aim of UNESCO is a practical aim, agreement among its members can be spontaneously achieved, not on common speculative notions,

but on common practical notions, not on the affirmation of the same conception of the world, man, and knowledge, but on the affirmation of the same set of convictions concerning action. This is doubtless very little, it is the last refuge of intellectual agreement among men. It is, however, enough to undertake a great work; and it would mean a great deal to become aware of this body of common practical convictions.

I should like to note that the word "ideology" and the word "principle" can be understood in two different ways. I have just said that the present state of intellectual division among men does not permit agreement on a common "speculative" ideology or common "principles." However, when it concerns the basic "practical" ideology and the basic principles of "action," implicitly recognized today, in a vital if not formulated manner, by the consciousness of free peoples, it constitutes *grosso modo* – a sort of common residue, an unwritten common law, at the point of practical convergence of extremely different theoretical ideologies and spiritual traditions. To understand that, it is sufficient to distinguish properly between the rational justifications, inseparable from the spiritual dynamism of a philosophical doctrine or religious faith, and the practical conclusions which, separately justified for each, are, for all, analogically common principles of action. I am fully convinced my way of justifying the belief in the rights of man and the ideal of freedom, equality, and fraternity is the only belief solidly based on truth. That does not prevent me from agreeing on these practical tenets with those who are convinced their way of justifying them, entirely different from mine or even opposed to mine in its theoretical dynamism, is likewise the only one based on truth. Assuming they both believe in the democratic charter, a Christian and a rationalist will, nevertheless, give justifications incompatible with each other, justifications to which their souls, minds, and blood are committed, and over which they will fight. And God keep me from saying it is not important to know which of the two is right! That is essentially important. They remain, however, in agreement on the practical affirmation of that charter, and they can formulate together common principles of action.[6]

Simply put, Maritain is saying that people can agree on practical conclusions while disagreeing on theoretical means for justifying those conclusions. To use a geographical metaphor, many roads lead to the same practical destination, or as he put it in the subtitle quoted above, "Men mutually opposed in their theoretical conceptions can come to a merely practical agreement regarding a list of human rights." The word "merely," as in "merely practical agreement," is a key word and reveals Maritain's attitude towards what we would now, in retrospect, call a remarkable achievement. Maritain's attitude seems to be dismissive, whereas I think it would be important to pursue first the issue of how such agreement was possible in the first place, and then figure out how to apply these rights in the everyday world in which we live. Maritain does not pursue these questions here.

While he grants that on the practical level it is possible to come to agreement "by a collective effort of comparing, recasting, and perfecting the drafts in order to make them acceptable to all as points of practical convergence," he believes that "it is not reasonably possible to hope for more than this practical convergence on a set of articles drafted in common."[7]

In chapter four, Maritain moves on to explain his theoretical basis for human rights. This is important as it will help us understand Maritain's own particular philosophy which, as we saw in the lengthy passage above, he considers "the only one which is solidly based on truth." I will follow Maritain's argument to see if perhaps some of his insights may be helpful with the practical problems posed for human rights advocates today in the face of challenges coming from countries like China and Malaysia. Such difficulties are reflected in the above quotation from Tum Diam Zamudin.

3. Maritain's Own Theoretical Basis for Human Rights

For the rest of chapter four, Maritain sets out his theoretical basis for human rights based on a version of Aquinas's Natural Law theory. He says "the philosophical foundation of the Rights of man is Natural Law." Since Maritain grounds human rights in natural law, we must examine his natural law theory to get at his view of human rights. Maritain is careful to distinguish his version of natural law from other natural law doctrines which he believes went wrong,[8] especially those deriving from Pascal through to Rousseau and Kant. He wrote:

> Through a fatal mistake, natural law – which is *within* the being of things as their very essence is, and which precedes all formulation, and is even known to human reason *not* in terms of conceptual and rational knowledge – natural law was then conceived after the pattern of a *written* code, applicable to all, of which any just law should be a transcription, and which would determine *a priori* and in all its aspects the norms of human behavior through ordinances supposedly prescribed by Nature and Reason, but in reality arbitrarily and artificially formulated."[9]

Maritain viewed these natural law theories as window-dressing for justifying arbitrarily imposed laws. He saw this as founding law on an illusion and depreciating the rights of the human person. For Maritain, natural law theory "compromised and squandered these rights, because it led men to conceive their rights in themselves divine, hence infinite, escaping every objective measure, denying every limitation imposed upon the claims of the ego, and ultimately expressing the absolute independence of the human subject ..."[10] The impossibility of this rationalist approach turned people against human rights. Maritain, therefore, embarks on a journey to set things right again and to rebase human rights on a true philosophy and a true idea of natural law – based on an analogical perspective.

Let us break out Maritain's argument found on pages 85–87 of *Man and the State* into steps:[11]

1. "[T]here is a human nature."
2. "[T]his human nature is the same in all men."
3. "[M]an is a being gifted with intelligence."
4. Man "acts with an understanding of what he is doing."
5. Man has "the power to determine for himself the ends which he pursues" (Free Will).
6. "[M]an possesses ends which necessarily correspond to his essential constitution and which are the same for all;" just like a piano has a particular end of producing certain sounds.
7. Because man is intelligent and determines his own ends, " it is up to him to put himself in tune with the ends necessarily demanded by his nature."
8. Therefore, natural law is "an order or a disposition which human reason can discover and according to which each human will must act in order to attune itself to the essential and necessary ends of the human being."
9. Now according to Maritain, "every being has its own natural law as well as its essence." And this is what he calls "the *normality of its functioning*" or further, "the proper way in which, by reason of its specific construction, it demands to be put in action." or further how "it should achieve fullness of being either in its growth or behavior."
10. The "should" is a moral ought. He says it has "*moral* meaning, that is, to imply moral obligation" for humans who are "free agents."
11. Therefore,"[n]atural law for man is *moral* law, because man obeys or disobeys it freely, not necessarily."

Maritain sets it up as such to avoid the predestination found in natural law theories like that of Leibniz (where, for example, "every event in the life of Caesar was contained beforehand in the idea of Caesar"). For Maritain, man is an existential being and not predetermined in some essential way.

To summarize his argument, we note that Maritain starts from the idea that there is a human nature, and just like other things that have a nature, humans have specific ends. (His analogy is to a piano, which has as its end to produce certain sounds.) So he sees natural law as human beings "attuned" to the "essential and necessary ends of the human being." He says "every being has its own natural law, as well as its own essence." He calls this "the *normality of its function*, the proper way in which, by reason of its specific construction, it demands to be put in action."[12] Maritain believes everything that exists in nature has its normality of function, that is, he thinks of natural law as the "ideal formula of development of a given being."[13] His notion of natural law is an empirical notion as opposed to a rationalistic one. It is something discovered over time, not through a priori means, but by experience. As humanity progresses in its knowledge, its conception of natural law also progresses. Here he is following Thomas Aquinas's teachings. Maritain argues that when Aquinas says "that human reason discovers the regulations of natural law through the guidance of the *inclinations* of human nature, he means that the very mode or manner in which human reason knows natural law is not rational knowledge, but knowledge *through inclination*."[14]

It is worth quoting more of Maritain here to be clear on what he is claiming. Going back in the text, Maritain wrote:

> Natural law is unwritten law. Man's knowledge of it has increased little by little as man's moral conscience has developed. The latter was at first in a twilight state. Anthropologists have taught within what structures of tribal life and in the midst of what half-awakened magic it was primitively formed. This proves merely that the knowledge men have had of the unwritten law has passed through more diverse forms and stages than certain philosophers or theologians have believed. The knowledge which our own moral conscience has of this law is doubtless still imperfect, and very likely it will continue to develop and to become more refined as long as humanity exists. Only when the Gospel has penetrated to the depth of human substance will natural law appear in its flower and its perfection.[15]

Ontologically, Maritain talks of natural law in terms of the proper functioning of a thing. From the epistemological point of view (how we come to know the natural law), he thinks that as humanity progresses, its knowledge of the natural law progresses. So from the one side, ontologically "there is immutability as regards things."[16] This is the first point he makes about natural law. Second, from the epistemological point of view, there is progress and hence relativity with respect to natural law. As a consequence, this affects the human rights grounded in natural law. Indeed he says "new rights" fight to gain their place against "old rights."[17] Hence, for Maritain, there is a progressive development of rights. He says

> Thus in human history no "new" right, I mean no right of which common consciousness was becoming newly aware, has been recognized in actual fact without having had to struggle against and overcome the bitter opposition of some "old rights."[18]

The reverse can also happen whereby "new rights" can downgrade "old rights." In Maritain's view, we need to get away from the rationalistic view of rights because it does not allow for competing or conflicting rights. On the rationalist view, rights were like a "divine attribute" and exclusive of any limitation, and so there would be no way of deciding a dispute involving two so-called inalienable rights. He tells us this is particularly so with economic and social rights. By example he says that "the right to a just wage and similar rights had to fight against the right to free mutual agreement and the right to private ownership."[19]

The rights derived from the rationalist natural law, while universal in application, went too far and left no room for resolving conflicts among rights considered inalienable. Maritain's solution was to construct a theory, based on Aquinas's natural law theory, whereby human rights were ontologically necessary, and yet had an empirical aspect, that is, in the discovery of what natural law entailed. Ontologically based in natural law, human rights acquired necessity and so applied to all beings with human nature. Yet at the same time, they were not immutable (at least at the human level) in the sense that humans gradually discovered natural law and, consequently, the human rights based on natural law. Humanity is still gradually discovering "new" human rights and reconciling them with "old" human rights and vice versa. Part of the thrust of Maritain's theory is geared to leave room for free will. While there is a necessity (ontological) to the nature of the human being and the ends human beings can pursue, they have the power to determine the ends which they pursue.

The epistemological aspect of Maritain's natural law theory creates problems when applying his theory in a practical situation. For me, the true test of a theory is how it contributes to judging proper action or in making practical decisions in everyday life. According to Maritain's theory, knowledge of natural law is increased "little by little as man's moral conscience has developed."[20] So practically speaking, humanity's moral development is a matter of discovery and growth. Early man had a primitive (undeveloped or underdeveloped) understanding of the precepts of natural law. Maritain argues that even in today's world " the knowledge which our moral conscience has of this law is doubtless still imperfect."[21] For Maritain, our knowledge of the natural law will always be incomplete and will never be fully developed. He says our knowledge of natural law (and presumably derivatively, human rights) "will continue to develop and to become more refined as long as humanity exists."[22] Our moral knowledge will always be imperfect.

To take Maritain's argument a step further, we must ask how we discover what natural law holds for us. How do we discover how to behave morally? How do we discover our "normality of functioning?" Unlike the rationalists who claim they can discover the precepts of natural law rationally (or by deduction like theorems from axioms) or in what Maritain calls an "abstract and theoretical manner," Maritain says "human reason discovers the regulations of natural law through the guidance of the *inclinations* of human nature."[23] Thus, Maritain writes,

> The judgements in which Natural Law is made manifest to practical Reason do not proceed from any conceptual, discursive, rational exercise of reason; they proceed from that *connaturality* or *congeniality* through which what is consonant with the essential inclinations of human nature is grasped by the intellect as good; what is dissonant, as bad.[24]

In his paper "Can there be moral knowledge?" William Sweet clarifies this concept of knowledge through inclination or connatural knowledge. Sweet says, "We 'pick-up' such knowledge by the experience of living and *via* self-observation (through direct and immediate awareness)." Further, he tells us, connatural knowledge according to Maritain (and Aquinas) "gives us first principles of morality and, specifically, the first principle 'Good is to be done and sought after, and evil is to be avoided' ... all other precepts of the natural law are based on this ... It serves as a first principle in the same way in which, Aquinas writes, the law of non-contradiction serves as a first principle of speculative reason."[25]

For Maritain, then, this so-called knowledge through inclination is "obscure, unsystematic, vital knowledge by connaturality or congeniality in which the intellect, in order to bear judgment, consults and listens to the inner melody that the vibrating strings of abiding tendencies make present in the subject."[26] This is certainly beautiful and poetic in its expression, but what does it mean practically speaking? How do we resolve a dispute if someone's inner melody differs from someone else's inner melody? Practical issues are important in the everyday world, and Maritain's theory does not help. It is well and good to take a historical approach and say humankind's moral knowledge is in a state of flux and is progressively growing. However, this approach creates a kind of relativity in moral knowledge that in practice could allow human criminals to get off the moral, as well as legal, hook.

4. A Practical Problem

At the 1997 fall meeting of the Canadian Jacques Maritain Association, a practical issue was raised during the question period following William Sweet's paper "Persons, Connatural Knowledge and the Universality of Natural Law."[27] In that same week, the United States was preparing for the visit of the new President of China, Jiang Zemin, and the current newspapers and news magazines all had articles concerning the 1989 Tiananmen Square incident and human rights in China. Consequently, it came up as an example in the question period as we sought help with how to resolve a conflict of precepts in Maritain's philosophy. (To be clear, it was Premier Li Peng, and not Jiang Zemin, who imposed martial law at the time of the Tiananmen incident, which resulted in the killings of the protesters.) We were looking for ways to decide cases of right or wrong where particular political systems are in a different state of development. Maritain would argue, according to Sweet, "Do what reason demands." The point was made by the questioner that if the spokesperson for the government of China were following Maritain's theory, he might argue the Tiananmen Square crackdown was necessary because reason demanded political and social stability, which would lead ultimately to further protection of human rights and democracy. As Jiang Zemin stated in a 1997 interview with *Time* magazine,

I believe the most important, the fundamental human right is how to ensure that the 1.2 billion Chinese people have adequate food and clothing. The rights and freedoms that our people enjoy today are unprecedented. Our consistent policy is to protect human rights according to law. Human rights and the system for the protection of human rights in China are advancing. These are the facts for everyone to see.[28]

An American, however, might argue that reason demanded that the revolution should have taken its course, because it would have led to the overthrow of the totalitarian regime and make way for democratic rule. Maritain's theoretical basis does not clarify what reason would demand. Some would say we should act in accordance with the first principle of natural law, which is, "Do good and avoid evil."[29] The question is how do we know that we are acting in accordance with the first principle of natural law? How do you decide what reason dictates? What does the situation demand? From a practical point of view, how do you decide what reason dictates? Maritain might say, "Do what is good!" or "Do what is reasonable!" But we could then ask, "What was good in this situation? And how do we find it out, especially when each party has a different point of view as to what is good or what is reasonable?" In the Tiananmen Square case, the Chinese rulers argued that retaining political order and stability to continue developing the common good is good for the Chinese people, otherwise all political and economic advances made to date would be destroyed by a revolution. So there was need to move quickly to suppress the revolution in the making in Tiananmen Square.

5. Other Practical Problems in Today's World

In today's world, people face practical situations where moral (and legal) decisions have to be made. In April 1994, one of the late twentieth century's worst genocides began in Rwanda. It is alleged that within a few weeks, between half and three-quarters of a million Tutsis were killed by Hutu rebels. An International Criminal Tribunal for Rwanda was established in November 1994 to try individuals for crimes of genocide, crimes against humanity, and crimes of sexual violence. In a 1998 article in the *Ottawa Citizen*,[30] Mike Blanchfield discusses the trial of Jean-Paul Akayesu, mayor of a small community in northwestern Rwanda. (At the time of the article, this was only one of three trials that had started.) To account for this, Blanchfield notes, "A February 1997 report by the UN inspector general uncovered a series of problems it said hampered the ability of the court to dispense justice. Among them: faulty accounting practices, cronyism that led to unqualified applicants landing jobs, and shortages of supplies such as law books." Mr. Okali, who has since taken over as the tribunal's chief administrator, is quoted as saying that he's "serious about reversing the tribunal's fortunes and proving that an international court of law can overcome some fundamental obstacles – the inevitable clashes of language, culture and legal traditions – and function as a credible forum for dispensing justice." (A problem similar to that in our discussion above.) Blanchfield says the success of this international tribunal and the one in the Hague ("which is trying war crimes cases related to ethnic cleansing in the former Yugoslavia") is important. He writes, "An international court is viewed as a way of deterring serious crimes such as genocide, a way for the world to finally live up to the pledge of 'never again' that has gone unfulfilled since the full extent of the Nazi Holocaust was uncovered five decades ago." If the tribunals are unable to function, it removes the intended deterrence factor. In his article, Blanchfield reported,

> So far, the Arusha tribunal has done little to deter ethnic killing in Rwanda. Massacres continue on a regular basis. In December, Hutu extremists based in the neighbouring Democratic Republic of the Congo killed more than 1,600 Tutsis in a single raid on a camp in northwestern Rwanda. Raids continued throughout January with hundreds more lives claimed.[31]

So, how do we deal with the massacres in Rwanda? Does Maritain's view make room for the Hutu who committed genocide to go unpunished because his/her moral consciousness is in an earlier stage of development and his/her inner melody is not as developed as our inner melody? Consider Canada's Louise Arbour and the International Tribunal in the Hague attempting to prosecute war criminals from the former Yugoslavia. How can they make use of the sort of theory that Maritain proposed? Currently, there is a lively movement to establish an International Criminal Court (ICC). Given Maritain's theoretical approach, we can ask on what basis can an ICC condemn someone if his/her moral development or his/her community has not reached a stage of moral development akin to those in the Western European context?

For Maritain, we come to know natural law through connatural knowledge, which is neither a priori like axiomatic or rational knowledge nor scientific like empirical knowledge. Connatural knowledge is somewhere in between. We come to know it by discovering the inherent nature of things. This is a process of discovery. By discovering the proper ends of human nature, we discover how the natural law applies to human beings. However, human nature is complex and humans have inclinations and propensities to all kinds of different things and, more important for our discussion, these can conflict from one human to another. There is room for considerable disagreement concerning the make-up of human nature. Indeed, each religion, each ideology, each cultural group has a different perspective on what constitutes human nature. Humans have capacity for different goods and different evils. What one human grouping (social, cultural, or religious, for example) may view as good and proper, another human grouping may view as evil or sinful. Think of the variations in different societies in the roles of women and girls, on attitudes to both male and female circumcision, and on tolerance for other religious beliefs.

Maritain describes a hierarchy of laws – starting with Eternal Law and moving through Natural Law to the Law of Nations and Positive Law (customary or statute law). Yet when you get down to it, regardless of Maritain's own faith in Catholic philosophy based on St. Thomas Aquinas, which is reflected in his metaphysical approach, all of these laws (except, of course, the Eternal or Divine Law) come from humans discovering or formulating them and putting the force of the state or society behind them as rules for keeping good behavior (good order and good government). Maritain seems to recognize this at the beginning of chapter four in *Man and the State* when he recognized that agreement on something like the UDHR was only possible at a practical level. The only way we progress in recognizing what is required by natural law is by sitting around a table (or exchanging written documents, debating issues) and searching for agreement. From the historical examples Maritain provides, we progress in our discovery of Natural Law as we discover more about human nature and human inclination. This agreement is gradual, but still possible on a practical level (regardless of how a given person may justify it from a particular cultural or philosophical perspective).

Adopting Maritain's own metaphysical position on Natural Law may give him and members of the Catholic faith comfort, but it does not give them prior or special access to the contents of Natural Law. Natural Law is also veiled in our own particular cultural/linguistic/religious categories and we can have no special (unadulterated) access to it, independent of these categories.

While this comment reeks of relativism (and I think we are doomed to some such relativism by virtue of our humanity and our human form of reasoning), we can find ways out of this quandary. This comes through a kind of Hobbesian/ Lockean social contract – of people agreeing to be subject to ordering principles – certain laws, codes to live by. As humans, we condemn those who try to live outside our moral codes and legal systems. People agree among themselves that these laws and codes apply to particular groupings – be they individuals or corporations, within states or states themselves, bound by international law. These agreements permit us to hold people responsible for violations of law – even in situations like Rwanda and the former Yugoslavia – because while state law may have broken down in those situations, certain norms of human dignity and survival have been violated. These norms are no longer arbitrary or vague. Instead, they are norms, principles, values, laws, and codes that people have discussed, debated, written down, and agreed to in documents like the UDHR and the International Human Rights Covenants and Conventions. They have been agreed to by representatives of states, cultures, religions, and linguistic traditions and can serve as the basis for trying individuals for violations or crimes against humanity. International tribunals, such as the one Canadian Louise Arbour directed, play an important role. The justice they set out for violations against humanity is viable and justified, because the laws they are enforcing have an objectivity determined in a forum applicable to virtually all humanity – the United Nations. In this past century, humankind has made tremendous progress in developing such a forum and the basis for developing the kind of law that permits us to go behind states' boundaries to enforce international law for crimes against humanity. The world is now ready for the next major step. This is the creation of an International Criminal Court (ICC), agreed to in 1998, where individuals are brought to justice for crimes that could not be adequately dealt with by the laws of a particular state, such as genocide, war crimes, and crimes against humanity.

The movement for such a court began some fifty years ago at the beginning of the United Nations. In the 1960s, there was again some impetus for establishing an ICC. A subsequent process towards establishing an ICC was started in 1995 at the instigation of the International Law Commission. The major question facing the Commission was how to design an effective and just court. The ICC would try individuals (as opposed to states) for crimes against humanity, war crimes, and genocide. (At the present time, the International Court of Justice's jurisdiction is restricted to states.) Where the Rwandan and Yugoslavian War Crimes Tribunals were limited geographically and chronologically, an ICC would be global in scope and would have an international jurisdiction that would complement national legal systems. There are a number of technical and jurisdictional issues involved in establishing the court. The jurisdictional issues revolve around what crimes are to come under the ICC's jurisdiction and the relation of the ICC to national courts. Regarding the complementarity of courts, the general sense is that if a crime is to be tried in a fair and just way under the national court, the first right to trial would rest with the national court, but if that is not a viable or fair process, then the ICC can step in. As you can expect, there are problems in developing the criteria.

With respect to the crimes to be covered under the Court, some of those under consideration are crimes of aggression, genocide (as in Rwanda), violation of laws and customs of war, crimes of terrorism, rape or other sexual abuse, forced prostitution, acts of piracy, drug trafficking, attacks against UN and associated personnel, hostage-taking, enforced transfer of population or deportation, and slavery. The crimes against humanity category has generated debate on whether or not to include only those crimes committed during war or to also include those committed during peace time.

Maritain was right to note that human society is still progressing in its discovery process and that there is still a long way to go. This progress has been most dramatic since the Second World War as we gradually have been removing states borders as barriers for applying human rights law.

6. The Universality of Human Rights

Above, I have argued that Maritain's Natural Law theory, while constructed to appear objectively grounded, is in practice subject to different interpretations based on the level of development of a given society or individual within that society. However, I don't think we should abandon our search. There is considerable merit in following certain paths that Maritain suggested in his chapter four of *Man and the State*. I want to place emphasis on the insight he offered in his speech to UNESCO's second General Conference and used to begin the chapter "The Rights of Man" in *Man and the State*.

> In the domain of practical assertion ... an agreement on a common declaration is possible by means of an approach that is more pragmatic than theoretical, and by a collective effort of comparing, recasting, and perfecting the drafts in order to make them acceptable to all as points of practical convergence, regardless of the divergence in theoretical perspectives.[32]

Human beings are alike in a number of ways independent of their religious, cultural or linguistic, or ideological orientations. From a practical point of view, we all require food, water, and air (oxygen) to survive. We need shelter from the elements and a place to sleep. To survive childhood, we require the care of others. I can go on with a list of needs that reflects many of the rights in the UDHR. These practical needs are common to all human beings for individual survival. If we can begin our discussion with the dignity of every human being, then establish the rights a human being must have if he/she is to have a dignified life, we can move into an agreement on a list of rights such as we find in the UDHR. This list of rights can be derived independent of our views on the existence of God or laws that derive from some divine realm. This derivation of rights has evolved over many years and probably will continue to evolve as we mature in our joint vision of what humanity is and can become. This vision may be informed by many different views of the way things are in terms of religion, culture, and ideology, so long as these views do not depart from according human dignity to every person. Using this approach, the scholars and diplomats who met around the various committee tables at the newly formed United Nations in the mid- to late 1940s were able to agree upon the UDHR. Their work was so successful, they obtained agreement among the approximately 40 countries that assented to the UDHR on 10 December 1948, and the over 150 nations that have assented to the UDHR since then and ratified the many International Covenants and Conventions derived from the UDHR.

Maritain's work on deriving these basic rights (albeit from his natural law perspective) was probably useful in helping the Committee draw up the list of human rights. Maritain was on the scene in 1947 as head of the French delegation, and he was writing influential books and papers on the subject prior to that time. No doubt René Cassin, who was awarded the Nobel Peace Prize for his work drafting the final version of the UDHR, not only knew Jacques Maritain, but probably read Maritain's book *The Rights of Man and Natural Law*.[33] (This is not to say Maritain was the only influence; the French have been talking about human rights long before the Declaration of the Rights of Man in 1789.)

While Maritain's theory does not allow us to determine the right way to proceed in a given situation (such as the Tiananmen Square situation), it can be used as an argument for tolerance. In the discovery of the precepts of natural law and the human rights based in natural law, Maritain's theory leaves room for discussion among people who do not share ideologies, cultural backgrounds and values, languages, and religions. They can discuss practical issues and arrive at mutual agreement.

Maritain's speech to the UNESCO General Council in 1947, a year before the United Nations's endorsement of the Universal Declaration of Human Rights, probably had an effect on the UDHR's acceptance by representatives of states with different cultures, values, languages, ideologies, and religions. Maritain's insight is that on a practical level (perhaps we might call it the survival level), people tread on common ground. To survive, each of us requires food, oxygen (clean air), and clean water. As human beings, we share basic needs. Proponents of other religions and ideologies will not agree with Maritain's natural law theory based on the Catholic philosophy of St. Thomas Aquinas (what Maritain believes is the true philosophy). However, Maritain leaves the door open for discussion on practical issues. (Maritain is clear about his preferences, but he leaves the door open for other interpretations). In the latter part chapter four of *Man and the State*, Maritain believes that rights rise above ideologies.

> [T]he recognition of a particular category of rights is not the privilege of one school of thought at the expense of the others; it is no more necessary to be a follower of Rousseau to recognize the rights of the individual than it is to be a Marxist to recognize the economic and social rights.[34]

For Maritain, the important thing is to recognize that human rights are "like everything human, subject to conditions and limitation, at least ... as far as their exercise is concerned."[35] Maritain's message is that we need to be open and flexible in our approach to human rights. Rights are not immune from limitation. We need to be flexible in our application of rights in order to resolve conflicts among the various rights. He says, "If each of the human rights were by its nature absolutely unconditional and exclusive of any limitation, like a divine attribute, obviously any conflict between them would be irreconcilable."[36] Maritain's approach is positive in that it opens the door to resolving differences and antagonisms where previous rationalist approaches to natural law tended to close the door to discussion. It is not easy. As Maritain says, advocates of different ideologies "will lay down on paper similar, perhaps identical, lists of the rights of man. They will not, however, play that instrument in the same way."[37]

Here is the challenge for the United Nations and the work they carried out since 10 December 1948. Having laid down the lists of rights in the UDHR, the UN must strive to keep the door open for discussion among the proponents of the different ideologies. Each ideology harbors a different hierarchy of values which determine for their proponents which rights get the most play.

Everything depends upon the supreme value in accordance with which all these rights will be ordered and will mutually limit each other. It is by virtue of the hierarchy of values to which we thus subscribe that we determine the way in which the rights of man, economic and social as well as individual, should, in our eyes, pass into the realm of existence.[38]

At the time Maritain was writing, he was concerned with three schools of thought with different values and different ways of interpreting the list of rights. These were the liberal-individualistic, communistic, and personalistic. Each had its own way of interpreting what constitutes human dignity. Today, with approximately 180 states in the United Nations, many more schools of thought, ideologies, cultures, languages, and religions are represented. Each has its own interpretation of the rights in the UDHR. The practical challenge for philosophers today is to devise ways and means to help states and peoples discuss their differences and lead to peaceful resolution of the difficulties of interpretation. The various fora in the context of the United Nations provide common ground for the peoples of the world to listen to the various perspectives and work out instruments that assure human dignity for each and everyone of us regardless of ideological persuasion.

In conclusion, it may be appropriate to quote from UNESCO's Constitution (an organization Maritain helped shape and where he was an influential player). "That since wars begin in the minds of men, it is in the minds of men that the defenses of peace must be constructed."[39]

Notes

1. See Article 1 of *The International Covenant on Civil and Political Rights* (1966) and *The International Covenant on Economic, Social and Cultural Rights* (1966), in *Human Rights, A Compilation of International Instruments*, 4th ed. (New York: United Nations, 1983) pp. 3, 8.

2. Tum Daim Zamuddin, "Rhetoric and Reality of Human Rights," acceptance speech for Honorary Doctorate of Philosophy (Management) from Universiti Utara Malaysia (28 July 1997); text supplied by the Malaysian Embassy in Ottawa, Canada.

3. Jacques Maritain, *Man and the State* (Chicago: University of Chicago Press, 1951), p. 76.

4. John P. Humphrey, *Human Rights and the United Nations: A Great Adventure* (New York: Transitional Publishers Inc., 1984), p. 37.

5. Ibid., pp. 39–40.

6. Maritain, *Man and the State*, pp. 77–79.

7. Ibid., p. 79.

8. William Sweet, "Maritain's Criticisms of Natural Law Theories," *Maritain Studies* 12 (1996), pp. 33–49.

9. Maritain, *Man and the State*, pp. 82–83.

10. Ibid., p. 84.

11. Ibid., pp. 85–86.

12. Ibid., p. 86.

13. Ibid., p. 88.

14. Ibid., p. 91.

15. Ibid., p. 90.

16. Ibid., p. 103.

17. Ibid.

18. Ibid.

19. Ibid.

20. Ibid., p. 90.

21. Ibid.

22. Ibid.

23. Ibid.

24. Jacques Maritain, *The Range of Reason* (London: G. Bles, 1953), pp. 22–29.

25. William Sweet, "Can there be moral knowledge?" *Maritain Studies*, 11 (1995), pp. 181–183.

26. Maritain, *Man and the State*, pp. 91–92.

27. William Sweet, "Persons, Precepts, and Maritain's Account of the Universality of Natural Law," *Maritain Studies*, 14 (1998), pp. 141–165.

28. "U.S. and China: Ups and Downs: an exclusive interview with Jiang Zemin," *Time*, Canadian edition (27 October 1997), pp. 32–34.

29. Maritain, *Man and the State*, p. 98.

30. Mike Blanchfield, "Rwanda: On trial for genocide," *Ottawa Citizen* (1 February 1998), p. F8.

31. Ibid.

32. Maritain, *Man and the State*, p. 79.

33. Maritain, *The Rights of Man and Natural Law*, trans. Doris Anson (New York: C. Scribner's Sons, 1943); see *Les droits de l'homme et la loi naturelle* (New York: Éditions de la Maison Française, 1942).

34. Ibid., p. 105.

35. Ibid., p. 106.

36. Ibid.

37. Ibid.

38. Ibid., pp. 106–107.

39. *Constitution of the United Nations Educational, Scientific, and Cultural Organization*, Preamble (adopted in London on 16 November 1945).

Eight

THE UNIVERSAL DECLARATION OF HUMAN RIGHTS IN THE SUPREME COURT OF CANADA

Jack Iwanicki

The Universal Declaration of Human Rights (UDHR), passed by the General Assembly fifty years ago, is an international document of immense importance. That importance could be developed and examined along a number of dimensions to gain an over all appreciation of its significance. I suggest considering it along the political, moral, educational, and legal dimensions. My plan for this chapter is to discuss briefly the first three dimensions, but then concentrate on the legal. More specifically, I plan to examine in detail cases that have come before the Supreme Court of Canada since the Canadian Charter of Rights and Freedoms (Charter) was enacted, in which reference is made to the UDHR. My reasons for doing so will become apparent from the text. I will also include some references to the International Covenant on Economic, Social and Cultural Rights, 1966 (ICESCR), the International Covenant on Civil and Political Rights, 1966 (ICCPR), and the Convention Relating to the Status of Refugees, 1951 (CSSR). I mention the political, moral, and educational dimensions, however, because even a brief discussion of them shows that an adequate examination of the significance of the UDHR must include a detailed examination of all of them.[1]

When we consider the political dimension of the UDHR, we are looking at the influence of the UDHR on governments and their enactments. In Canada, we could review the Bill of Rights and the Charter and examine reliance on the UDHR in those documents. The framers of the Charter relied on the UDHR because of the similarity in the terminology of the documents especially sections 9 and 12 of the Charter. These sections read as follows: "Everyone has the right not to be arbitrarily detained or imprisoned"; "No one shall be subjected to arbitrary arrest, detention, or exile"; "Everyone has the right not to be subjected to any cruel or unusual treatment or punishment"; and "No one shall be subjected to torture or cruel, inhuman, or degrading treatment or punishment."[2]

When we turn to the moral dimension, we are looking at the importance of the UDHR for the work of non-governmental agencies. One example, Amnesty International, will suffice to show the importance non-governmental agencies attach to the UDHR. In a recent issue of *The Activist*, Amnesty International Canada announced the launch of its "From Declaration to Dedication" campaign.[3] Among the activities listed for the campaign was the launch on "Parliament Hill in Ottawa where Amnesty hosted a gathering of more than 35 non-governmental organizations (NGOs) and civic officials."[4] A number of prominent citizens, including Marion Dewar, head of Oxfam Canada, and Lloyd Axworthy, Minister of Foreign Affairs, signed a campaign pledge to defend human rights. Other events held across Canada are listed, including candlelight processions and vigils, to bring to the attention of communities the importance of human rights, their abuse, and the protections set out in the UDHR.

Other dimensions, like the educational, could be considered, for example the role played by UDHR in making people around the world aware of the provisions of the UDHR and the implications of them for communal life. I will return to this briefly later.

To explore the legal dimension, I plan to examine cases that have come before the Supreme Court of Canada in which reference is made to the UDHR.[5] When I first started this project, I expected to find frequent references to the UDHR. When I reviewed the reports[6] I was surprised to discover that since the enactment of the Charter few cases refer to the UDHR. This need not be surprising since the UDHR is only a "standard-setting"[7] document of the United Nations. By contrast, other documents, such as the International Covenant on Economic, Social and Cultural Rights, 1966 (ICESCR), the International Covenant on Civil and Political Rights, 1966 (ICCPR), and the Convention Relating to the Status of Refugees, 1951 (CSSR), address "implementation" as well as standards. Since these generally have their roots in the UDHR, I have included some in my discussion.

I now turn to my main project, the examination of cases. The Supreme Court shows itself to be comfortable with reliance on international materials in *Canada (Attorney General) v. Ward.*[8]

Justice La Forest, on behalf of the Court, framed his discussion as follows: "This case raises for the first time in this court several fundamental issues respecting the definition of a 'Convention refugee' in s. 2(1) of the Immigration Act, 1976."[9]

The provisions of the Act follow substantially the provisions of the Convention Relating to the Status of Refugees, 1951.[10] The Covenant, in its preamble, provided in part that "Considering that the Charter of the United Nations and the Universal Declaration of Human Rights approved on 10 December 1948 by the General Assembly have affirmed the principle that human beings shall enjoy fundamental rights and freedoms without discrimination ."[11]

The court is comfortable with the international material because it has been incorporated by the appropriate legislative body into domestic legislation.[12] As we shall see, the courts have more difficulty assigning weight to international materials where there is no incorporation, even though Canada was a signatory to and ratified the convention in question.

To turn to the details of the case, in 1983, the Ireland-born Ward joined the Irish National Liberation Army (INLA), a paramilitary organization. One of his first jobs with the organization was guarding two hostages. The next day, the INLA ordered their execution. Ward allowed them to escape for moral reasons without revealing to the INLA his involvement in their escape. Later, the INLA suspected Ward and he was confined and tortured. He was subsequently tried by a kangaroo court and sentenced to death. He escaped and sought the protection of the authorities. They charged him with forcible confinement of the hostages to which he pleaded guilty and was sentenced to three years in prison. His wife and children were held as hostages by the INLA to prevent him from leaking information to the authorities. He never did. Towards the end of his confinement he sought the assistance of the prison chaplain, who helped him obtain a passport and airline tickets to Canada. Once there, he claimed the protection of the Act as a "Convention refugee."

> "Convention refugee" means any person who
> a) by reason of a well-founded fear of persecution for reasons of race, religion, nationality, membership in a particular social group or political opinion,
>> (i) is outside the country of the person's nationality and is unable or, by reason of that fear, is unwilling to avail himself of the protection of that country ...[13]

Ward, through his counsel, claimed refugee status on the grounds of a well-founded fear of persecution for reasons of membership in a particular social group.[14] In the Supreme Court, Justice La Forest rejected the membership ground because membership in the IMLA did not meet the requirements of the definition of a particular social group developed by the courts in a series of earlier cases.[15]

However, this case is interesting from the international perspective for two reasons. The United Nations High Commissioner for Refugees was allowed as an intervener before the Court. Second, for the first time, the Commissioner raised the ground of political opinion as a reason for Ward's fear of persecution. La Forest stated, "The additional ground was ultimately accepted by the appellant during oral argument."[16] Finally, La Forest referred to the UNHCR Handbook, paragraph 66, which provided that it was not the duty of a claimant to identify the reasons for the persecution. It was for the examiner to decide whether the Convention definition was met.

La Forest concludes, "While political opinion was raised at a very late stage of the proceedings, the court has decided to deal with it because this case is one involving human rights and the issue is critical to the case."[17] La Forest went on to allow Ward's appeal on the grounds of political opinion.

R. v. Oakes[18] is a fundamental case for the interpretation of sections 1 and 11d of the Charter. Section 1 of the Charter "guarantees the rights and freedoms set out in it subject only to such reasonable limits prescribed by law as can be demonstratively justified in a free and democratic society." Section 11 states that "any person charged with an offense has the right to be presumed innocent until proven guilty in a fair and public hearing ... by an independent and impartial tribunal." Oakes was found guilty of possessing a narcotic. A section of the

Narcotic Control Act provided that anyone found guilty of possession would be "presumed" guilty of possession for purposes of trafficking, an offense carrying a much more serious penalty. Oakes challenged the legislation claiming his Charter rights under Section 11d were violated. The Court ruled in his favor setting out the elements of the now famous Oakes test. With reference to international materials, Chief Justice Dickson observed, "Further evidence of the wide-spread acceptance of the principle of the presumption of innocence is its inclusion in major international documents."[19] He mentioned the UDHR Article 11,1 in which "Everyone charged with a penal offense has the right to be presumed innocent until proved guilty according to law in a public trial at which he has had all the guarantees necessary for his defence."[20]

He also mentioned Article 14,2 of ICCPR, where "Everyone charged with a criminal offense shall have the right to be presumed innocent until proved guilty according to law."[21]

Here we see international materials used to confirm an interpretation of a section of the Charter, even though there has been no incorporation of the materials.

R. v. O'Connor[22] was a case in which a priest was charged with rape. On the priest's behalf, Counsel applied for the disclosure of medical records and records of the therapy sessions, which many of his victims had undergone as a result of the rapes. Crown counsel could not assure the court that all such records were made available to the accused. Counsel, on O'Connor's behalf, claimed that his Charter right to a fair trial was violated.

Justice L'Heureux-Dubé, in her judgment addressing the principles governing the production of records held by third parties, noted that three constitutional rights were involved, "(1) the right to full answer and defense; (2) the right to privacy; and (3) the right to equality without discrimination."[23]

L'Heureux-Dubé went on to note, "An individual who is deprived of the ability to make full answer and defense is deprived of fundamental justice."[24] However, that right had to be considered in context. She also observed that, "although fairness of the trial and, as a corollary, fairness in defining the limits of full answer and defense, must primarily be viewed from the point of the accused, both notions must nevertheless also be considered from the point of view of the community and the complainant."[25]

In elaborating the importance of the right to privacy, L'Heureux-Dubé noted the Supreme Court had earlier acknowledged that section 7 of the Charter included a right to privacy. Section 7 reads, "Everyone has the right to life, liberty and security of the person and the right not to be deprived thereof except in accordance with the principles of fundamental justice." L'Heureux-Dubé cited the discussion of Wilson J. in *Morgentaler*[26] examining the relationship between liberty and security of the person. She went on to refer to the U.S. Supreme Court decision in *Roe v. Wade*.[27]

She then referred to international materials to support her conclusion, Article 12 of the UDHR, "No-one shall be subjected to arbitrary interference with his privacy, family, home or correspondence, nor to a tax on his honour and reputation. Everyone has the right to the protection of the law against such interference or attacks."[28] She also referred to Article 17, 1 and 2 of the ICCPR, identical to Article 12 just quoted.

As a result of her analysis, L'Heureux-Dubé found that the misconduct of the Crown did not constitute abuse that would warrant a stay of proceedings. She agreed with the Court of Appeal that a new trial should be ordered.

Here then, we have a case where international materials are used to help interpret Charter provisions in light of the conflicting values involved. In contrast to *Oakes*, no specific provision directly addresses privacy, but the Court finds the roots of privacy in section 7. The international materials give an understanding of the content of the right to privacy.

Kindler v. Canada[29] is unusual in that international materials are referred to by both the majority and a dissenting minority. Briefly, the facts of the case are that Kindler was found guilty of murder in the United States, escaped to Canada, and was arrested. Extradition was applied for and granted. The Minister did not request the death penalty not be imposed. Kindler argued his Charter rights had been violated, specifically sections 7 and 12. Section 12 reads, "Everyone has the right not to be subjected to any cruel and unusual treatment or punishment." The Supreme Court decided that Kindler's Charter rights were not violated. In what follows, I concentrate on the international materials referred to in the case.

Justice La Forest, in his majority judgment, indicated that "the Minister's decision in the present case operates in a specific case where the particular facts are critical to constitutional evaluation. More important, it takes place in a global setting where the vast majority of the nations of the world retain the death penalty."[30] He acknowledged a growing and welcome trend to abolish the death penalty, but also observed that some nations, notably the United States, had gone against the trend. He further acknowledged that a number of major international agreements supported the trend for abolition, but added, "except for the European Protocol No 6 to the Convention for Protection of Human Rights and Fundamental Freedoms Concerning the Abolition of the Death Penalty, Europe, T.S. No 114, all fall short of actually prohibiting the use of the death penalty. This contrasts with the overwhelming universal condemnation that has been directed at practices such as genocide, slavery and torture ..."[31] As an example, La Forest referred to articles 6 and 7 of the ICCPR.

Thus, for the majority of the Court, the international documents did not unambiguously support the abolition of the death penalty, and La Forest could find that Kindler's Charter rights were not violated.

Justice Cory, in his dissent, provided an extensive historical review of the imposition of the death penalty. In a section on twentieth-century developments, he reviewed in detail the international documents supporting abolition. He referred to the UDHR, its preamble, and its relevant provisions:

> Whereas recognition of the inherent dignity and of the equal and inalienable rights of all members of the human family is the foundation of freedom, justice and peace in the world ...
> Article 1. All human beings are born free and equal in dignity and rights ...
> Article 3. Everyone has the right to life liberty and security of the person.
> Article 5. No one shall be subjected to torture or to cruel inhuman or degrading treatment or punishment.[32]

Cory went on to list the relevant provisions of the ICCPR. I quote parts of Article 6, 2: "In countries which have not abolished the death penalty, sentence of death may be imposed only for the most serious crimes ... and not contrary to the provisions of the present Covenant ..."[33]

When Cory turns to Canada's international commitment, he refers to the provisions of the Second Optional Protocol:[34]

> The States Parties to the Present Protocol,
> Believing that abolition of the death penalty contributes to the enhancement of human dignity and progressive development of human rights,
> Recalling article 3 of the Universal Declaration ... and article 6 of the International Covenant on Civil and Political Rights ...
> Noting that article 6 of the Covenant on Civil and Political Rights refers to the abolition of the death penalty in terms that strongly suggest that abolition is desirable,
> Convinced that all measures of abolition should be considered as progress in the enjoyment of the right to life,
> Desirous to undertake hereby an international commitment to abolish the death penalty have agreed as follows:
> Article 1 No one within the jurisdiction of a State party to the present Optional Protocol shall be executed.
> Article 2 Each State party shall take all necessary measures to abolish the death penalty within its jurisdiction.[35]

Cory observes that Canada supported the Second Optional Protocol. In a summary section to his judgment he said, "Except for the United States, the western world has reinforced this commitment, both internationally and nationally through the express abolition of the death penalty. Canada's actions in the international forum affirm its own commitment to the preservation and enhancement of human dignity and to the abolition of the death penalty."[36]

Cory was therefore prepared to find that Kindler's Charter rights had been violated. The international materials he presented contributed significantly to his conclusion.

Sheena B., Re[37] was a case in which a blood transfusion was given to a child whose parents were Jehovah's Witnesses. The parents claimed that their Charter rights under section 7[38] had been violated. The Supreme Court denied their claim. In his judgment, Chief Justice Lamer stated, "To summarize my opinion, I would simply say that extending the scope of the word 'liberty' to include any type of freedom other than that which is connected with the physical dimension of the word 'liberty' would not only be contrary to the structure of the Charter and of the provision itself, but would also be contrary to the scheme, the content and manifest purpose of s. 7."[39]

Lamer went on to observe, "The approach that I am adopting also appears to me to be supported by the human rights instruments on which the framers of our Charter drew extensively."[40] In that context, Lamer quoted a statement by then Minister of Justice Jean Chrétien in the Charter debate that some of the rights in sections 7 to 14 in the Charter derive from the ICCPR.[41]

Lamer quoted Article 9.1 of that Covenant. "Everyone has the right to liberty and security of the person. No one shall be subjected to arbitrary arrest or detention. No one shall be deprived of his liberty except on such grounds and in accordance with such procedure as are established by law."[42]

He also went on to refer to Art. 3 of the UDHR, "Everyone has the right to life, liberty and security of the person."[43]

Later he observed, "I am fully aware that the weight to be given to the foregoing may be uncertain, but nevertheless I believe that it provides an additional indication, at least, of the scope that the framers of the Charter may have intended to give the expression right to 'liberty' in the context of s. 7."[44]

Miron and Valliere v. Trudel et al.[45] was a case involving a provision in the standard automobile insurance policy that extended benefits to a spouse. The insurer denied benefits to common law spouses. A majority in the Supreme Court found that the provision violated section 15,1 of the Charter and could not be saved by relying on section 1. (Section 15,1 of the Charter reads: "Every individual is equal before and under the law and has the right to equal protection and equal benefit of the law without discrimination and in particular, without discrimination based on race, national or ethnic origin, colour, religion, sex, age or mental or physical disability.")

Justice Gonthier, in his dissent, argued there was a violation of section 15,1, which could be saved by appeal to section 1:

I conclude from the foregoing that a distinction deemed irrelevant because based on an enumerated or analogous ground and thus discriminatory under s. 15 (1) may nevertheless be rationally connected to furthering a larger social purpose and hence be judged reasonable under s. 1.[46]

Gonthier then went on to analyze jurisprudence in the United States and referred to Article 16 of the UDHR, which he said was "binding on Canada." Article 16 provided that, "Men and women of full age, without any limitation due to race, nationality or religion, have the right to marry and to found a family. They are entitled to equal rights as to marriage, during marriage and its dissolution."[47]

Gonthier concluded, "[my] brief review of domestic and international law confirms what in my view requires little if any confirmation, namely that marriage is both a basic social institution and a fundamental right which states can legitimately legislate to foster."[48]

Given the fundamental importance of the institution of marriage, Gonthier was prepared to uphold the constitutionality of the provision in the insurance policy, even though it could be taken to be discriminatory under section 15,1 of the Charter.

Milne v. Canada[49] is another case in which the Supreme Court was not prepared to give international materials much weight.

In *Milne*, the accused pleaded guilty to five counts of gross indecency. He was then found to be a dangerous offender and sentenced to indefinite detention. Some years after his sentencing, the dangerous offender legislation was amended, and gross indecency was removed from the list of offenses for which a prisoner could be indefinitely detained. The prisoner appealed, arguing that his detention violated section 9 of the Charter, arbitrary detention, and section 12, cruel and unusual punishment.[50] To support his position, the prisoner relied on article 15 of ICCPR, which read in part, "If subsequent to the commission of the offense, provision is made by law for the imposition of the lighter penalty, the offender shall benefit thereby."[51]

About that provision, Justice La Forest, speaking for the majority, said, "Counsel concedes that it [the ICCPR] has not been adopted as part of the law but he submits that the court should use the provision as an aid in interpreting sections 9 (arbitrary detention) and 12 (cruel and unusual punishment) of the Charter ..."

He went on to conclude, "It is difficult to see how such an approach could be taken in light of the fact that specific attention was given to this matter in sec. 11 (i) of the Charter[52] which limits the rights of an accused in this regard to the benefit to a reduction in sentence made between the time of the commission of the offense and the time of sentencing."[53]

Justice Estey, in his dissent, argued the punishment now could be considered cruel and unusual given that it would be impossible to indefinitely detain the prisoner given the amendments to the Criminal Code. He would have referred the matter back to the trial judge.[54]

On the more general question of the reliance on international materials, the Court seemed settled that given the specific exemption provided for by section 11, a more extended exemption, made possible through the international document would be rejected even though it would seem unfair to a prisoner. While the broader exemption would complicate the interpretation of criminal law, it would not be an adequate reason for its rejection. Consider another example. When the death penalty was repealed in Canada, should those found guilty of murder before the repeal still be put to death? I suggest not.

Finally, one of the more interesting uses of international materials by the Supreme Court occurred in *Reference Re Compulsory Arbitration.*[55] The international materials were used by Chief Justice Dickson in his dissenting judgment (Justice Wilson concurring). Dickson's judgment appears toward the end of my comments on this case.

The general question addressed in the case was whether a number of Alberta statutes,[56] requiring binding arbitration and prohibiting strikes and lockouts in the event of a labor dispute violated section 2,d of the Charter. That section of the Charter states that everyone has certain fundamental freedoms, including freedom of association. Justice LeDain, in his judgment (Justices Beetz and La Forest concurring), argued that the provisions prohibiting strikes and lockouts did not violate the Charter since freedom of association did not include the right to strike. With reference to the meaning of freedom of association, he stated that

> it is essential to keep in mind that this concept must be applied to a wide range of associations or organizations of a political, religious, social or economic nature ... It is in this larger perspective and not simply in regard to the perceived requirements of a trade union, however important they may be, that one must consider the implications of *extending a constitutional guarantee* ... on the ground that the activity is essential to give an association meaningful existence.[57] [emphasis mine]

By way of comment, we could argue that what is at issue is what is meant by "freedom of association" in the different contexts in which it can be interpreted, and thus how we are to understand "freedom of association" within the labor context or the work situation. For further discussion see Chief Justice Dickson's judgment in what follows.

LeDain rejected the premise "that without such additional constitutional protection (of rights to lockout or strike) the guarantee of freedom of association would be a meaningless and empty one." He added, "Freedom of association is particularly important for the exercise of other fundamental freedoms such as freedom of expression and freedom of conscience and religion."[58]

He also noted that freedom of association connected with work was recognized and protected by labor relations legislation. This led him to conclude that the issue before the court was not a challenge to the more general sense of association applying to all kinds of associations (political, religious, social, or economic), but to its application within a particular context, the workplace. On that score he observed that the modern rights to bargain collectively and to strike, involving correlative duties or obligations resting on an employer – are not fundamental rights or freedoms. They are the creation of legislation, involving a balance of competing interests in a field which has been recognized by the courts as requiring specialized expertise.[59]

He went on to note, ironically, that while in labor relations cases the Court had developed a principle of judicial restraint, so arbitrators could develop labor relations law, here the Court was asked to constitutionalize fundamental features of labor relations rather than allow legislators to develop these features of the law. He therefore held that the legislation did not violate section 2,d of the Charter. Since that was the case, it was not necessary for him to consider section 1.[60]

Justice McIntyre, in a separate judgment upholding the constitutional validity of the provisions, outlined a further important interpretational problem that would arise if the right to strike were constitutionalized.

In every case where a strike occurs the question of the application of sec. 1 of the Charter may be raised to determine whether some attempt to control the right may be permitted. The section 1 enquiry involves the reconsideration by the court of the balance struck by the Legislature in the development of labor policy.[61]

He then gave examples of the types of question a court would have to settle, for example which governmental services are essential and whether the alternative of compulsory arbitration is adequate compensation for the right to strike. He concluded, "None of these issues is amenable to principled resolution. There are no clearly correct answers to these questions. They are of a nature peculiarly apposite to the functions of the Legislature."[62]

While we might admit that there may be no clearly correct answers to all of the questions, surely some should be "amenable to principled resolution." Further, when legislatures address the issues they will have to resolve them on the basis of principles. At stake, therefore, is what issues, if any, are essential to associating in the workplace.

I turn now to Chief Justice Dickson's judgment. He noted, "Freedom of association is the cornerstone of modern labour relations. Historically, workers have combined to overcome the inherent inequalities of bargaining power in the employment relation to protect themselves from unfair, unsafe or exploitative working conditions."[63]

He noted four lines of authority to be examined, Canadian, American, British Commonwealth, and international law. I will concentrate on the latter. With reference to the basic problem confronting the Court, he identified two questions to consider. The first question is whether trade unions were accorded any constitutional protection at all and the second, what is the appropriate definition adopted for "freedom of association." He distinguished two definitional approaches. Under the first, freedom of association entailed simply the freedom to combine together. Under the broader "constitutive" definitional approach, freedom of association not only embodied the freedom to combine together, but extended to the freedom to engage in the activities for which the association was formed. In this case, with the constitutive approach, we recognize that what was at stake was a particular type of associative activity and then we uncover the conditions necessary for its effective exercise.

Turning to the international materials, Dickson noted:

> International law provides a fertile source of insight into the nature and scope of the freedom of association of workers ... a body of treaties (or conventions) and customary norms now constitutes an international law of human rights ... the Charter conforms to the spirit of this contemporary international human rights movement, and it incorporates many of the policies and prescriptions of the various international documents pertaining to human rights.[64]

He concluded, "The various sources of international human rights law – declarations, judicial and quasi-judicial decisions of international tribunals, customary norms – must, in my opinion, be relevant and persuasive sources for the interpretation of the Charter."[65] He went on to take particular note of "the similarity between the policies and provisions of the Charter and those of international human rights documents."[66] He also added, "Furthermore, Canada is a party to a number of international human rights conventions which contain provisions similar or identical to those in the Charter."[67] He concluded,

> In short, though I do not believe the judiciary is bound by the norm of international law in interpreting the Charter, these norms provide a relevant and persuasive source for provisions of the Charter, especially when they arise out of Canada's international obligations under human rights conventions.[68]

Dickson then went on to list specific provisions in the ICESCR and the ICCPR. He noted, as we observed earlier, that these two covenants are rooted in the UDHR. A couple of extracts will be useful.

> ICESCR art. 8 1: The States Parties to the present Covenant undertake to ensure:
>> a) The right of everyone to form trade unions and to join the trade union of his choice ... No restrictions may be placed on the exercise of this right other than those prescribed by law and which are necessary in the interests of national security or public order for the protection of the rights and freedoms of others.

d) The right to strike, provided that it is exercised in conformity with the laws of the particular country.[69]

With respect to these covenants, Dickson noted, "Prior to accession the Federal Government obtained the agreement of the provinces, all of whom undertook to take measures for the implementation of the Covenants in their respective jurisdictions."[70]

He went on to point out that the provisions of Convention No. 87 of the International Labour Organization (ILO) were more explicit and telling. The ILO is an international agency with representatives from labor, management, and government. Article 2 of Convention 87 provides in part that "workers and employers without distinction whatsoever shall be able to establish associations." Article 3 provides:

1. Workers and employer organizations shall have the right to draw up their constitutions and rules, to elect their representatives in full freedom, to organize their administration and activities, and to formulate their programs.
2. The public authorities shall refrain from any interference which would restrict this right or impede the lawful exercise thereof.[71]

Finally, Dickson referred to decisions of the various agencies established by the ILO, the Committee on Freedom of Association, the Committee of Experts, and Commissions of Enquiry. A quotation taken from a report of the Committee of Experts reflects the international attitude towards interfering with the right to strike.

In the opinion of the Committee, the principle whereby the right to strike may be limited in the public service or in essential services whether public, semi-public or private, would become meaningless if the legislation defined the public service or essential services too broadly. As the Committee has already mentioned in previous general surveys, the prohibition should be confined to public servants acting in their capacity as agents of the public authority or to services whose interruption would *endanger the life, personal safety or health of the whole or part of the population.*[72] [emphasis mine]

By way of conclusion, we see Dickson use the international materials to show that the words "freedom of association," as they appear in the Charter, must be given a much broader reading than the majority of the Court was prepared to do. As well, the federal government's obtaining of the undertakings of provincial governments, before acceding to the materials, surely must justify a broader reading. Finally, the right to strike and lockout must be seen as the most fundamental right of associations of either employers or employees.

Confining the government's authority for restricting the right to strike brings labor law in line with other basic areas of the law (for example, the criminal law), which find their roots in the harm condition. Thus, one fundamental condition, which should constrain resort to the law in areas of fundamental conduct affecting others, is that the conduct constrained must have the effect of harming or endangering others or the public.

Dickson shows that the international materials provide good supporting grounds for finding the legislation unconstitutional. Indeed, this case is probably the best example of international materials leading the way for the development of Canadian law.

By way of conclusion, I hope that the detailed discussion of some of the cases referring to the UDHR will allow readers to draw their own conclusions about the importance of the UDHR for the Supreme Court of Canada.

The division between those cases in which judges of the Court see themselves as acting within their constitutional jurisdiction and those where they are asked to go beyond it is worth noting. In cases like *Ward* and *Thompson*, where the provisions of the international conventions have been specifically incorporated by the appropriate legislative authority, the Court goes on to provide a detailed, comprehensive, and defensible analysis of the relevant provisions. Beyond that in *Ward*, where the Court decides who can appear before it and what defenses may be presented, the Court is liberal in its approach. Allowing the High Commissioner for Refugees to appear as an intervener in *Ward*, allowing the Commissioner to present new defenses was generous and just. The Court, however, was careful to require that the appellant (Ward) was prepared to accept those new defenses before relying on them to allow the appeal.

In cases where disagreement occurred within the Court about the significance and importance to be attached to international materials, while individual judges would find such materials persuasive, the majority of the Court was reluctant to allow them to prevail over national materials like the Charter and legislation generally. *Milne* and *Reference Re Compulsory Arbitration* are good contrasting examples. *Milne*, the reader will recall, was the case where legislation was amended so gross indecency no longer constituted grounds for indefinite detention. The Court rejected the international provision where it conflicted with the specific wording of section 9 of the Charter. In defense of the Court, no action was taken by the government, beyond ratification, that the international provision was acceptable.

By contrast in *Compulsory Arbitration*, Dickson showed that the federal government had taken a number of important steps to allow the Court to conclude that the right to strike, while not specifically mentioned in the Charter, could legitimately be interpreted into the relevant Charter provision. The majority of the Court was not prepared to do that.

I offer one final general conclusion. For Canada, it seems the initiative for implementing provisions of international conventions will lie mainly with legislative bodies rather than the courts.

Jack Iwanicki

Appendix A

The complete list of cases mentioning the UDHR:

1. *Canada (Attorney General) v. Ward*, 153 N.R. 321
2. *Singh v. M.E.I.*, 58 N.R. 1
3. *Sheena B. Re.*, 176 N.R. 161
4. *Ruffo (Juge) v. Conseil de la magistrature*, 190 N.R. 1
5. *Reference Re Compulsory Arbitration*, 74 N.R. 99
6. *Qué. (Cur. Pub.) c. Syndicat nat'l employés*, 202 N.R. 321
7. *R. v. O'Connor*, 191 N.R. 1
8. *R. v. Oakes*, 65 N.R. 87
9. *Mooring v. National Parole Board*, 192 N.R. 161
10. *Miron and Valliere v. Trudel*, 181 N.R. 253
11. *R. v. Mills*, 67 N.R. 241
12. *Lavigne v. Ont. Public Service Employees Union*, 126 N.R. 161
13. *Kindler v. Canada (Minister of Justice)*, 129 N.R. 81
14. *R. v. Keegstra*, 117 N.R. 1
15. *Gould v. Yukon Order of Pioneers*, 194 N.R. 81
16. *Edmonton Journal v. Alberta (Attorney General)*, 102 N.R. 321
17. *Chan v. Minister of Employment and Immigration*, 187 N.R. 321
18. *R. v. Big M Drug Mart Ltd.*, 58 N.R. 81
19. *2747-3174 Québec v. Régie d'alcool*, 205 N.R. 1

Notes

1. See *The Universal Declaration of Human Rights, A Commentary*, ed. Asbjorn Eide, et al. (Oslo: Scandinavian University Press, 1992; New York: Oxford University Press, 1992).

2. Canadian Charter of Rights and Freedoms, Section 9; The Universal Declaration of Human Rights, Article 9; Canadian Charter, Section 12; and Universal Declaration, Article 5. See Maxwell Cohen, "Towards a Paradigm of Theory and Practice, The Canadian Charter of Rights and Freedoms B International Law Influences and Interactions," *Canadian Human Rights Yearbook* (Toronto: Carswell, 1986).

3. *The Activist* (February/March 1998), pp. 4–5.

4. Ibid.

5. For more information see *National Reporter*, [N.R.] (Fredericton, N.B.: Maritime Law Book Ltd.).

6. See Appendix A.

7. For terminology see Ian Brownlie, "Table of Contents," *Basic Documents on Human Rights* (Oxford: Oxford University Press, 3rd ed., 1992); for contrast, see I.A. Shearer, *Starke's International Law* (London: Butterworths, 11th ed., 1994), p. 330.

8. 153 N.R. 321.

9. Ibid., 325.

10. Brownlie, *Basic Documents*, pp. 64–69.

11. Ibid., p. 64.

12. See also, "Thompson v Thompson," 173 N.R. 83; Section 17.2 of The Manitoba Child Custody Enforcement Act.

13. 153 N.R. 321.

14. For Justice La Forest's interpretation of other terms crucial to Ward's position, see 153 N.R. 340–361.

15. For La Forest's detailed discussion, see 153 N.R. 361–385.

16. Ibid., 385.

17. Ibid.

18. 65 N.R. 87.

19. 65 N.R. 106.

20. Brownlie, *Basic Documents*, p. 23.

21. Ibid., p. 130.

22. See *R. v. O'Connor*, 191 N.R. 1.

23. 191 N.R. 54.

24. Ibid.

25. Ibid., 54–55.

26. *R. v. Morgentaler, Smoling and Scott*, (1988), 1 S.C.R. 30; 82 N.R. 1.

27. (1973), 410 U.S. 113 (S.C.).

28. Brownlie, *Basic Documents*, p. 24.

29. *Kindler v. Canada (Minister of Justice)*, 129 N.R. 81.

30. 129 N.R. 89.

31. Ibid.; See also, Articles 6, 7, and 8 of the International Covenant on Civil and Political Rights.

32. Note similarities in the Canadian Charter, Sections 7 and 12.

33. 129 N.R. 140.

34. Second Optional Protocol to the International Covenant on Civil and Political Rights, 129 N.R. 143; See also, *United Nations Yearbook*, Vol. 43 (The Hague: Martinus Nijhoff, 1989), pp. 484-485.

35. 129 N.R. 123-124; 129 N.R. 144.

36. 129 N.R. 145.

37. *Sheena B., Re*, 176 N.R. 161.

38. Canadian Charter, Section 7; *Singh v. M.E.I.*, 58 N.R. 1.

39. 176 N.R. 256.

40. Ibid., 258.

41. Ibid.

42. Ibid.

43. Brownlie, *Basic Documents*, p. 23.

44. 176 N.R. 259.

45. (1995), 181 N.R. 253.

46. 181 N.R. 340.

47. Ibid.

48. Ibid.

49. 81 N.R. 37.

50. See Canadian Charter, Sections 9 and 12; The Universal Declaration of Human Rights, Articles 5 and 9.

51. Brownlie, *Basic Documents*, p 131.

52. Canadian Charter, Section 11.

53. 81 N.R. 51–52. Bracketed references added.

54. 81 N.R. 54–55.

55. 74 N.R. 99.

56. The Alberta statutes were the Public Service Employee Relations Act, the Labour Relations Act and the Police Officer's Collective Bargaining Act.

57. 74 N.R. 105.

58. Ibid. Bracketed phrase added.

59. 74 N.R. 106.

60. Canadian Charter, Section 1.

61. 77 N.R. 140.

62. 74 N.R. 140.

63. Ibid. 154.

64. 74 N.R. 170.

65. Ibid.

66. 74 N.R. 171.

67. Ibid.

68. Ibid. 172.

69. 74 N.R. 173. For similar language, see, Article 22 of International Covenant on Civil and Political Rights.

70. Ibid. 172.

71. Ibid. 176.

72. 74 N.R. 179.

Nine

HUMAN RIGHTS AND THE SURVIVAL IMPERATIVE: RWANDA'S TROUBLED LEGACY

Philip Lancaster

We can understand the enthusiasm of the drafters of the Universal Declaration of Human Rights (United Nations General Assembly resolution 217A of 10 December 1948) by considering the historical context of their deliberations. After two cataclysmic global wars, the psychological urge to peace may have overwhelmed philosophical reservations that might have prolonged debate indefinitely.[1] Some may even have been blind to the weakness of the Kantian logic that I believe is clearly evident in the preamble or may have found their own reasons to support it.[2] The diplomatic bargaining involved in composing a declaration to which all could agree is, we now see, a testimony to the applicability of Weberian *zweckrational* to world politics rather than a philosophical accomplishment.[3] At the time, the declaration may have seemed to be what was needed. It was greeted with great hope – but it was a hope which has since come to seem naive.

In the complex world we have created at the beginning of the third millennium, all roads do not lead to Rome, nor do all arguments about rights lead to the conclusions expressed in the Declaration. Yearning for peace is not, in and of itself, a valid ground for a conclusion that is proclaimed as universally applicable. The existing arguments sometimes leave their proponents sounding like missionaries for a world view that is profoundly unattainable to the inhabitants of the more violent parts of our world. In this essay, I want to present a case study to argue that the Universal Declaration of Human Rights fails to compel allegiance, not only because it lacks the compulsion of law, but also because it is lodged in the world as a conclusion to a poorly formed normative argument. I will consider the force of the most plausible argument I can invent, and then take the argument into the ugly little world of mass murderers to test its limits. I will argue that the Declaration does not warrant the semi-religious awe it sometimes inspires and that there is a pressing need to develop convincing arguments for it if we ever hope to use it effectively as a basis for international political action aimed at achieving world peace.

The case of Rwanda provides us with a clear example of how survival imperatives and the Declaration operate in separate worlds. The current regime has drawn criticism that, while well intentioned, may be grounded in an overly confident interpretation of the logic of the Declaration. By reviewing the events in

Rwanda, I will show that people's actions must be read against a backdrop of threats particular to a time and place not well understood by some of the more vocal proponents of human rights.[4] I do not intend to act as an apologist for the current regime, but only to argue that a careful consideration of its situation ought to shake our certainty in the universality of the logic underlying the Declaration, and therefore ought to temper some of our criticism.

1. Some Ruminations on the Logic of Human Rights Theory

The underlying premise of the Universal Declaration is that respect for human rights constitutes the most likely hope for global peace. The preamble states that "disregard and contempt for human rights have resulted in barbarous acts which have outraged the conscience of mankind," and "it is essential, if man is not to be compelled to have recourse, as a last resort, to rebellion against tyranny and oppression, that human rights should be protected by law." The general claim here is that contempt for human rights is bad primarily because of the violent reaction it provokes. While this might be accepted as the basis for a general negative claim that lasting peace is unlikely without respect for rights, it is not strong enough to warrant the more positive claim that respect for human rights necessarily leads to peace.[5]

To put this in Rawlsian terms, the negative version of the argument to rights is that all reasonable beings, capable of disinterested rational thought and concerned with their own long-run best interests, would arrive at the list of rights in the 30 articles of the Universal Declaration.[6] Rawls's argument runs into the standard objection that people are interested in their lives and generally unwilling to abstract from their own interests. Why, for instance, would any self-interested rational powerful person want to go behind Rawls's veil of ignorance in the first place? The argument is compelling if, and only if, we are confident all other persons will be willing to abstract away from whatever present interests they have. Since people in strong positions have no reason to give up their present interests, those in weak positions have little grounds for confidence that everyone will act the same way.

We might state Rawls's argument more simply as the common-sense claim that, in the long run, reasonable people will inevitably see that more is gained from cooperation than from conflict. Anatol Rapaport's famous Tit for Tat strategy for the Prisoner's Dilemma[7] might even be enlisted to provide some theoretical support for this claim, providing that we are able to match the highly controlled conditions of the game in real life – particularly conditions of rough mutual vulnerability. But again, there seems little hope for achieving cooperation through Tit for Tat if there is an acceptable alternative strategy open to one of the players that does not require cooperation. Ample historical evidence exists for use of such thinking. Rome's treatment of Carthage might be the best known, but we find many cases, going back as far as prehistoric times, when fortune seemed to favor the ruthless.[8]

The fundamental idea in the Declaration resonates both with Aquinas's dictum that law is "an ordinance of reason for the common good" and with Hobbes's claim that all men have reason to seek peace, if only to avoid the greater evil of war. But such theories appeal to agents in the real world if and only if there is something that would limit their hope of victory in any conflict that might arise – a Hobbesian sovereign for instance. After all, why worry about the common good if you are strong enough to get your own way? More importantly for my argument, why should we trust in the efficacy of the Declaration to restrain our enemies if there is no sovereign? I doubt that Hobbes would see the virtue in putting down our weapons before the advent of an effective sovereign power.

Despite these potential objections, the "reason to rights" argument seemed to enjoy broad support among the signatories of the Universal Declaration, who agreed to the positive formulation of the argument with the statement, "recognition of the inherent dignity and of the equal and inalienable rights of all members of the human family is the foundation of freedom, justice and peace in the world." Suffice to say, the Declaration follows from and feeds into an argument with a long and honorable tradition. But, does the logic of the argument hold in all cases; does it hold against the possibility of radical evil? What can be said about a decision to cooperate when faced with an absolutist ideology that threatens annihilation of your group or with an enemy who has no visible need to cooperate? Would it not be true in such cases that the pious hope in the ultimate efficacy of disembodied reason is suicidal? We have witnessed enough genocide to know that the meek may fare badly when the strong believe they can win. Such examples show us the wide gap between the moral insight and the political realities the Declaration was designed to bridge.

We need, therefore, to seek a stronger argument for rights.

2. Kant's Codicil

In working out his logic of rights, Kant argues that the disagreement between morals and politics can be resolved by considering the logic of amoral politics from a purely practical point of view. He says that while "[he] can imagine a moral politician, i.e. someone who conceives of the principles of political expediency in such a way that they can co-exist with morality, [he] cannot imagine a political moralist, i.e. one who fashions his morality to suit his own advantage as a statesman."[9] To reverse the order in favor of political expediency has the unfortunate consequence of locking its exponents into a perpetual contest for dominance. Kant explains that a politician who subordinates his moral behavior to his political goals necessarily stumbles over the problem of uncertainty.[10] Since no human can have perfect knowledge of human nature or of the causal laws of human interaction, no politician can know for sure how his plans will turn out.

On the other hand ... political wisdom [conceived of as respect for right], presents itself as it were, automatically; it is obvious to everyone, it defeats all artifices and leads straight to its goal, *so long as we prudently remember that it cannot be realized by violent and precipitate means, but must be approached as favourable opportunities present themselves.*[11]

The usual interpretation of Kant's views is that since no empirically reliable argument for immoral politics exists, reason leads us necessarily to the conclusion that moral principle, rightly conceived according to the categorical imperative, is the only possible guide to perpetual peace left open to the prudent person. Morality, interpreted as respect for human rights, is thus a necessary condition of peaceful politics – provided it is applied non violently and opportunistically. Kant does not claim it is sufficient to the task, but instead gives us a weak, *faute de mieux* argument. Since the political archer does not know with reliable certainty where his or her arrow will fall, he or she must at least aim well away from unintended targets.

Now, Kant does say that two peoples may enter into conflict with each other without doing injustice, if both sides accept the rules of the game they play. "For if one party violates his duty towards another who is just as lawlessly disposed towards him, that which actually happens to them in wearing each other out is perfectly just."[12] The only trouble is that the two parties will be unable to end the perpetual war that Kant sees as the necessary result of competitive maneuvering for advantage. At the very least, he suggests that the two parties may serve as an example for others of the dangers of immoral politics.

I would contend that this strand of reason undoes far more than the necessity for morality in political dealings. It also indicates the difficulty of reaching peace without sufficient confidence that the other is doing so as well. With apologies to Kantian scholars who may be aware of an argument I cannot find, Kant offers no explanation of how the desire for peace is sufficient to quench one group's hope that in a given conflict it might win or how to quell the fear that it might lose. Surely a viable alternative to perpetual struggle is total victory, or its opposite. If that is so, then the logical claim for the universality of human rights as a dictate of self-interested reason is extremely weak. It works only in the case that all parties to a conflict are sufficiently timid to avoid all risk. Where this is not the case, Kant's codicil advising prudent use of favorable opportunity suggests that it might be time to prepare to fight in self-defense.

There is one other concern that ought to be stimulated by consideration of the limits of the Kantian argument. The idea that all peoples ought to recognize the rights of all other peoples may have some logical force where it is anticipated that radical evil will not interfere with the supposedly natural tendency towards cooperation, which the Declaration proclaims as a dictate of reason. But consider for a moment the plight of highly moral Orthodox Jews living in the Warsaw ghetto in the days before it was reduced to rubble and its survivors carted off to extermination camps. Any cooperation shown by Jews just helped their murderers. In this case, the political dynamic of the Third Reich stood as radical evil, as complete negation of the possibility of reasonableness. In such conditions, Kantian logic – urging that "the true courage of virtue ... does not so much consist ... in standing up to the evils and sacrifices which must be encountered, as in facing the evil principle within ourselves and overcoming its wiles" – is suicidal.[13] If the right to survive is part of the bundle of normal human rights, then survival imperatives may arise in any desperate situation that ought to prevail over considerations of long term ideals. In Nazi Germany, passive resistance founded on a belief in the ultimate "good" of the other just failed. Tragically, it was not the last time.

3. Rwanda

In May 1998, the United Nations Human Rights Field Operation in Rwanda was suspended by the Rwandan Parliament because, in the government's view, the United Nations had failed to understand Rwandan reality.[14] The current administration had been accused by at least one credible agency of gross violations of human rights, including extra-judicial executions, arbitrary detention, and inhuman treatment of detainees.[15] The picture painted by many observers is far from flattering to the regime. Rwandan resentment of external criticism reached a crisis point when the UN spokesperson in Rwanda openly condemned the government for publicly executing convicted perpetrators of genocide.

While an in-depth analysis of Rwanda's history is beyond the scope of this paper, I would like to pick up the story near the end of the genocide of 1994.[16] The character of the killings was certainly different from what went on during the Holocaust. Absent was the highly structured administrative apparatus to carry out the dirty work on behalf of the old regime. Africa Watch has compiled convincing graphic testimony of massacres organized as community events in which large numbers of people used farm implements to dispatch their neighbors.[17] The most significant implication of the method of killing was that in order to murder and dispose of nearly one million people in such a short period without the aid of high technology, a massive social mobilization was required. The other significant difference from previous genocides is that it was no secret. Yet despite the determined coverage of some of the world's most prominent international journalists and the persistent efforts of the commander of the United Nations Assistance Mission in Rwanda, no serious international effort was launched to stop the killing. Only the Rwandan Patriotic Front (RPF) seemed to have both the will and the power to stop the killing.

In mid-June 1994, a French-led coalition established a buffer between the RPF and the remnants of the rapidly crumbling government forces. This had the unfortunate effect of providing a screen behind which the government could regroup its forces, both regular and militia. In July 1994, the Rwandan government, formed largely of Hutu extremists, fled west into Zaire using the army and militia to "persuade" approximately two million citizens to flee with them. The CNN pictures of the horror of the flight into Goma moved the world's humanitarian agencies to a massive effort to succor the refugees, regardless of their possible complicity in a genocide. Meanwhile, the survivors inside Rwanda crawled out of their hiding places and tried to put their lives back together with relatively little outside help.[18] But the battle had not been decisively won, and a large number of former government members, regular forces, and militia operating inside the refugee camps in Zaire were imbued with the belief that they could still win. They were able to control access to food and medical assistance delivered by international agencies.[19] A desperate choice faced them: return to Rwanda to face retribution from the survivors of the genocide, flee deeper into Zaire, or fight their way back home. One consequence of the conviction that they could win was that a sufficient amount of aid destined for their own people was siphoned off to buy weapons to execute guerrilla raids into Rwanda.

The human rights problem at this point is interesting from a number of perspectives. First, there is no legal or diplomatic mechanism for dealing with the collective actions of stateless groups. They are simply assumed to be in need of international protection because of their lack of a state structure. The refugee populations of the Zairean camps fell into this category and so were seen by the world community as helpless victims and deserving of international protection of their human rights, regardless of what they had done or were still doing. That they could organize themselves to redirect aid resources to fund military activities inside Rwandan territory failed to catch the attention of anybody but the victims of their attacks. Sadly, the attacks were often aimed at survivors of the genocide to silence their testimony. (The United Nations High Commission for Human Rights report E/CN.4/1997/52, dated 17 March 1997, paragraph 10, gives the figure of 54 genocide survivors killed during the period January to mid-February 1997.)

From Rwanda's perspective, the existence of armed elements just beyond its borders posed a persistent threat to efforts to rebuild the country. Aside from the destabilizing effect of guerrilla raids on a country whose entire administrative class had either fled or been killed, the existence of a large group of Rwandan citizens under the coerced control of the perpetrators of the genocide posed a long-term risk that could not be ignored, particularly not by people who left had a generation earlier and who fought their way home. The refugees had already demonstrated their military potential, and the Rwandan regime was a long way from having either the administrative efficiency or military force necessary to deal with it. Now this is interesting from a human rights perspective because of the political organization of the refugee community. Refugees did not act as individual stateless victims needing international protection, but as members of a political collectivity prepared to convert international sympathy into military force. Since they were members of the majority ethnicity, they already had a large potential support base deep within Rwandan borders. This raises the interesting issue of whether the inhabitants of the refugee camps in eastern Zaire were really captives of their own leaders.

The survival imperatives of the new regime in Rwanda left the refugees little room for maneuver. The Rwandan People's Army represented the surviving minority in a country whose majority ethnicity still outnumbered them by about four to one. Few survivors felt safe in the company of those from the majority ethnicity who they did not know as having clean hands. The genocide was a messy affair in every sense, resulting in survivors living cheek by jowl with perpetrators in conditions that offered no physical security. However, the defeated regime had shown itself ruthless, cunning, and remorseless in the conduct of operations prior to and during the genocide. It had effectively conned the entire world community, along with their Tutsi compatriots, into believing that cooperation was just around the corner.

The situation at the end of 1994 was desperate. To survive, the new regime needed international help, and therefore could not openly pursue too hard a policy with its own people. But it also needed internal order to deal with the threat of armed revolt. The international community seemed blind to the problems and launched a veritable invasion of well-meaning humanitarians interested in protecting the rights of all people, without distinction. This "blindness" left large numbers of survivors feeling vulnerable to their neighbors, with no reason to trust the international community's willingness to protect them if things went wrong again and no reason to put faith in the good will of the majority.

To add one more chapter to the tale of Rwandan woe, in November 1996, nearly a million refugees returned in a wave that overloaded the capacity of the new regime in Rwanda to screen out the dangerous elements of the former regime. International agencies in Rwanda documented a significant increase in security problems during the ensuing months and were highly critical of government reaction. The current administration seems to have acted as if the classification victim/refugee excused all culpability and legitimated all actions against those who had perpetrated the genocide. How else can we explain the regime's blindness to the fact that the inhabitants of both prisons (with admittedly horrendous living conditions) and refugee camps stood accused of collective and individual complicity in genocide, and yet continued to be the subject of international sympathy and aid? How else can we account for the fact that guerrilla raids into Rwanda, carried out from internationally supported refugee camps during the period November 1995 through November 1996, caused no interruption in the flow of refugee aid?

What prudent course was open to a legitimate authority wanting to protect its people against the predations of an invisible power whose only manifestation seemed to be organized paramilitary raids? Given the Mafia-like structure and conduct of the militant elements embedded in the refugee community prior to and since their return to Rwanda, the Rwandan government had few reasonable options that fit within the spirit of the Universal Declaration or met the constrained conditions of the remaining pieces of the state. This brings us back to Kant's codicil.

4. Survival

There seems at the moment no way of reaching into the Rwandan dynamic to find the kind of "favorable opportunities" for human rights that Kant suggested. The argument that the current regime should ease up on its repressive measures in favor of a genuine respect for rights ignores both Rwanda's recent history and the Tutsis' reasonable sense of continuing vulnerability to the majority ethnicity with whom they share a country. We need to remember that the Tutsis had put their faith in the good intentions of the deposed regime, assisted by the good offices of the United Nations, only to fall into a genocidal trap. (I refer here to the so-called Arusha Accord which had been the blueprint for a negotiated return of the RPA to Rwanda, agreed to prior to the genocide.) The deposed regime tried and failed at an end game strategy that left nearly a million dead and the perpetrators free to exploit international sympathy to arm themselves anew. Our judgment of the current actions of the present regime should focus not so much on its apparent inability to respect human rights as on its insecurity in the face of what it sees as a survival imperative. If it lets down its guard, if it agrees to prioritize respect for individual human rights, then it may gain moral superiority but leave itself powerless to deal with the continuation of genocidal policies by other means. Given the history of the past few years, any sign of reasonableness is likely to be read as a sign of weakness by the militant remnants of the former regime. Given that these same remnants are drawn from the majority Hutu population and given that many hands among them held machetes during the genocide, lending legitimacy to the eliminationist goals they espouse is not a reasonable option for the surviving minority.

Kant argues for the necessity of respect for human rights as a precondition of peace. His argument secures some empirical support from history if we consider how aboriginal peoples on the Great Plains of Canada and the United States responded to contact with European settlers.[20] But the universality of Kant's argument, and indeed the universality of the Declaration, must give way in practice to pressing survival concerns in cases where the sufficient condition of trust is still too far off for prudence to operate. To persist in expecting a vulnerable people to respect the rights of members of a political collectivity with proven genocidal intentions and the continued, if diminished, capacity to execute them is to ask far more than we have a right to ask of others. In view of the present conditions in Rwanda, such a demand is unreasonable.

This case study may well illustrate the central weakness of the Kantian-based logic, which I believe is the best that can be produced in support of the Universal Declaration, but fails to adequately recognize the negative claim of necessity that

I believe gives the Declaration its strength. However, if respect for human rights is a necessary, but not sufficient, condition of peace, then we must consider more carefully how the sufficiency conditions might be met. If, as I have argued above, there are times when the acknowledgment of necessity is overwhelmed by particularly unfavorable circumstances, then we need to turn our attention to the nature of those circumstances. Perhaps this case illustrates most clearly the eventual troubles that may arise when political agreement based on compromise leads to declarations that are not supported by coercive force of the kind usually considered necessary to enforce such agreements within sovereign states. Perhaps it provides nothing more than the beginnings of an argument for meaningful international law. It will be interesting to see if the current climate of international uncertainty will favor the development of political will among sovereign states to generate the next logical step in the chain of reasoning from the Universal Declaration.

Notes

1. Stephen P. Marks, "From the 'Single Confused Page' to the 'Decalogue for Six Billion Persons': The Roots of the Universal Declaration of Human Rights in the French Revolution," *Human Rights Quarterly*, 20 (1998), pp. 459–514.

2. "Perpetual Peace," *Kant's Political Writings*, ed. Hans Reiss, trans. H.B. Nisbet (Cambridge, England: Cambridge University Press, 1970), pp. 120–125.

3. Jacques Maritain, *Man and the State* (Chicago: University of Chicago Press, 1951), p. 76.

4. See "Rwanda, Ending the Silence," *Amnesty International Report, AFR 47/32/97* (25 September 1997).

5. See Alan Gewirth, *Human Rights: Essays on Justification and Applications* (Chicago: University of Chicago Press, 1982), ch. 1.

6. John Rawls, *A Theory of Justice* (Cambridge, MA: Harvard University Press, 1971), sec. 25.

7. See *Fights, Games and Debates* (Ann Arbor: University of Michigan Press, 1960).

8. Lawrence H. Keeley, *War Before Civilization* (New York: Oxford University Press, 1966).

9. Kant, "Perpetual Peace," p. 118.

10. Ibid., p. 122.

11. Ibid. Emphasis mine.

12. Ibid., p. 124.

13. Ibid.

14. See "Statement by Mary Robinson, United Nations High Commissioner for Human Rights" (9 May 1998).

15. See "Ending the Silence," Amnesty International Report 47/32/97 (25 September 1997).

16. Gérard Prunier, *The Rwanda Crisis 1959–1994: History of a Genocide* (London: Hurst & Company, 1995); Alain Destexhe, *Rwanda: Essai sur le génocide* (Brussels: Editions Complexe, 1994); Francois Bugingo, *Africa Mea* (Montreal: Editions Liber, 1997).

17. African Rights, *Rwanda: Death, Despair, Defiance* (London: African Rights, 1995).

18. Witnessed by the author while in charge of the largest sector of United Nations Assistance Mission in Rwanda (UNAMIR), Gitarama and Butare Prefectures, during period December 1994 to May 1995.

19. Field notes, October 1994, UN assessment team to eastern Zaire.

20. Keeley, *War Before Civilization,* p. 154.

PART III

RIGHTS AFTER THE UNIVERSAL DECLARATION

Ten

RECONCILING INDIVIDUAL RIGHTS AND THE COMMON GOOD: AQUINAS AND CONTEMPORARY LAW

Paul Groarke and J.L.A. West

The following paper is divided into three sections. The first section briefly reviews the history of the concept of rights and its significance in the ongoing debate between liberals and communitarians. The contemporary literature has overlooked the possibility of constructing a theory of rights on Thomistic principles, which would reconcile individual rights with the common good. The second section reviews Aquinas's position with respect to unjust laws in the *Summa Theologiae* and draws attention to the prominence of the principle of equality in his discussion. This principle is sufficient to provide the basis for a viable theory of individual rights within an understanding of law that is ordained to the common good. The final section discusses the implications of the Thomistic position in the context of the existing law and general constitutional theory.

1. The Evolution of the Concept of Rights

Anyone who has read the contemporary philosophical literature might be forgiven for thinking that the modern understanding of rights rests on the belief in the inherent value of the individual. According to Elaine Pagels, this interpretation is fundamentally wrong.

> Much more common, and far more universal, in historical and geographical terms, is the opposite idea: that society confers upon its members whatever rights, privileges or exemptions they enjoy. According to this concept, ultimate value derives from the social order.[1]

In this context, the concept of rights has a distinctly legal flavor. This is evident in the development of the term, which can be seen historically as an attempt to give the moral claims of the individual a supervening authority over ordinary laws.

The prominence of the idea of natural rights in our philosophical tradition is usually attributed to Thomas Hobbes and John Locke. Earlier yet, its origins can be traced to Francisco Suarez and other philosophers in the Catholic tradition. Some of the elements of a social contract can be found in the work of these philosophers, who recognized that circumstances exist in which a king could lose his right to govern the people. This possibility did not threaten the relationship between the sovereign and the individual, since individual rights existed within the constraints necessary for the good of the whole community.

Francisco de Vitoria, the predecessor of Suarez, wrote:

> if all men would be equal and subject to no power, with each one tending by his own choice and opinion in a different direction, without some providence which would have common care and concern for the common good, the republic would necessarily be pulled apart and the state would be destroyed.[2]

This view is firmly within the Thomistic tradition. Vitoria is not questioning the notion of equality per se. He is arguing that it is meaningless to speak of the equality that exists between members of a community outside the social framework of the larger community in which the individual resides.

Although Hobbes was influenced by the work of Suarez, the Thomistic influences on the concept of rights were eventually supplanted by a strong liberal notion of autonomy. We do not derive our rights from membership in society; quite the contrary, society derives its legitimacy from the fact that it protects and furthers the rights of individual persons. This view has persisted until the present day and seems to have reached its apogee in some of the more extreme contractarian views in the contemporary ethical literature.

The modern concept of rights finds some similarities with the theory of natural law, at least constitutionally, since the natural law derives its legal efficacy from the fact that it can be used to determine the validity of human laws. However, considerable debate has occurred about whether the origin of modern rights is found in medieval thought. Authors such as Maritain, Finnis, and Tully have argued that modern rights theories are either developments of the earlier approach or complementary to it, whereas Macpherson and Strauss have maintained that the two are incompatible.[3] Elaine Pagels also denies a continuity between the two approaches, when she writes that the modern concept of pre-political rights is of relatively recent origin.

> Not until the 17th and 18th centuries is expression given to the notion that every human being has rights that are to be recognized – not conferred – by society. In the civil war in England, in the tradition that formed the United States Constitution and in the revolution in France, fought in the name of "liberty, equality and fraternity," we find a new theory of "inalienable" human rights as the constitutive principle of political order. Following this declaration of human rights, a new statement of the purpose of government appears: "to ensure these rights, governments are instituted among men."[4]

The historical events in France and the United States help to explain how the concept of rights achieved such prominence in the constitutional apparatus of modern liberal democracies.

Although the limited concept of natural rights has been replaced by a broader concept of "human rights," the inalienable or constitutional status of the concept of rights has singled it out for such acclaim. This is evident as early as the Déclaration des droits de l'homme et du citoyen in 1789, which holds in article 2:

> The aim of every political association is the preservation of the natural and inalienable rights of man; these rights are liberty, property, security, and resistance to oppression.[5]

The general scheme of such constitutional rights is simple enough. The entrenchment of individual rights is designed to place moral limits on the legal authority that a civil government can exercise over the individual. This idea has proved remarkably attractive in the popular imagination, and it is one of the ironies of our intellectual history that the present use of the concept of rights turns its original meaning on its head.

No doubt such documentary utterances are important in the history of ideas. Nonetheless, the meaning of such declarations is easily overstated and the notion of inalienable rights has always been advanced, at least in a legal context, with important qualifications. Article 5 of the same Déclaration, for example, attempts to limit the power of the state by holding that the law "has the right to forbid only actions which are injurious to society." Rather than limit the power of the state, this recognizes that the concept of inalienable rights presupposes a social context in which individual rights are subject to constraint. This is a necessary fixture of any legal order, which issues from the sovereign power and cannot exist without an identifiable source.

Much the same insight can be found in the work of those contemporary philosophers who reject the argument that individual rights are morally ascendant. The question of whether or not we can speak properly of individual rights outside a social context could be used as a convenient dividing line between liberals and communitarians. The argument against liberals is essentially that rights do not exist within a community unless there is a community with the moral and legal authority that any community exercises over individuals. The contest between the two views has polarized the more general discussion of rights, at least in the Anglo-American tradition, and the term appears to have been appropriated by liberals in the course of the ongoing debate. One notable result of this is that the philosophical discussion of even group rights has usually taken place within a liberal framework. This is despite the fact that the Marxist critique of natural rights has had a discernible effect on the use of the term "rights" in an international context, where it has been extended to social and economic claims.

Many philosophers within the communitarian camp are inclined to dismiss the moral use of the term "rights" as a rhetorical device for asserting moral demands. Morton Winston captures the skepticism among communitarians as well as anyone. Alasdair MacIntyre, he writes, rejects Alan Gerwirth's move, "from the claim that all purposive agents need or want freedom and well-being in order to function successfully as agents to the conclusion that they have 'rights' to these goods."[6] According to MacIntyre, in making this step, Gerwirth has "illicitly smuggled in" a conception of the rational agent functioning within a social context in which the notions of entitlement and having a right are intelligible ones. "Lacking any such social form, the making of a claim to a right would be like presenting a check for payment in a social order that lacked the institution of money."[7] Hence, there is no need to accept the narrow concept of individual rights found in liberal thought, and the present paper essentially argues that the work of Aquinas provides the social context needed to construct a meaningful theory of rights.

2. Aquinas on Law, the Common Good, and Individual Rights

The previous section has shown that the modern liberal notion of "inherent rights" differs from the traditional notion of rights as arising from membership in a political community. In a fairly broad statement, Pagels puts virtually all of Christian, Muslim, and Jewish thought into the latter category, in which "Society confers upon its members whatever rights, privileges or exemptions they enjoy. According to this concept, ultimate value derives from the social order."[8] While the distinction she is making is useful in some cases, it requires certain qualifications. The purpose of the present section is to illustrate that Aquinas's position is actually in neither of these camps, but indeed provides a *via media* between the positions she identifies, which we see as two extremes.

In Aquinas's theory of law, his use of the principle *lex iniusta non est lex* (an unjust law is not a law) reveals the problem with the view that political privileges arise solely from society. This view has, of course, a long history. Aquinas attributes it to Augustine, and it can be found in Cicero and other Roman authors.[9] There is a rather obvious sense in which this principle seems to support the notion of individual rights. On the surface, it can be taken to mean that if a law treats an individual unjustly, then it is not really a law, and we have no obligation in conscience to obey it. In certain cases, we may actually be obliged to break it.

According to Aquinas, a law may be unjust in two ways. First, it may be contrary to the human good. This injustice occurs with respect to the end or purpose of the law, when the law imposes upon subjects burdens that do not further the common good, but advance the lawmaker's personal desires or vanity. This kind of injustice is found in a number of contemporary cases where laws are the result of conflict of interest. In democracies such injustice might well include decisions calculated to increase voter support at critical times, at the expense of the common good, for example, handing out excessive government grants or contracts and deciding whether or not to invoke conscription in a war situation. A law can also be contrary to the human good on the part of the authority of the lawmaker when he or she makes laws concerning matters that exceed his or her power or jurisdiction. Finally, a law may be unjust due to its form, "as when burdens are unequally distributed, *even if they are ordered to the common good.*"[10] Laws of this kind, Aquinas notes, are more like outrages (*violentiae*) than laws. He then quotes Augustine's famous passage and makes the crucial point:

> As Augustine says, a law which is not just does not seem to be a law. Hence, such laws do not bind in the court of conscience; except perhaps on account of avoiding a scandal or disturbance for the sake of which a man ought to yield even his right.[11]

The second way a law may be unjust is by being contrary to the divine good. This happens, for example, when a tyrant demands his subjects commit idolatry or an act contrary to the divine law. Such laws, Aquinas maintains, should not be observed at all. In summary, a law can be unjust either because it is contrary to the human good – either by the end or by the form (that is, because of something about the authority or because it imposes disproportionate burdens) – or, because it is contrary to the divine good, by violating divine law.

For pragmatic reasons, this chapter is restricted to Aquinas's arguments concerning laws contrary to the human good. Within this category, the criterion that a law is unjust if unequal burdens are imposed is of special concern for the argument to follow. To understand this criterion, we must recall Aristotle's account of equality from the *Politics,* which provides a helpful nuance to Aquinas's view. In his discussion of distributive justice, Aristotle noted that we must distinguish between numerical equality and proportionate equality. On the basis of numerical equality, each person receives exactly the same share, regardless of his or her contributions or merits. However, the distribution is proportionately equal where those who have made an equal contribution receive an equal share.[12] Applying this to Aquinas's view, we can see that when the burdens are unequally distributed, disproportionate, the law is unjust. Of utmost importance is that unequal distribution of burdens makes a law unjust, even if the law is for the common good. Thus, we see that with Aquinas, equality can override consideration of the common good.

Still, Aquinas thinks law must be directed towards the common good.[13] This principle has understandably led liberals to view Thomistic political theory with suspicion, as giving the common good priority over the good of the individual. Such a priority allows a dangerous form of holism, in which leaders appeal to the good of the state to justify repression of individual rights. This is a serious concern indeed. However, a careful reading shows that Aquinas's theory does include principles that yield important safeguards for individual rights.

In the Aristotelian tradition, the appeal to the common good does not originate in an attempt to justify the state's impositions upon the individual. Instead, the appeal to the common good shows that rulers should not govern for personal gain, but in the interest of the community. This latter feature of the common good is also found in Aquinas where, following Isidore of Seville, he argues that since laws are framed for the common good, they should not benefit only private individuals. Instead, laws should be established because they are useful for the community as a whole.[14] A central aim of appealing to the common good, far from enshrining the rights of rulers over and above those of subjects, is to show how use of political authority should not be for the private benefit of the ruler.

Grounds for the liberal concern can nevertheless be found in Aquinas's text. In the same article where he discusses the illegitimacy of unjust laws, he argues,

> Since a man is a part of a community each man, in that which he is and in what he has, is the community's. Just as every part in that which it is, is the whole's. Hence, nature inflicts some injury on a part in order to save the whole.[15]

Taken in isolation, such texts give credence to the liberal critique. However, Aquinas immediately adds an important qualification, "And on account of this, laws of this kind, *imposing proportionate burdens*, are just, and they bind in the court of conscience, and are legal laws."[16] Hence, as we argued in the previous section, an important qualification upon the rulers' right to impose burdens upon citizens is that the burdens imposed must be proportionate.

This seems to give rise to two competing principles, the common good and equality. In reality it does not. In this context, Aquinas articulates the three principles discussed above twice in the same key article from the *Prima Secundae*.[17] At the beginning of the *respondeo*, he puts them forward as the criteria a law must meet to be just, while he repeats them later in the same passage, in order to explain when a law is unjust. In both accounts proportionate equality is mentioned; however, a careful reading shows a fundamental shift in emphasis between the two.

When discussing just laws, Aquinas emphasizes that the lawgiver is entitled to impose proportionate burdens upon individuals for the sake of the common good. Yet, when he turns to the issue of unjust laws, he tells us that laws which impose disproportionate burdens do not bind a person in conscience, even if they are ordered to the common good. When combined, these qualifications provide a moderate position that incorporates the most attractive features of the liberal and communitarian camps. Such a position must allow for both the individual, as a part of the community, to contribute to society by accepting burdens for the common good and the fair distribution of demands made upon individuals in the name of the common good.

Finally, the liberal view that community and individual interests are fundamentally at odds does not necessarily hold. In Aquinas's view, they ought to be harmonious. If the lawgiver's intention in framing the laws is "fixed upon the true good," namely the common good, then the laws will be set with the aim of aiding the citizens in pursuit of the good life. Since living such a life is the natural end of each human being, we have no need for the interests of the state and the citizens to be at odds. Indeed, in Aquinas's view, the presence of such discord would indicate a misguided attempt to pursue some private good, at the expense of the common good, on the part of either the ruler or the citizen.[18]

Aquinas addresses the issue of compatibility of community and individual interests while discussing whether the virtue of prudence includes the governing of many. In *Summa Theologiae* II–II, q. 47, a. 10, an objector says that prudence concerns seeking the good for oneself, whereas those who seek the common good deny their own interests and, therefore, are imprudent. Aquinas replies, "he who seeks the common good of the multitude also seeks his own good as a consequence." He gives two reasons for this. The first is that "one's own good is impossible without the common good of either the family or the community or the kingdom." Aquinas, citing Valerius Maximus, says that for this reason the Romans were said to prefer being poor in a rich empire than rich in a poor empire. Second, since a person is a part of a home and a community, "it is necessary that he consider what is good for him in terms of what is prudent concerning the good of the multitude." Aquinas supports this by arguing that the well-being (*bona dispositio*) of the parts depends upon their relation to the whole.[19]

Aquinas's arguments show the misguided character of the liberal assumption that the individual good is incommensurable with the common good. We have is no reason to think the two are not harmonious, for the individual's good is only attained in the context of attaining the common good of his or her family and community. We find this point explained by Jacques Maritain, who fully recognized that since the good of the body politic is the good of human persons, the common good and that of the individual are mutually conducive. Hence, he writes,

> The common good is the good *human* life of the multitude, of a multitude of *persons*; it is their communion in the good life; it is therefore common *to the whole and to the parts*, on whom it flows back and who must all benefit from it. Under the pain of being denatured, such a good implies and demands the recognition of the fundamental rights of the person. It involves as its chief value, the highest possible accession (an accession compatible with the good of the whole) of persons to their life as persons ...[20]

3. Implications for Constitutional Theory: The Canadian Example

The Thomistic theory is significant from a legal point of view for a number of reasons. One of the interesting features of legal argument in the constitutional sphere is that it refuses to see the dichotomy between the liberal and communitarian positions, which are so prevalent in the philosophical literature. This refusal may be a reflection of the pragmatic nature of legal discourse, which generally seeks a practical accommodation between the public interest and individual rights. It may also be a consequence of the fact that, from a legal perspective, individual rights are always exercised in a social context. Legal or constitutional rights derive from the community at large, which has purportedly expressed its aspirations in a constitution. If the Thomistic view is accepted, and law is ordained to the common good, we have the possibility that individual rights might derive from the common good.

In this part of the chapter, we accordingly consider the Thomistic theory of law and a Thomistic concept of rights in the context of the existing law. The Canadian law is of interest in such a discussion, since it incorporates elements from both a conservative and a liberal tradition, and we have restricted our discussion to the Canadian constitution. After discussing the nature of the constitutional jurisprudence, we consider two ways in which the Thomistic position seems to help in explaining the operation of the current law. The more contentious issue is the introduction of the principle of the common good as an over-arching principle governing the application of more specific constitutional provisions. Such a possibility is noteworthy in the context of the Canadian Charter of Rights and Freedoms, which has appended a liberal set of individual rights to a relatively conservative body of constitutional law. The Thomistic position also seems helpful in the area of rights, where the concept of proportionate equality enters the case law in a straightforward manner.

First, then, we should consider the discussion in Aquinas. As we have seen, the use of the principle of equality in the *Summa Theologiae* seems to provide the necessary basis for a working theory of rights, which is much in line with the egalitarian tradition in contemporary liberal thought. This basis is evident in *Summa Theologiae* II–II, q. 57, a. 3, ad 3, where Aquinas says that "right" (*ius*) is the object of justice. The notions of justice and right rest on the principle of equality. Aquinas writes, "That is called just in our work which corresponds to some kind of equality with another, for instance, the payment of a wage owed for a service rendered."[21]

In article four of the same question, Aquinas says, "Right or just depends on commensuration with another person." This might seem at odds with the Thomistic view that law "is ordained to the common good" and protects the interests of the whole community, even to the injury of its parts. Nonetheless, we have no reason to believe that Aquinas would have perceived any difficulty in reconciling these two aspects of his theory of law.

The theory of rights which emerges from the Thomistic model of law suggests a possible amalgamation of some of the main features of a communitarian and liberal view in the same constitutional theory. The position Aquinas takes can be characterized as conservative and communitarian, since the individual appears to derive his fulfillment from his function as part of the community. At the same time, however, the principle of *lex inuista non est lex* provides Aquinas with the necessary foundation for a theory of individual rights within the broader context of the community.

Not only does a Thomistic perspective see no inherent conflict between a theory of individual rights and a theory of law which rests on the common good, but it supports the much stronger argument that individual rights derive from the common good and participate in it. This perspective is attractive for the legal theorist because it does not seem possible to speak of a constitutional theory of rights without presupposing the existence of the society from which they are claimed. While we may want to argue that rights emanate from our inherent value as individuals, rather than our membership in the community, this is an unsatisfying explanation in a constitutional context, because it does not catch the essential point that rights have the form of a demand. A constitutional right is meaningless unless it is addressed to an authority over the individual, who has the capacity to enforce it in some manner.

This leads us to the other point noted, that of the usefulness of a Thomistic concept of rights in the context of the law. The position Aquinas takes is significant from a legal perspective because it provides a practical model of rights, which we can use to examine the law. Although this position has implications for all constitutional jurisprudence, the Canadian tradition is of particular relevance in elaborating such a theory. This is because the historical foundations of Canadian jurisprudence lie in the British principle of parliamentary supremacy, which places an emphasis on the needs of government. Canadian law also reflects the British positivist tradition, manifested in John Austin's argument that the law is a command. The King or Crown is the source of the law, and so is above the law. This explains why in the Canadian tradition, the actions of the Governor General were the subject of convention rather than law. It also explains why it was so difficult to sue the Crown.

Some think this interpretation goes too far. Former Chief Justice Brian Dickson suggested that the importance of the doctrine of parliamentary supremacy in Canadian law has been exaggerated, for Canadian courts have traditionally exercised some control over the substantive powers of government.[22] Although undoubtedly the claim has some truth, Canadian jurisprudence has been distinguished historically by its deference to the authority of Parliament and a strong sense of the public good. Although many concessions to individual rights have been made in the British tradition, those rights did not impinge upon the authority of the sovereign. The principle of "equality before the law" is a good example of a procedural doctrine that did not limit the substantive powers of government.[23]

While we may see advantages and disadvantages to the British/Canadian tradition, questions naturally arise, for example, "What controls the sovereign power?" Likely the actions of the sovereign are restricted by the principle of the common good. Although the theoretical question as to who should enforce such a restriction remains unanswered, some aspects of the issue would seem to fall naturally within the constitutional mandate of the courts. Without investigating the matter, we might speculate that traces are found of such a criterion in the rules of statutory interpretation and other technical restrictions in the law. In past practice, few constraints were placed on Parliament. The older tradition, however, seems to run contrary to the constitutional protections which have been extended to individual rights under the Canadian Charter of Rights and Freedoms. This tension remains even today, since the Charter is only one part of the Canadian constitution and there is always the possibility of a conflict with constitutional prerogatives, like the authority of the federal government to pass legislation with respect to "peace, order and good government."

Such tensions may be a strength rather than a weakness of the system, since the divergent features of the Canadian constitutional system have put the Canadian courts in an unusually good position to reconcile the liberal and communitarian positions in a single legal framework along the lines suggested by Aquinas. The Canadian tradition still safeguards the common good, even as it provides a series of guarantees of individual rights and freedoms. Thus, Justice Dickson writes that the Charter of Rights "is profoundly sensitive to the fact that on some occasions rights have to be balanced with competing values."[24] This is evident, he argues, in the wording of section 1 of the Charter, which states that the rights protected by the Charter are subject to reasonable limitations:

> This introduces the need to balance the right of the individual against society's reasons for restricting that right in the context of a given case. Thus, although the arrival of the *Charter* has meant a new role for Canadian courts, that role is well rooted in a heritage that has long displayed sensitivity to the need for government to get on with the business of governing. Unless the impugned legislation runs counter to what can be justified in a free and democratic society, the legislatures have the plenary right to identify important policy objectives and implement them by law.[25]

Although the Charter is undoubtedly a liberal document, it reflects a strong conviction that individual rights are subject to the limits placed upon them by the public interest.

Although the "rights" in the Charter have a higher constitutional status than the ordinary law, the inclusion of section 1 gives the general principle of government precedence over individual rights. The Charter of Rights also differs from the Bill of Rights of the United States and many other constitutional declarations in that it contains the elements of a legal framework intended to protect the values of a specific community. As Dickson writes, the *Charter* serves to make it clear that liberty in Canada is but one component of a much larger matrix of values. Interpretive sections in the *Charter* such as section 25 ... section 27 ... and section 28 ... all affect the interpretation of *Charter* rights in ways that reflect important features of the Canadian social and political fabric. These provisions, along with others regarding the important matters of language and educational rights, reflect the unique history of Canadian society. [26]

We can infer from the interpretive provisions to which Dickson refers that individual rights are to be interpreted in a manner consonant with the good of the larger community. This should be enough to rebut any legal assumption that individual rights and the common good are necessarily in conflict.

Having set out some of the parameters of the Canadian jurisprudence, and its incorporation of conservative and liberal elements, we can turn to the more specific issues arising in the context of a Thomistic theory of rights. We must consider if the Thomistic principle that the law is ordained to the common good can be imported into a convincing constitutional theory. The advantage of introducing a Thomistic theory of law in this context is that it brings individual rights under the scope of an inquiry into the common good. One interesting aspect of adopting such a position is that the Charter of Rights is a part of the Constitution Act and possesses the character of law. As a result, the question which initially arises is whether the Charter is ordained to the common good? This kind of question is not as hypothetical as it might seem, because of the conflict between the principle of the common good and a theory of unlimited individual rights.

The decisions of the Supreme Court on hate literature and obscenity are relevant in this context, since they represent areas where the Supreme Court is willing to place moral limits on the scope of the Charter. In *R. v. Keegstra*, [1990] 3 S.C.R. 697, for example, the Supreme Court held that the criminal offence of promoting hatred was a justifiable limit on freedom of expression. This places significant limits on individual rights and freedoms: the case establishes that the guarantee of freedom of expression does not extend to speech that is antithetical to the common good. This is a conservative view, which is difficult to justify on the basis of the liberal views presently available in the academic marketplace. However, the Supreme Court gave a liberal rationale for its decision in the case and expanded it in *R. v. Butler*, [1992] 1 S.C.R. 452, where the court upheld the offence of obscenity on the basis of the principle of harm.

The use of the harm principle is an awkward strategy, legally, if only because it leads to difficult and, even intractable, evidentiary issues. Nor is evidence necessarily conclusive; expert evidence is usually partial and moral standards are not subject to the normal standards of proof. The Supreme Court of Canada avoided these difficulties by adopting a notional rather than a substantive doctrine of harm, arguing that Parliament is entitled to a reasonable apprehension that obscene material would cause harm to society. Yet then another question arises.

"Why should we assume that such material would cause harm?" The answer is apparently that it is inherently immoral, and for that reason, it seems evident the Supreme Court relied on moral grounds to justify its decision. For any practical purposes, at least, the *Butler* decision makes it clear that moral contingencies are operating as a condition precedent to the operation of the Charter.

The decision in *Butler* presents a good example of a set of circumstances in which the Supreme Court was prepared to adopt a restricted concept of individual rights and freedoms in order to protect the moral fabric of society. Still unclear, in this context, is whether the concept of harm provides anything more than a liberal rationale for an underlying conception of the public good. The Supreme Court has explicitly, in a number of cases, rejected the liberal approach that gives individual rights predominance over social constraints. This result may well be an inevitable part of any body of constitutional law, but its significance is that it permits a government to restrict personal liberties in order to protect the interest of the community. The most plausible interpretation of the present situation is that the constitution was never intended to provide a guarantee of unrestricted individual rights, and the rights and freedoms in the Charter must be construed in accordance with an over-arching principle like the common good. This view is also consistent with the concept of rights and the theory of law that emerges in the *Summa*.

A further matter calling for attention is the question of proportionate equality, which would seem to govern a Thomistic theory of rights. It is significant that the term "rights" in Canadian law bears resemblance to the concept of rights that emerges from the discussion in the *Summa*. We see this, for example, in section 15 of the Charter of Rights, which enshrines "the right to the equal protection and equal benefit of the law" in the constitution. Section 15 is notable because it subjects the actions of government to the substantive principle that everyone is equal before and under the law. We also find some similarities to the Thomistic view in the general assumption of equality in provisions like section seven, which gives everyone the right to life, liberty, and security of the person, and the right not to be deprived thereof except in accordance with the principles of fundamental justice. The judicial interpretation of these rights, like the case law dealing with the rights of an accused person, canvasses the same fundamental concerns that arise in the *Summa*.

A further illustration of the similarities between the Charter and the *Summa* is given in the law relating to section one, which holds that the state must first establish that the objective of the legislation meets a "pressing and substantial" concern.[27] On the Thomistic explanation, section one can be read as a stipulation that the purpose of the legislation must be directed to the common good. Once that has been established, the courts turn to the next task, to determine whether the means used to achieve the objective are "proportional." Such a determination is more complex than on the Thomistic analysis, and encompasses issues which relate more directly to the question of whether the law is in keeping with the common good. The essential issue is "does the measure achieve a proper balance between the interests of the individual and the interests of the community as a whole?" The courts have placed a good deal of value on personal freedom, but their primary concern is to determine if the legislation treats a certain class of individuals or groups unfairly. This implicitly raises a fundamental issue of equality and asks the courts to decide whether the legislation is discriminatory.

The assertion of a moral or a legal right is often presented as a conclusion. This is particularly true in the constitutional arena, where a right is generally appealed to in making an argument: since other individuals – certain kinds of persons or human beings – enjoy a particular prerogative, and since I share the relevant characteristics of those individuals, the law must grant me the same prerogative. The essence of the claim is the contention that individuals or groups with the same essential features have not been treated equally. Similar claims arise under the Canadian Human Rights Act and other human rights legislation, which introduce a general principle of equality into the law regulating the private relationships between individuals. Although such legislation is not, strictly speaking, part of the constitution, it has been accorded "quasi-constitutional" status by the courts.

Such constitutional or quasi-constitutional claims extend beyond a moral demand, since they suggest that society has a legal obligation to provide the prerogative in question. This role of society is crucial because it establishes the broader concept of constitutional rights, which rests on a fundamental demand that the community defer to individual rights. Undoubtedly, this aspect of the concept of rights appeals to those who wish to advance compelling moral claims. Yet there is another feature of the law involved, which seems to undermine the liberal premise that individual interests are somehow prior to the interests of the community. This feature is the question of standing: the person or persons who claim they have a right to a particular prerogative must first satisfy the court that they are entitled to advance a constitutional claim. This approach is interesting, in the context of inalienable rights, since it is tantamount to a recognition that the community determines whether an individual has the status to claim the rights in question.

The law is far more sensitive than is the academic literature on the question of standing. The issue of standing usually enters the philosophical debate in the context of applied ethics, where feminists have argued that the concept of rights has been of little help in redressing the historic inequalities within Western society. Legal and constitutional rights were usually granted to legal persons, a concept generally excluding those who suffered from entrenched inequalities. This exclusion was not always a simple matter of discrimination, since the law has to deal with such awkward categories of claimants as unborn children, dependent adults, prisoners, corporate personalities, and resident aliens. The common law is given to complications on difficult questions and does not hesitate to provide partial answers to such questions, as it did in the instance of a child who had been injured *in utero*.

The embarrassments of history likely reflect the failings of a particular community rather than a deficiency in the structure of the law. Although many prominent issues of standing still require resolution, an individual's claim to a right must be addressed to the community at large. Of course, this does not imply that the community will be morally correct or will adequately apply the criteria when deciding to extend rights to a class or group of individuals in specific cases. However, such situations illustrate that individual rights cannot be understood outside a community, and they suggest that a party who applies for redress from the community and rejects its authority has adopted an inconsistent position.

The question of standing leads to the substantive issue of discrimination. Since the language in the Charter of Rights and human rights legislation is decidedly inclusive, the question of comparison has given rise to the primary issue in most complaints under human rights legislation. That issue is whether the individual asserting the right shares the relevant features of the category of individuals who already enjoy the prerogative or benefit in question.

The significance of this issue is evident because the predominant concern of the courts under the Charter of Rights and the Canadian Human Rights Act is whether the law distributes its benefits and burdens equally. As Justice McIntyre wrote, in *Law Society of B.C. v. Andrews*, [1989] 1 S.C.R. 143, at p. 165,

> the admittedly unattainable ideal should be that a law expressed to bind all should not because of irrelevant personal differences have a more burdensome or less beneficial impact on one than another.

Such a concern naturally raises the question of proportionate equality, which seems to govern the legal inquiry into the significant characteristics of the relevant "comparators," the individual or group with which the claimant is asserting equality. The issue of proportionality arises on both sides of the question, since the courts have recognized that a law which fails to draw relevant differences – and treats individuals who are fundamentally different in an equal fashion – may also attract a complaint of inequality under human rights legislation. If the burdens are unequally distributed, in the sense that they are disproportionate, then the law is unconstitutional.

This brief examination of two major concerns in Canadian law shows some of the issues that arise in bringing a Thomistic theory into contact with existing jurisprudence. Many further issues could be explored in such a context, but they lie beyond the scope of this chapter. A Thomistic theory of rights would, however, provide a helpful model in examining some of the concerns that arise under the Canadian constitution. Such a theory is particularly significant because the jurisprudence under the Charter of Rights is relatively undeveloped and we do not have a constitutional theory that properly explains the manner in which the Charter should be interpreted. Providing such a theory is a fundamental issue in the

Canadian jurisprudence, which deserves further attention from the legal, academic, and philosophical community.

Notes

1. Elaine Pagels, "The Roots and Origins of Human Rights," *Human Dignity: The Internationalisation of Human Rights*, ed. Alice H. Henkin (New York: Aspen Institute for Humanistic Studies, 1979), p. 2.

2. Francisco de Vitoria [*Relectio de potestate civili, Obras de Francisco de Vitoria: Relecciones teologicas*, ed. Teofilo Urdánoz (Madrid: Biblioteca de Autores Cristianes, 1960), n. 5, p. 157] quoted in John P. Doyle, "Vitoria on Choosing to Replace a King," *Hispanic Philosophy in the Age of Discovery*, ed. Kevin White (Washington, DC: Catholic University of America Press, 1997), p. 47.

3. Jacques Maritain, *The Rights of Man and Natural Law* (New York: Scribners, 1943); *The Person and the Common Good* (Notre Dame: University of Notre Dame Press, 1966); John Finnis, *Natural Law and Natural Rights*, (Oxford: Clarendon Press, 1980); J. Tully, *A Discourse on Property: John Locke and his Adversaries* (Cambridge: Cambridge University Press, 1980); C.B. Macpherson, *The Political Theory of Possessive Individualism* (Oxford: Oxford University Press, 1962); Leo Strauss, *Natural Right and History* (Chicago: Chicago University Press, 1953), pp. 181–183; see also Ernest L. Fortin, "Human Rights and the Common Good," ed. J. Brian Benestad; *Ernest Fortin: Collected Essays,* 3 vols (Lanham: Rowman & Littlefield, 1996), vol. 3, p. 20; and Ernest Fortin, "On the Presumed Medieval Origin of Individual Rights," ed. J. Brian Benestad; *Ernest Fortin: Collected Essays*, ed. J. Brian Benestad, 3 vols. (Lanham: Rowman & Littlefield, 1996), pp. 243–264.

4. Pagels, "Roots and Origins," p. 6.

5. "The French Declaration of the Rights of Man and Citizen (1789)," *The Human Rights Reader*, ed. and trans. Walter Laqueur and Barry Rubin (New York: Meridian/Penguin, 1990), pp. 118–120.

6. Morton E. Winston, "Introduction," *The Philosophy of Human Rights*, ed. Morton E. Winston (Belmont, California: Wadsworth, 1989), pp. 1–42.

7. Ibid., p. 29.

8. Pagels, "Roots and Origins," pp. 2–3.

9. See Norman Kretzmann, "Lex iniusta non est lex: Laws on Trial in Aquinas' Court of Conscience," *The American Journal of Jurisprudence,* 33 (1988), pp. 99–122.

10. S. Thomae Aquinatis, *Summa Theologiae*, 3 vols. (Taurini: Marietti, 1952), I–II, q. 96, a. 4.

11. Ibid.

12. Aristotle, *Politics*, 1280 a 15 ff.

13. *Summa Theologiae*, I–II, q. 90, a. 2.

14. Ibid., I–II, q. 96, a. 1.

15. *Summa Theologiae*, I–II, q. 96, a. 4, resp.

16. *Summa Theologiae*, I–II, q. 96, a. 4.

17. Ibid.

18. *Summa Theologiae*, I–II, q. 92, a. 1, resp.

19. *Summa Theologiae*, II–II, q. 47, a. 10, ad 2.

20. Jacques Maritain, "The Human Person and Society," *Challenges and Renewals: Selected Readings,* ed. J.W. Evans and L.R. Ward (Notre Dame: University of Notre Dame Press, 1966), pp. 293–294.

21. *Summa Theologiae,* II–II, q. 57, a. 3, ad 3.

22. See Brian Dickson, "The Canadian Charter of Rights and Freedoms: Context and Evolution," *The Canadian Charter of Rights and Freedoms,* ed. Gérald A. Beaudoin and Errol Mendes (Scarborough, ON: Carswell, 1996), pp. 1-1 – 1-19, at pp. 1-12.

23. Ritchie J. in *Attorney-General of Canada v. Lavell* (1973), [1974] S.C.R. 1349 at 1373; see *Stephen's Commentaries on the Laws of England,* quoted in Dickson, "The Canadian Charter," at 1366.

24. Dickson, "The Canadian Charter of Rights and Freedoms," p. 1-12.

25. Ibid., pp. 1-12 ff.

26. Ibid., pp. 1-13.

27. See Supreme Court of Canada, *R. v. Oakes,* [1986] 1 S.C.R. 103.

Eleven

MODERATING THE PHILOSOPHY OF RIGHTS

Ralph Nelson

Surely one of the most remarkable occurrences in the last half of the twentieth century was the revival of human – formerly natural – rights theory. The Universal Declaration of Human Rights of 1948; the emergence of notions of human rights in political philosophy, especially liberal political philosophy; the use of the rhetoric of rights in international relations; the entrenchment of rights in the Canadian Charter of Rights and Freedoms; and last, but not least, the adoption by Pope John Paul II of the language of human rights bear testimony to this renewed interest.

We know that declarations may not be followed by implementation, especially when some categories of rights are contested. We know, as well, that liberal political philosophy has become, in the words of one liberal, "rights-obsessed."[1] Sometimes, the rhetoric of rights in international relations is more for domestic consumption than to improve matters in other states. Sometimes, entrenching charters in constitutions changes political systems in unforeseen and unpopular ways. And while the language of human rights offers a bishop an apt idiom for condemnation of abuses, it may not be a basis for the governance of a church.

If we accept that attention to human rights – a concern for the lives, liberties, and well-being of our fellow creatures – is a good thing, we may still be concerned that the emphasis on, and the scope of, these rights have been exaggerated. To describe the effect of natural law on *ius gentium*, as Hugo Grotius wrote, moderation (*temperamentum*) is needed.[2]

Jacques Maritain played a key role in the revival of human rights theory after John Dewey consigned the concept of human rights to the museum of antiquities.[3] In a relatively short period of time, Maritain's thought underwent a transformation, perhaps owing to the influence of Mortimer Adler, and Maritain set himself the task of grafting a doctrine of natural rights onto Thomism. He writes, "A genuine and comprehensive view would pay attention *both* to the obligations and the rights involved in the requirements of the natural law."[4] If Maurice Cranston were correct, Thomas Aquinas already has a doctrine of rights, so apparently no graft is needed.[5] However, Cranston's position is not tenable.[6]

Maritain, with his proposal for a personal and communitarian philosophy, attempted to combine the conception of the common good with the attribution of rights to the human, civic, and working person. Now a notable representative of the new communitarian current has set out an antinomy between "the politics of rights" and "the politics of the common good."[7] Maritain's project means that we do not have to choose; we can have both. Some critics of Maritain have always rejected any attempt to graft human rights to a Thomistic philosophy, because such a philosophy is a duty-ethic; or because Maritain would then have to accept elements of modern philosophy that he has elsewhere rejected (Kantian themes, for instance); or because, in integrating an account of rights, he has leaned toward the personalist pole and away from the communal one. (Personalism differs from individualism in name only.)[8]

The position of *The Rights of Man and Natural Law* must be combined with that of *The Person and the Common Good*, as well as other writings aimed at safeguarding two kinds of values: one about justice and the other about community. The problem is one of method. On a number of occasions Maritain tried to "distinguish in order to unite." This approach distinguishes concepts, like science and wisdom, and then shows how they become integrated in a broader perspective. If we begin with community, common good, and duty, how are we led to rights? As I see it, because of the nature of his publications during the 1940s, some kind of reconstruction is called for. Fortunately, Yves R. Simon, Maritain's former student and later friend, has provided a more systematic elaboration in which the priority of the common good is maintained and a defense of human rights emerges.[9] Simon's approach is a corrective to Maritain's, since he provides the background of what is lacking in the latter, an account of a Thomistic political philosophy that begins with the primacy of the common good. Simon, through an examination of the governing process, shows how our duties emerge and only subsequently deals with the question of rights. Through Simon, then, we can show how Thomistic political philosophy can come into contact with modern political discourse. Simon's democratic philosophy assigns an appropriate place to rights, without letting politics be consumed by them, as might happen through a one-sided emphasis on Maritain's adoption of rights. Simon's approach avoids the danger of the legalization of political thought, a constant temptation in the Thomist tradition. Accepting an American version of human rights also means acquiring a lot of other baggage, specifically the power assigned to the judiciary.

Maritain's broad conception of human rights is a salient feature of the Universal Declaration of Human Rights of 1948. That document outlines two sets of rights: political and civil rights and economic and social rights. Since I am mainly concerned with the stages in the development of the present preoccupation, I have selected a number of markers that bring out the main issues. I begin with Maurice Cranston's critique of the Declaration and several responses to it.

Cranston holds that the only real human rights are political and civil, arguing that the other set of claims, economic and social, are logically distinct from the first set. He claims that the theory underlying the Universal Declaration does not make sense and "hinders the effective protection of what are correctly seen as human rights."[10]

Sociologist Raymond Aron challenges this critique. But Aron's view is particularly interesting because of its commentary on the relation of the French

Declaration of 1789 to the Universal Declaration of 1948. Writing twenty years after the Universal Declaration, he observes,

> [The Declaration] was not accepted by member states as a basis for either legislation or judicial principles; it remains today as it was yesterday, a simple, solemn – and perhaps vain – enumeration of the rights that states judge theoretically desirable to grant to individuals but that they shun considering as imperatives ...[11]

In it, personal and political rights are enlarged by economic and social rights, as if liberals and socialists have been brought together. Yet he notes the devaluation of certain rights, such as the right of property – once "sacred and inviolable."

Aron classifies the Universal Declaration into four categories: the egalitarian principle, the democratic formula, individual and intellectual liberties, and the administration of justice. He believes that in the modern state, in contrast to what he calls the nomocratic state, "achievement of social and economic rights is accorded a higher place than respect for individual rights."[12] What we now have is "the dialogue between liberals and socialists relative to economic and social rights."[13] Aron's assessment of the Declaration is severe.

> The crux of the debate seems to me essentially theoretical: can or should economic and social economic and social rights be placed on the same level as the rights I have termed traditional – those that express universalism, the democratic formula, and personal and intellectual freedoms?[14]

The relative importance of one set of rights or another depends on the situation. In some instances, "the *objectives* that a social order should set for itself" are beyond its means, and so "there is no corresponding duty since no one can be held to the accomplishment of what he *cannot* accomplish."[15] We think of the provision of a basic living standard, work, and education, rest, and leisure in poorer countries. The Marxist stance that the so-called formal freedoms (the first set of rights) must be postponed until real freedom is achieved must be addressed.[16] In this regard, Aron notes that "the producer does not always gain in real freedom what the citizen loses in formal freedom."[17]

Aron then turns to what is common to all sociological thought in dealing with human rights. A philosophy of human rights "that tends to limit the power of the state" is contrasted with a philosophy of human rights "which assigns to the state the crushing, perhaps unrealizable task of transforming the condition of man in society in compliance with certain requirements that were never manifested in the course of preceding centuries."[18] He speaks of the establishment of equality in education and the means that might be used to bring it about, mentioning quotas specifically, and anticipating affirmative action. If sociological thought concedes that economic and social rights enjoy the same status as traditional rights, then sociological thought accepts "historic relativism," in which "the rights of man, stripped of their false universality, recover a historic significance, indeed a historic efficacy."[19] Aron conjectures that "the enlargement of rights has been accompanied by a compensating depreciation."[20] So that when a precious few rights were asserted, they were more highly valued than now. Such a hypothesis must be tested in an age of rights inflation.

For Aron, the 1948 Declaration, involving as it does "a synthesis between a Marxist-Leninist conception and a liberal conception" of rights, is problematic.[21] He notes that

> the 1948 declaration, through its very ambiguity, fulfills the historic function of any such declaration: it criticizes modern society in the name of the ideals that this society has set for itself. According to sociological thought, any philosophy of natural right expresses and denies at the same time the society from which it emanates.[22]

I have reported at some length on Aron's reflections, because they highlight the political and economic implications that partisans of a human rights philosophy either fail to give proper attention to or ignore completely.

Another commentator on Cranston's thesis, Sidney Hook, shares some of Aron's conclusions.[23] Hook's alternative, however, runs into complications. Why should we continue to refer to certain rights as human rights if they have a historical character? A human right would seem to be one that human beings possess, essentially, even though our knowledge of such rights is subject to progress. We discover these rights; we do not invent them. Hook supports rights by relativizing them, like Aron, when he refers to "the historical character of human rights" and the expansion of the list of such rights to include economic and social rights.[24] The dilemma is that if rights are historical, they are not human rights, and if they are human, they are not specifically historical. Perhaps Hook's difficulty is that he wants to embrace simultaneously Dewey's historicism and the advantages of protecting a number of rights and freedoms.

Hook's main point concerns acceptance of the two sets of rights – Aron's position – while asserting the priority of the first set over the second. Like Aron, he deals with the Marxist distinction between formal and real freedoms. "If civil and political rights are, as I believe, of paramount importance, it is not for the reasons given by Cranston."[25] What, then, are the reasons? Hook replies "that without them all other rights could be easily ignored, abused, corrupted, and ultimately lost."[26] Civil and political rights are of strategic importance. Unless civil rights and liberties are regarded as of *strategic* importance and become, so to speak, the ribbed frame of the ship of state and its political order, the social and economic rights that define the social order lack the proper safeguard against erosion, or still worse, perversion into support for tyranny.[27]

After this historic relativism or historicizing of human rights, found in the analysis of Aron and Hook, John Finnis's *Natural Law and Natural Rights*[28] not only returned to the earlier terminology and perspective, but also offered a fresh defense of the content of human rights. Before examining Finnis, I offer some reflections on the development up to now. It is one thing to set down a number of objectives regarded as desirable, it is quite another to set down these objectives as rights that impose duties on public officials. Certain officials in a liberal democracy are deemed particularly adept at dealing with issues of rights: jurists and lawyers. For some time, constitutionally entrenched rights have been the primary means by which the law provides for judicial power. Finnis quite correctly addresses this fact.

With John Finnis, we once again find an attempt to blend classical natural law and key elements of contemporary liberal political philosophy. His account of incommensurable goods is reminiscent of Isaiah Berlin's well-known thesis on irreducible value pluralism. He incorporates ideas from Ronald Dworkin's legal theory, using rights as counters as opposed to rights as trumps; incorporates Rawlsian formulations about life plans; and defends the notion of absolute rights (shades of Blackstone!). Without going into a complete evaluation of Finnis's theory of natural law, I shall confine myself to his discussion of rights and the common good, since this reveals the extent to which his view of the common good is liberal rather than classical, or Thomistic.

Finnis pays his respects to the United Nations Declaration by describing its enumeration of rights as "simply a way of sketching the outlines of the common good, the various aspects of individual well-being in community."[29] Finnis "places duties before rights and makes the duty not to choose against basic values the ground for absolute rights."[30] For Finnis, rights-talk is essential – it is either essential to or an important aspect of practical reasonableness.[31]

Yet even Finnis's view is unsatisfying. By now we should expect that some of the shopworn terms of human rights theory, often ambiguous, would have been retired. One adjective we can do without is "inalienable," the current meaning of which is a considerable departure from the French Declaration with its distinction between inalienable and imprescriptible.[32] (There are moments when a dose of Benthamite linguistic analysis would be helpful.) The possession of the fundamental rights is absolute, not limited even in exercise.

Considering Finnis's remarks about the United Nations Declaration, we can ask why the language of goods should be translated into the language of rights. Inevitably in such a theory, the trail leads to a consideration of the common good and whether any conflict between goods and rights might arise. Finnis denies that we should worry about such conflicts, for "we should not say that human rights, or their exercise, are subject to the common good; for the maintenance of human rights is a fundamental component of the common good."[33] I agree, but the state has other functions regarding rights, such as regulation and adjudication, which indicate that conflict is likely. Finnis does not reduce the common good to the maintenance function, because there are "other aspects of the common good."[34] The common good refers primarily to human flourishing.

A more significant feature of Finnis's account of the common good concerns the nature of the common good itself. How does his theory deal with the distinction between the common good as a means or an instrument and the common good as an autonomous good? How does Finnis deal with the two-sidedness of the common good, having a collective side and a distributive side? The answer to these queries determines to what extent Finnis offers us a liberal or classical solution. Here is the main formulation of the common good.

> in the case of the political community ... the point or common good of such an all-round association was said to be the securing of a whole ensemble of material and other conditions that tend to favour the realization, by each individual in the community, of his or her personal development.[35]

Subsequently, when he rejects the notion of common aims or tasks, we are justified in drawing two conclusions: he offers only an instrumental conception of the common good, and his theory is one-sided in emphasizing only the distributive factor. Together these assertions lead us to the conclusion that Finnis's account, in the final analysis, is liberal instead of classical. The stress on rights might tend to an identification of rights with the common good, in fairness to him, a step he did not finally take. The eclipse of the collective – some would say constitutive – side of the common good is a major departure from the tradition to which he claims attachment. What happens when community and rights are identified, and when both the distributive and constitutive side of the common good are encompassed?

We find one answer to this question in Alan Gewirth's recent *The Community of Rights*.[36] By examining some central themes in this important contribution to human rights theory, I will show how Gewirth aims at conserving the two facets of the common good, finding a place for each. However, in the final analysis, the priority is given to the distributive facet, explaining in part why Gewirth describes his position as ethical/liberal individualism.

The initial problem for Gewirth is how to respond to the communitarian critique of liberal political philosophy. Gewirth's answer, and the aim of his book, is to show that both rights and community are mutually implied in what he calls the community of rights. However, in certain instances, he seems to rely on something other than rights to provide the social bond (such as love or a feeling of solidarity). A second aim of his study is to incorporate the social and economic rights of the United Nations Declaration with the civil and political rights already assured in his previous account of rights.[37] He does not hesitate to call this effort socialism, surely an untimely meditation.

I will not address the validity of Gewirth's argument for generic rights to freedom and well-being here, having done so in earlier works.[38] Conclusions about the nature and extent of rights emphasize the role of government in securing economic and social rights. The rights are "positive" (involving active assistance), and "negative" (involving forbearance). Gewirth is convinced that "the conciliation of rights and community has been established,"[39] through the mutuality entailed in human rights. He refers to solidarity and mutuality.

To help us understand Gewirth's position, we have to look at his use of the classical tradition – particularly Aristotle – and his employment of a vocabulary that allows us to compare his project with that of Maritain and Simon, especially concerning the distinction between the distributive and the collective (as when he says that "solidarity is a collective rather than a distributive relation"[40]), the recognition of collective as well as individual rights. However, in the final analysis, the distributive has priority over the collective, and hence it remains a liberal theory. The community of rights has "its primary basis in the community's protection of each individual's rights and its secondary basis of a more general affective outlook whereby persons have obligations to the community."[41] But if we use the term constitutive as we do collective, as Gewirth does, such a good must be constituted before it is distributed, thus leading to a different priority. Gewirth reiterates his understanding of the priority when he says that the term "common," "from its initial distributive meaning, takes on also the collective meaning of the community that is constituted by and is the protector of human rights."[42] It would be difficult to find a clearer statement of the difference between a liberal notion of community – there are only rights – and a Thomistic one (i.e., that of Maritain and Simon). Loyalty and devotion to the community are on the constitutive side, according to Gewirth. However, are they not values ignored by liberals? Elsewhere Gewirth says that "common" is an ambiguous term, with both a distributive and a collective meaning. So, while his account is superior to Finnis's in recognition of the two facets, it hesitates to identify the consequences of conceding a collective or constitutive facet.

As ethical individualism becomes reconciled with communitarianism in Gewirth's account, his liberal theory of rights leads us to a socialist destination. Socialism, in the sense of economic democracy, becomes a right. Gewirth summons up the cooperative model of capitalism and borrows many elements from the arsenal of socialist ideas: full employment, equal rights to property, use of the fiscal system for redistribution, corporate taxation, producers cooperatives, and worker control. Much of the work examines studies concerning the feasibility of such policies, addressing to some extent Aron's reflections on the desirability-possibility issue. Gewirth insists that these outcomes are to be seen,

> not as utopian hopes for a better world, but as requirements of justice whose moral mandatoriness has been established on the basis of the principle of human rights. These outcomes, moreover, are readily available through resources that are presently within the reach of Western democratic societies.[43]

Some institutional implications of this economic democracy, such as the considerable expansion of the bureaucracy, are scarcely mentioned. Instead, Gewirth considers the implications of the community of rights for democratic decision-making, when he muses as to "whether, or to what extent, moral rights and other important values should be left vulnerable to the empirical, optional, decision-making procedures of democratic electorates."[44] The reader begins to realize that the expansion of economic democracy might be paid for by placing curbs on legislative democracy and correspondingly assigning a greatly increased role for judges, who are the real guardians of rights-talk. How typical of liberal political philosophers to view the growth of judicial power with equanimity, if not fervent approval.

We may be astonished when we see that Gewirth addresses the charge "that there has been an unjustified expansion of what people are held to have rights to"[45] with a rather curt dismissal. Surely, he must be aware that he is participating in a "rights inflation." However, one of the least appealing aspects of Gewirth's thought is its tendency to brush aside critics and play down the extent to which rights have swallowed everything else. Children, the mentally handicapped, and animals are simply excluded from the list of rights-bearers, and we now have the now prevalent practice of awkwardly listing as rights in the passive voice what are more fittingly seen as duties in the active voice.[46]

Despite what Gewirth says, the new minting of rights seems to be a flourishing industry among political philosophers. Here is a partial list of these coinings: the right to suicide and voluntary servitude, the right to moral independence, the right to recognition, the right to difference, and most recently, the *amicus curiae* brief submitted to the United States Supreme Court in favor of physician-assisted suicide, signed by a distinguished group of liberal political philosophers.[47] Taking the long list of new rights, not necessarily compatible with each other, I am tempted to paraphrase Ecclesiastes: there is a time for the right to life and a time for the right to die; there is a time for the right to liberty and a time for the right to voluntary servitude; there is a time when children have rights and a time when they do not; a time for the right to identity (we are all basically alike) and a time for the right to difference. We come to understand the great advantage of a duty theory, since hardly anyone is likely to want more duties imposed upon them than currently exist.

Far from rights talk including mutuality, the psychology of rights tends to stress our separate selves. Even if one agrees that rights imply duties, it is easy in an egocentric society to see rights as a private, untouchable property. So it is not what you may claim, but what I may.

Mary Ann Glendon, in her *Rights Talk: The Impoverishment of Political Discourse*,[48] identifies some of the consequences of the over-emphasis on rights: the illusion of absoluteness, the lone rights bearer, the missing language of responsibility, the missing dimension of sociality, and rights insularity (the failure to pay heed to decisions made in Europe and elsewhere when similar problems were at stake). A similar study of the Canadian political system since the Constitution Act of 1982 would be in order, pulling together many of the commentaries and criticisms of the new political order and the role of the judiciary in it. The appeal of a Charter of Rights and Freedoms to ordinary Canadians is strong, even if they have not been the main beneficiaries of it. The entrenchment of rights increased judicial power in a dramatic way, and only the weak reed of the notwithstanding clause preserves the vestige of parliamentary supremacy, another name for democratic decision-making. The power of the judiciary has expanded constitutionally and judges have not been slow to exercise creativity. Take, for instance, the practice of "reading into" the Constitution what is not stated there. In some instances, the decision may be congenial, in some cases not, but in any case this is a sorry substitute for judicial reasoning – and ignores the distinction between *dicere* and *dare legem*. The tendentious historical research carried on by judges in key cases concerning aboriginal land claims is but another instance of the overweening ambitions of members of the judiciary to settle complex issues.

Since we have little chance of changing the new constitutional order, it is salutary to find a vigorous criticism of the Supreme Court. We cannot elect its members, though we can make every effort to bridle judicial hubris and inculcate an attitude of restraint and deference. In addition, we should encourage our parliamentarians to place more controls over Human Rights Commissions, tribunals that indulged in rights creation and, given their makeup, are strongly inclined to do so. If they cannot be mended, they perhaps should be ended. For they too are part of the overreaching philosophy of rights that needs to be moderated. Behind this plea is the belief that democratic decision-making, and not judicial decision-making, should be the exemplar of public reason.[49]

Notes

1. Alan Ryan, *John Dewey and the High Tide of American Liberalism* (New York: W.W. Norton & Co., 1995), p. 366.

2. See Hugo Grotius, "Rules of Moderation," *De Jure Belli ac Pacis, Libri Tres*, Introduction by James Brown Scott, trans. Francis W. Kelsey (New York: Oceana Publications, 1964), pp. 723–782.

3. John Dewey, *Freedom and Culture* (New York: Capricorn Books, 1963, 1939) pp. 156–164.

4. Jacques Maritain, *The Rights of Man and Natural Law*, trans. Doris C. Anson (New York: Gordian Press, 1971).

5. *Western Political Philosophers: A Background Book*, ed. Maurice Cranston (London: Bodley Head, 1964), p. 35.

6. Louis Lachance, O.P., *Le droit et les droits de l'homme* (Paris: Presses Universitaires de France, 1959), pp. 164–170.

7. *Liberalism and Its Critics*, ed. Michael Sandel (New York: New York University Press, 1984), pp. 6–7.

8. Cf. Etienne Borne, "L`apport de Jacques Maritain à la philosophie des droits de l`homme," *Droits des peuples, droits de l`homme: Paix et justice sociale internationale*, ed. Roberto Papini (Paris: Editions du Centurion, 1984), pp. 108–121; Ralph McInerny, *Aquinas on Human Action: A Theory of Practice* (Washington: Catholic University of America Press, 1992), pp. 212–219.

9. See, Yves R. Simon, "Thomism and Democracy," *Science, Philosophy, and Religion, Second Symposium*, ed. L. Bryson and Louis Finkelstein (New York: Conference on Science, Philosophy and Religion in Their Relation to the Democratic Way of Life, 1942), pp. 258–272.

10. Maurice Cranston, *What are Human Rights?* (London: Bodley Head, 1973), p. 65.

11. Raymond Aron, "Sociology and the Philosophy of Human Rights," *Politics and History: Selected Essays*, trans. Miriam Bernheim Conant (New York: Free Press, 1978), p. 122.

12. Ibid., p. 125.

13. Ibid., p. 126.

14. Ibid., p. 130.

15. Ibid., p. 132.

16. Ibid., p. 134.

17. Ibid.

18. Ibid.

19. Ibid., p. 136.

20. Ibid.

21. Ibid., p. 137.

22. Ibid., pp. 137–138.

23. Sidney Hook, "Reflections on Human Rights," *Philosophy and Public Policy* (Carbondale: Southern Illinois University Press, 1980), pp. 67–97.

24. Ibid., p. 88.

25. Ibid., p. 93.

26. Ibid.,

27. Ibid., p. 95.

28. John Finnis, *Natural Law and Natural Rights* (New York: Oxford University Press, 1980).

29. Ibid., p. 214.

30. Kent Greenawalt, "Review of Natural Law and Natural Rights," *Political Theory*, 10:1 (February 1982), p. 135.

31. John Finnis, *Natural Law*, pp. 198, 221.

32. *Les déclarations des droits de l`homme: Du Débat 1789–1793 au Préambule de 1946*, ed. Lucien Jaume (Paris: Flammarion, 1989), pp. 49–52.

33. John Finnis, *Natural Law*, p. 218.

34. Ibid.

35. Ibid., p. 154.

36. Alan Gewirth, *The Community of Rights* (Chicago: University of Chicago Press, 1996).

37. Alan Gewirth, *Reason and Morality* (Chicago: University of Chicago Press, 1978).

38. Ralph Nelson, "Between Inconsistent Nominalists and Egalitarian Idealists," *Maritain Studies*, 12 (1996), pp. 129–132.

39. Alan Gewirth, *Community of Rights*, p. 20.

40. Ibid., p. 305.

41. Ibid., p. 86.

42. Ibid., p. 93.

43. Ibid., p. 311.

44. Ibid., p. 320.

45. Ibid., pp. 102–103.

46. See, Gewirth, *Community of Rights*, pp. 45, 66, 77.

47. See, Robert Nozick, *Anarchy, State, and Utopia* (New York: Basic Books, 1974), pp. 58, 331; Ronald Dworkin, *A Matter of Principle* (Cambridge: Harvard University Press, 1985), p. 353; Charles Taylor, *Reconciling the Solitudes: Essays on Canadian Federalism and Nationalism* (Montreal & Kingston: McGill-Queens University Press, 1993), pp. 45, 55, 58, 88, 142-143; Luc Ferry, *Homo Aestheticus: The Invention of Taste in the Democratic Age,* trans. Robert De Loaiza (Chicago: University of Chicago Press, 1993), p. 258; and Michael J. Sandel, "Last Rights," *The New Republic* (14 April 1997), p. 27.

48. Mary Ann Glendon, *Rights Talk: The Impoverishment of Political Discourse* (New York: Free Press, 1991).

49. See, John Rawls, *Political Liberalism* (New York: Columbia University Press, 1993), p. 216; Bob Woodward and Scott Armstrong, *The Brethren: Inside the Supreme Court* (New York: Avon Books, 1981).

Twelve

MACINTRYE OR GEWIRTH?
VIRTUE, RIGHTS, AND THE PROBLEM OF
MORAL INDETERMINACY

Gregory J. Walters

Within the history of Western ethics, we find both the teleological approach, exemplified by Aristotle's ethics of virtues, and the deontological approach, heralded by Kant's ethics of duty, rule-utilitarianism, and divine will/command conceptions of morality. Usually, we assume that these two approaches are incompatible and we must follow either the "good" or the "right."[1] In this essay, I am concerned with what I believe is the most significant contemporary manifestation of the virtue-rights debate. Alasdair MacIntyre's work in virtue ethics is now well known, but rarely discussed is MacIntyre's critique of Alan Gewirth's theory of morality as a theory of human rights.[2] This is puzzling since MacIntyre admits that Gewirth represents the most sophisticated attempt to lay the foundations of a theory of human rights in a systematic analysis of the rational basis of morality. If Gewirth fails to provide adequate grounds for rejecting the emotivist and subjectivist accounts of morality that MacIntyre finds so prevalent today, then MacIntyre has strong evidence to conclude that other Kantian deontologists, such as John Rawls, Alan Donegan, and Bernard Gert, will not succeed either. MacIntyre's singling out Gewirth from among this eminent group of scholars would warrant the focus of this essay, but more is at stake in MacIntyre's critique of Gewirth. MacIntyre's critique raises the central and perennial question of how best to rationally justify moral theory. If MacIntyre is right and Gewirth wrong, then nothing less is at stake than the possibility of construing the difference between moral right and wrong as objectively knowable and universal for all persons who claim to use rational methods of reflection. If Gewirth is right and MacIntyre wrong, at stake is the problem of moral indeterminacy in virtue ethics and a rethinking of the role of human rights in contemporary moral theory. The MacIntyre-Gewirth debate raises fundamental questions about moral justification, ethical universalism, the determinacy of substantive moral norms, and the proper role of rights, responsibilities, and community in contemporary ethical theory.

My first business in this essay is to identify why MacIntyre believes the Enlightenment project of justifying morality failed, given its operative moral suppositions, and to highlight the implications for Gewirth's human rights theory. Second, I identify four key elements of MacIntyre's critique of Gewirth. Third, I present Gewirth's rebuttal to MacIntyre based on his argument to the "Principle of Generic Consistency" (PGC). Fourth, I highlight aspects of the moral indeterminacy, which Gewirth maintains plagues MacIntyre's virtue ethics. Finally, I ask: How are we to evaluate this debate, and what conclusions should we draw from it for Christian ethics?

1. The Failure of the Enlightenment Project and the New Teleology

MacIntyre's central thesis is that the moral projects of Kierkegaard, Kant, and Hume failed. However different their respective philosophical accents on choice, reason, and passion, their projects had to fail because they inherited a moral scheme whose internal incoherence guaranteed failure from the outset. The inherited scheme entailed both a certain view of human nature and a set of moral principles, rules, and injunctions divorced from their earlier teleological context. The pre-Enlightenment moral scheme, essentially derived from Aristotle, turned on three hinges: a conception of "untutored" human nature; a conception of the precepts of rational ethics or of divine law; and a conception of "human-nature-as-it-could-be-if-it-realized-its-*telos*."[3] The third element dropped out of the moral horizon just prior to and during the Enlightenment period, and requires reference to the other two dimensions if its status and function are to be intelligible. In the classical scheme, ethics is understood as a "science" that enables persons to move from raw nature to a nature realized in accordance with its essentially relational end. The precepts of rational ethics are constituted by different virtues and vices, which correct, improve, and educate the subject about how to move from human potentiality to action. To ignore the role of the virtues and vices in the moral life is to land ourselves in frustration, to miss the mark with respect to the good of rational happiness, a *telos* unique to the human species as such. Aquinas, Maimonides, and Ibn Roschd appropriated the classical scheme within their respective theistic frameworks, but did not essentially alter it. They brought teleology and deontology, virtue and law, together in a tensive synthesis. Thus, the theological virtues get added to the cardinal virtues, a doctrine of sin is added to the Aristotelean concept of error, and the human *telos* is transformed from the earthly city to the heavenly city and eternal life.

Several historical developments eroded the classical and mediaeval moral foundation. Both the secular rejection of Protestant and Catholic theology and the scientific and philosophical rejection of Aristotelianism eliminated the idea of "man-as-he-could-be-if-he-realized-his-*telos*." The Lutheran, Calvinist, and Jansenist Catholic theological supposition that the power of reason has been destroyed by original sin made man's true end unintelligible. Pascal is a key figure here, because he made links between fallible reason in theology and seventeenth-century philosophy and science. Pascalian reason does not comprehend "essences" or the transition from potentiality to action, as in the despised conceptual scheme of scholasticism. Pascal's anti-Aristotelian science set strict boundaries to calculative rationality. Reason can assess truths of fact and mathematical relations, but when it comes to practice it can only speak of means. Reason can neither discern ends nor refute skepticism. The central achievement of reason, according to Pascal, "is to recognize that our beliefs are ultimately founded on nature, custom and habit."[4] By the eighteenth century, the essentially sixteenth-century Protestant and Catholic Jansenist concept of reason became a completely secularized vision, marked by the forceful rejection of divine law morality. The view of "man-as-he-could-be-if-he-realized-his-*telos*" is gone. Because the role of moral precepts in the classical scheme was to teach untutored human nature how to reach its *telos*, such precepts could not be derived from descriptive accounts of human nature, once the teleological world view was forgotten. Now there can be no move from "is" to "ought." Hume's critique of the naturalistic fallacy became the great "epitaph" of the Enlightenment. Its tremors are still felt in modernity's myth of "bureaucratic expertise," with its false claim to value neutrality and the power to manipulate law-like generalizations. The Enlightenment moral scheme drove a wedge between is and ought, nature and morality, because it lost a functional concept of the "human person." Functional concepts entail a notion of good (or bad). Thus, Aristotle's *Nicomachean Ethics* can point out that the relationship between the human person and living well is analogous to the harpist playing the harp well.[5] But the "human person" as a functional concept is older than Aristotle, and is rooted in various forms of social life, for example, the "human person" as a family member, as a citizen, as a soldier, as a philosopher, or as a servant of God. "It is only when man is thought of as an individual prior to and apart from all roles that 'man' ceases to be a functional concept."[6] Conversely, a notion of good entails an essential purpose or function.

> The presupposition of this use of "good" is that every type of item which it is appropriate to call good or bad – including persons and actions – has, as a matter of fact, some given specific purpose or function. To call something good therefore is also to make a factual statement ... But once the notion of essential human purposes or functions disappears from morality, it begins to appear implausible to treat moral judgments as factual statements.[7]

But this is not all. The radical transformation in moral outlook was actually celebrated as liberating the Enlightenment self from a theism whose outmoded hierarchical, politico-ecclesiastical structures were ideologically legitimated by the earlier teleological world order. The social and political consequences of this change in moral horizon were embedded in the French and American revolutions. It is precisely here, on the historical cusp of the rallying cries for revolutionary praxis, that MacIntyre situates the origin of the modern self, the liberal individual who speaks "unconstrained by the externalities of divine law, natural teleology or hierarchical authority."[8] Morality would now have to find a new teleology and categorical status to fill the void left in the wake of modernity. It would run in a direct line from Bentham and Mill's utilitarianism, to Sidgwick and Moore's intuitionism, to American pragmatism – "another *praeparatio evangelica* for emotivism" – to present-day emotivism. Modern analytical philosophers, including Gewirth, essentially follow Kant in grounding the authority and objectivity of moral rules in reason. They are the modern representatives of categorical moral utterance. While the concept of "rights" was invented to serve one set of purposes and the concept of "utility" devised for another, both represent substitutes for the lost concepts of the older and more traditional morality.

2. Of Witches, Unicorns, and Rights: MacIntyre's Critique of Gewirth

For MacIntyre, as we have seen, modern rights are the deontological husk of the earlier divine command morality, but now alien to modern metaphysics. Utility has become the new, yet entirely inadequate, moral teleology whose claims are incommensurable with rights-claims. We must situate MacIntyre's fourfold critique of Alan Gewirth in the context of his argument about the failure of the Enlightenment project of justifying morality and about modern philosophy's efforts to deal with that failure.

First, MacIntyre challenges a central aspect of Gewirth's argument for a supreme principle of morality, the Principle of Generic Consistency. MacIntyre says that the following is the "key sentence" of Gewirth's book *Reason and Morality*: "Since the agent regards as necessary goods the freedom and well-being that constitute the generic features of his successful action, he logically must also hold that he has rights to these generic features, and he implicitly makes a corresponding rights-claim [*sic*]."[9] The introduction of the concept of "right" in the second part of this sentence needs justification, MacIntyre holds. Gewirth confuses claims about goods necessary for rational agency with claims to rights. The claim that I have a "right" to do or have some object X is different from the claim that I need, want, or will be benefitted by X. "From the first – if it is the only relevant consideration – it follows that others ought not to interfere with my attempts to do or have whatever it is, whether it is for my own good or not. From the second it does not. And it makes no difference what kind of good or benefit is at issue."[10]

Second, MacIntyre objects that rights-claims cannot derive claims about goods necessary for rational agency. Claims to the possession of rights presuppose the existence of a socially established set of rules. "The existence of particular types of social institution or practice is a necessary condition for the notion of a claim to the possession of a right being an intelligible type of human performance."[11]

Third, MacIntyre denies the universalism of rights on the grounds that rights-claims have a socially local character. Rights presuppose the existence of specific types of social institution. Where they lack such social form, he writes, "the making of a claim to a right would be like presenting a check for payment in a social order that lacked the institution of money." Thus Gewirth "has illicitly smuggled into his argument a conception which does not in any way belong, as it must do if his case is to succeed, to the minimal characterization of a rational agent."[12]

Fourth, as evidence for the non-universality of rights, MacIntyre notes that there is no expression in any ancient or mediaeval language that correctly translates the modern term "right" until near the close of the Middle Ages. "From this," he admits, "it does not follow that there are no natural or human rights, it only follows that no one could have known that there were." The truth appears plain to him: rights do not exist and belief in them is tantamount to a belief "in witches and in unicorns."[13] Here, MacIntyre is drawing a parallel between the assertion that human rights exist and the assertion that witches and unicorns exist. But the reason for "not" believing in rights is, in MacIntyre's view, the same reason for not believing in witches and unicorns: because "every attempt to give good reasons for believing that there *are* such rights has failed."[14]

3. Gewirth's Rebuttal to MacIntyre's *After Virtue*

Gewirth has responded to MacIntyre's critique,[15] although his rebuttal presupposes a good knowledge of the argument to the Principle of Generic Consistency, as set forth in *Reason and Morality.* In his rebuttal, Gewirth takes offense at the way in which MacIntyre attempts to assimilate the ontological status of human rights to the ontological status of witches and unicorns. Even if attempts to give good reasons for rights had failed in the past, this fact would not ground MacIntyre's assertion that an equivalency exists between the ontological status of rights and the ontological status of witches and unicorns. Rights are "normative entities," in a way that witches and unicorns are not. More to the point, Gewirth suggests "empirical correlates" for the existence of human rights. Here "existence" has a secondary meaning of social recognition and legal enforcement in a way that we cannot provide empirical correlates for the past or future existence of witches and unicorns. Thus, when we look at murderous or oppressive phenomena in Nazi Germany, the Soviet Union, Chile, or elsewhere, we are not seeing mere "fictions." These oppressions are empirical phenomena that are undeniably violations of human rights. Similarly, where certain basic freedoms and phases of well-being are protected, regardless of race or religion and so on, the referent is the empirical existence of socially recognized and legally enforced human rights.

But can we not rebut Gewirth on the grounds that his implicit criteria of "empirical correlates" could equally be used to prove the existence of the devil? Then the argument would be that the existence of tangible evil in human affairs is the empirical correlate of the devil's existence. This analogy does not hold, however, or at least it does not refute Gewirth's argument for the non-fictional status of human rights. Oppressive phenomena, such as rape, murder, and torture, and the liberating fulfillment of the protection of human well-being are not understood as "effects" of the existence of human rights in the same way that palpable evil is seen as an effect of the devil's work in the world. Instead, violations and fulfillment of human freedom and well-being are what is "meant," respectively, by the social nonexistence and existence of such rights. Gewirth does not need, in other words, to rely on a causal hypothesis, whose own existence cannot be empirically instantiated. Linking palpable evil to the work of the devil requires just such a causal hypothesis. And if we might further object that "the empirical phenomena of evil likewise constitutes what is 'meant' by the existence of the devil," then one important difference remains. The concept of the devil cannot be empirically instantiated, because it goes beyond available evidence.

Gewirth also rejects MacIntyre's blanket assertion that all attempts to give good reasons for believing in human rights have failed. MacIntyre has made an assertion without any extensive historical evidence to support it. Moreover, MacIntyre's discussion is limited to Gewirth's position or argument for human rights, which MacIntyre treats only in part. Gewirth uses a "dialectically necessary method" to argue to his principle of generic consistency. His method is "dialectical" because it deduces conclusions from statements made or accepted by a "prospective purposive agent" (PPA) about how they view things. PPAs are those who act voluntarily for purposes that they have freely chosen – purposive agents – as well as those who have the capacity to do so, which they have some disposition to exercise. The method is "necessary" in that statements made or accepted by every PPA logically derive from the generic features of purposive action. Gewirth contrasts his "dialectical" method with an assertoric method, and his necessary method with a contingent method in his book, *Reason and Morality*:

> it is one thing to say assertorically that X is good; it is another thing to say dialectically that X is good from the standpoint of some person, or that some person thinks or says 'X is good.' Where the assertoric statement is about X, the dialectical statement is about some person's judgement or statement about X. But whereas the dialectical method is relative to persons in this way, the dialectically necessary method propounds the contents of this relativity as necessary ones, since the statements it presents reflect judgements all agents necessarily make on the basis of what is necessarily involved in their actions ... The basis of this necessity is found in one or another aspect of the generic features of action and hence in the rational analysis of the concept of action. Thus, although the dialectically necessary method proceeds from within the standpoint of the agent, it also undertakes to ascertain what is necessarily involved in this standpoint. The statements the method attributes to the agent are set forth as necessary ones in that they reflect what is conceptually necessary to being an agent who voluntarily or freely acts for purposes he wants to attain.[16]

Gewirth's method, particularly its "necessary" side, does indeed seek to achieve categoricalness for moral judgements. Every agent, because he or she engages in purposive acts, is logically committed to the acceptance of certain evaluative and deontic judgments and, ultimately, of a supreme moral principle that he calls the Principle of Generic Consistency: "Act in accord with the generic rights of your recipients as well as of yourself."[17] Gewirth's revised neo-Kantian categorical imperative, now reinterpreted along the lines of action theory, requires that each agent respect his or her recipients' necessary conditions of action.[18] Like MacIntyre, Gewirth is concerned with the problem of moral emotivism and the interminable claims and counterclaims that arise in moral discourse. Gewirth also wants to bring this moral "dissensus" to a halt. He attempts to do so by recourse to facts and propositions that a PPA cannot reject because they are tied to the context of action itself. Gewirth has attempted to prove the normative structure of action in three broad steps:

> First, every agent implicitly makes evaluative judgments about the goodness of his purposes and hence about the necessary goodness of the freedom and well-being that are necessary conditions of his acting to achieve his purposes. Second, because of this necessary goodness, every agent implicitly makes a deontic judgment in which he claims that he has rights to freedom and well-being. Third, every agent must claim these rights for the sufficient reason that he is a prospective agent who has purposes he wants to fulfill, so that he logically must accept the generalization that all prospective purposive agents have rights to freedom and well-being.[19]

The general aim to which Gewirth aspires in these three argumentative steps is to show that the agent's pursuit of purposive action commits him or her to accept certain normative judgments on pain of self-contradiction. Purposive action requires a certain normative structure. The PGC is derived logically, Gewirth argues, from judgments that are necessarily constitutive of the normative structure of action. The fuller structure of Gewirth's argument may be diagrammed in the following fashion:[20]

STAGE I[21]
A PPA claims (by definition)
(1) I do (or intend to do) X voluntarily for some purpose E;
     By virtue of making this claim, the PPA rationally must consider that (claim) in logical sequence;
(2) E is good;
(3) My freedom and well-being are generically necessary conditions of my agency;
(4) My freedom and well-being are necessary goods;

STAGE II[22]
By virtue of having to accept (4), the PPA must accept

(5)   I (even if no one else) have a claim right (but not necessarily a moral one)
to my freedom and well-being. [Gewirth speaks of "generic rights" as
prudential rights, and not yet moral rights, at Stage II, since in order to
show that they are moral rights it has to be shown that each agent must
admit that all other humans also have these rights.]

STAGE III[23]
By virtue of having to accept (5) on the basis of (1), the PPA must accept
(9)   Other PPAs (PPAOs) have a (moral) claim right to their freedom and well
being.
If this is the case, then every PPA rationally must claim, by virtue of claiming
to be a PPA;
(13)   Every PPA has a (moral) claim right to its freedom and well-being,
which is a statement of the PGC [the Principle of Generic Consistency].

Now let us recall that MacIntyre's main objection to Gewirthian rights is that
rights-claims cannot be derived from claims about goods necessary for rational
agency. This derivation is implied in Gewirth's move from (4) to (5) in the above
steps of his overall argument. But Gewirth maintains that MacIntyre fails to
understand what is logically at stake in the move from (4) to (5). Gewirth
condenses his argument from Stage I to Stage II in his rebuttal of MacIntyre in the
following:

Since freedom and well-being are the necessary conditions of action and
successful action in general, no agent can act to achieve any of his purposes
without having these conditions. Hence, every agent has to accept (1) "I must
have freedom and well-being." This "must" is practical-prescriptive in that it
signifies the agent's advocacy of his having what he needs in order to act. Now
by virtue of accepting (1), he also has to accept (2) "I have rights to freedom
and well-being." For if he denies (2), then, because of the correlativity of claim-
rights and strict "oughts," he also has to deny (3) "All other persons ought at
least to refrain from removing or interfering with my freedom and well-being."
By denying (3), he has to accept (4) "Other persons may (i.e., It is permissible
that other persons) remove or interfere with my freedom and well-being." And
by accepting (4), he has to accept (5) "I may not (i.e., It is permissible that I
not) have freedom and well-being." But (5) contradicts (1). Since every agent
must accept (1), he must reject (5). And since (5) follows from the denial of (2),
every agent must reject that denial, so that he must accept (2) "I have rights to
freedom and well-being." I call them *generic rights*, because they are rights to
the generic features of action and successful action in general.[24]

MacIntyre focuses on what he thinks is the crucial difference between (1) and
(2). The upshot of Gewirth's rebuttal to MacIntyre is that MacIntyre has not fully

appreciated steps (3), (4), and (5) in the above outline of the argument. More precisely, MacIntyre overlooks the dialectically necessary character of Gewirth's argument. The argument must remain at the level of rational necessities. The "must" in (1) is not the same as someone saying that he or she "must" have a new car or chocolate cheesecake. Persons desire many particular things and even feel that they "must" have some of these. However, a "must" concerned with objects that are dispensable differs from Gewirth's understanding of "must" in relation to objects that are necessary conditions of action. "The latter objects," Gewirth writes of freedom and well-being, "unlike the former, have an ineluctableness within the context of action that reflects the rational necessity to which, in keeping with the dialectically necessary method, the argument must be confined."[25]

Now MacIntyre also objects that claims about the possession of rights, unlike rights-claims, presuppose the existence of a socially established set of rules that is historically contingent. Gewirth had raised this objection against himself in *Reason and Morality*.[26] But he then goes on to argue that an agent's right-claim is logically prior to, and independent of, a community or an existing set of social rules except in a quite minimalist sense. Gewirth reverses MacIntyre's accepted relation between rights and institutions, because rights-claims are, in some cases, demands that certain social rules or institutions actually be established. Thus, when slaves revolted against their masters, or revolutionaries against oppressive regimes, the prior issue concerned rights to the necessary conditions of human agency itself.

> These rights and the claims to them have a prior status because it is for their sake that the most important social rules should exist. Thus, from the agent's standpoint, a community will be legitimate only if it recognizes his rights. Hence, far from rights presupposing a community which recognizes them, the relation is rather that a legitimate community presupposes the claiming and respecting of rights.[27]

Finally, Gewirth responds to MacIntyre's charge that rights-claims are not "universal features" of the human condition and that, without an expression for human rights, "no one could have known" such rights exist. Just because persons do not have some single expression, such as human rights, it does not follow for Gewirth that such rights do not normatively exist. As long as persons have a "concept" of human rights, it can be shown that they exist. Gewirth chides MacIntyre for failing to acknowledge the extensive distinctions that bear on the ways persons and groups have used the concept of rights. MacIntyre also fails to acknowledge the extensive historical evidence for a "concept" of rights in ancient Greece, Rome, the Middle Ages, and even in non-Western societies.[28] We get the impression that Gewirth is asking MacIntyre to please read *Reason and Morality* before making such wild assertions and blanket historical generalizations.

To this point in his rebuttal, Gewirth has addressed the explicit criticisms raised by MacIntyre. Gewirth also notes, however, an "implicit" supposition in

MacIntyre's objection that every attempt to give good reasons for believing there are rights has failed. Namely, MacIntyre's premise entails an argument from "incommensurability" or "mutual incompatibility" with three spheres of applicability. The first concerns disagreement between analytic moral philosophers such as Hare, Rawls, Donagan, and Gert. The second concerns the putative incommensurability between rights and appeals to utility. The third concerns basic controversies over justice, which, MacIntyre maintains, "cannot be rationally resolved."[29] Let us look briefly at Gewirth's response to these applications of "incommensurability" in turn.

First, disagreement between modern analytic philosophers such as Hare, Rawls, Donagan, and Gert does not prove that human rights cannot be given rational justification. Indeed, MacIntyre would not accept the parallel contention that widespread disagreement among philosophers over the nature and content of the virtues proves that rational justification of the virtues is not possible. MacIntyre overlooks what these authors agree to, namely, "consistency, impartiality, and mutuality of consideration" as vital components of moral rationality. MacIntyre thereby gives a misleading impression about their putative "incommensurability," because he emphasizes only their "differences."[30]

Second, MacIntyre overlooks the extensive work carried out on the conflict between rights and utility as ostensibly incommensurable. Gewirth alludes to his own work and then makes two important points. First, utilities do not have the same primary status as human rights, because they "compromise objects of preference indiscriminately. Hence, any attempt to 'act' for the attainment of utilities must presuppose the objects of the human rights, while on the other hand, many utilities do not have this indispensability for agents." Second, Gewirth says that his principle of human rights has a rigorous rational justification insofar as any attempt to violate or deny the principle involves the agent in self-contradiction. In contrast, the principle of utility has no such rational justification. "Notorious fallacies are incurred by attempts to justify the principle through an appeal to each individual's desire for his own happiness." Along the same lines, Gewirth argues that his PGC has a better distributive element than utilitarianism. Whereas the PGC proceeds "by showing that each prospective agent logically must acknowledge that all other prospective agents have the same generic rights he claims for himself," utilitarians may be willing to submerge individual rights by an appeal to utility maximization.[31]

Third, Gewirth says MacIntyre does not see that the argument between Rawls's criterion of "need" and Nozick's criterion of "entitlement" can be rationally resolved by an appeal to the criterion of "degrees of necessity for action,"[32] which Gewirth derives from the PGC. This criterion entails that when two rights conflict with one another, the right whose "object" is more needed for action takes precedence. Thus, the rights not to be stolen from or lied to are overridden by the rights not to starve or be murdered, if the latter rights can be fulfilled only by infringing the former.[33] In the debate between Rawls and Nozick over the conflict of basic rights and Nozickian property rights, Rawls is correct. When basic needs of food, housing, and clothing cannot be filled, then the criterion of degrees of necessity for action makes taxation of others morally justifiable.[34]

4. The Problem of Moral Indeterminacy in MacIntyre's Virtue Ethics

Because MacIntyre rejects a morality of rights and duties in the name of a morality of virtues, Gewirth must also address MacIntyre's own positive doctrine of the virtues. Here we come to the crux of the virtue-rights debate. Gewirth critiques MacIntyre's use of historical material for his positive conception of the virtues. Gewirth points out that MacIntyre has reversed the traditional conception of the relation between moral virtues and rules. The traditional priority, "from moral rules to moral virtues," ensures that a moral virtue is disposed or habituated to act in accordance with the direction of moral rules, what St. Thomas would call *recta ratio*. Gewirth defines the moral virtues as "deep-seated traits of character whereby persons not only do what is morally right in the sense of obligatory but do it habitually, with knowledge that it is right and because it is right."[35] His ultimate criterion of this moral rightness is the PGC. However, MacIntyre sees the justification of rules and principles as radically problematic, and the order of priority as derived from the virtues to the function and authority of rules. But what is the criterion for a quality to be a virtue? MacIntyre's doctrine is confronted by a crucial difficulty, which Gewirth maintains besets any virtue ethics that does not base the virtues on moral rules for action, i.e. "moral indeterminacy." "A quality, rule, or judgment is morally indeterminate," Gewirth writes, "when its content allows or provides outcomes which are mutually opposed to one another so far as concerns their moral status. Thus the content in question may be morally wrong as well as morally right." When this is applied to MacIntyrean virtues as practices, "the criterion for a quality's being a virtue does not include the requirement that the virtue reflect or conform to moral rules, [and thus] there is no assurance that the alleged virtue will be morally right or valid."[36] In short, the question is whether the qualities that emerge as virtues in MacIntyre's account truly satisfy the fundamental condition of being a "moral" virtue, in which his practices are, in fact, morally right or valid.

Gewirth argues that MacIntyre's core concept of the virtues, defined by his notions of a "practice," the "narrative unity of life," and moral "tradition," fails to delineate the concept of a moral virtue. MacIntyre's notion of a practice is one of the most criticized aspects of his virtue theory.[37] Like others, Gewirth points out that the activities of the Ku Klux Klan and the Nazi Party would satisfy his vague notion of a practice, and do not meet the justificatory challenge of moral rightness.[38] Second, even though MacIntyre rejects Aristotle's metaphysical biology and reinterprets it along the lines of a teleological proceduralism for "the good," he does not specify its contents. Gewirth can rightly ask why a Hitler or

Stalin wouldn't fit MacIntyre's second stage. They both exhibited virtues of integrity and constancy in their "quest" for their *telos* or good. There is also the question of whether or not MacIntyre's conception of a tradition would not permit us to speak of traditions of slavery, racism, religious obscurantism, or the *ancien régime*. To be sure, MacIntyre emphasizes the important role of "argument," but leaves unanswered questions about methods, contents, and outcomes. He does not tell us what moral and intellectual criteria characterize his conception of argument.

The moral indeterminacy implicit in these three aspects of MacIntyre's concept of the virtues is "explicit" in his concept of community. While MacIntyre admits that communities may hold immoral practices and institutions,[39] he never specifies the criterion by which the "moral limitations" of communities might be defined. If his criterion is the virtues as he has defined them, then MacIntyre's argument is circular. He simply cannot appeal to the virtues for an "independent" criterion for a moral critique of community. MacIntyre cannot avoid the sort of universalism he finds so offensive in Kant and modern analytic moral philosophers like Gewirth.[40] Without providing some determinate content for "the good," MacIntyre's virtue ethics is as open to the charge of "formalism" as is Kant's. All three stages of MacIntyre's argument are infected with moral indeterminacy.

How might MacIntyre reply to Gewirth's charge of moral indeterminacy? First, MacIntyre distinguishes a morality of the virtues from the morality of law. The latter prescribes and proscribes certain harmful actions. In his morality of law MacIntyre, de facto, sets forth his basic morality. Gewirth is quick to point out the inherent contradiction here. For what it shows is that "for all his emphasis on the virtues and all his decrying of a morality of rules," MacIntyre "makes the latter morally prior because it provides for the protection of persons' most basic rights. But this contradicts his earlier 'rejection' of 'the modern view' according to which 'the justification of the virtues depends upon some prior justification of rules and principles.'"[41] Insofar as MacIntyre grounds the absoluteness of legal requirements to the goals of the community, he incurs the same problem noted above. If MacIntyre says his morality of law prohibits harms that would destroy the bonds of community, then we may rightly ask: "But which community? ... the Nazi community required the murder of Jews and others; the contemporary Afrikaner community requires the subjugation, economic and personal as well as political, of millions of blacks."[42] Second, MacIntyre might reply that the virtue of justice can answer the problem of moral indeterminacy, since it requires treating others in respect to their merit or desert. The crucial question for Gewirth is what constitutes merit or desert. Justice must be more than the virtue of sharing in practices or the good or goods of the telos of a whole life. And, if desert is tied to sharing in the human community, then what does MacIntyre mean by "human community?" Is it an egalitarian conception of community? Gewirth can conclude that, just as MacIntyre "gives no clear answer to the substantive question of what are the goods which persons ought to pursue, so he also gives no clear answer to the distributive question of who should have these goods, and in what proportion they ought to be 'shared.'"[43] The dialectical nature of Gewirth's theory of human rights overcomes some of the contingency that besets formal, non-substantive criteria for evaluating moral principles, and thus provides an advance beyond mere proceduralism that leaves the substantive requirements of morality underdetermined.[44]

5. Concluding Remarks

In this essay, I have been concerned with what I believe is the most significant contemporary manifestation of the virtue–rights debate. I have tried to listen carefully to the positions of MacIntyre and Gewirth, in order to give their respective concerns the attention they deserve. What conclusions may we draw from this important debate?

First, permit me to violate scholarly protocol with an anecdotal remark. At a philosophy conference, I asked Professor MacIntyre if he had ever responded to Gewirth's critique of his virtue ethics. He informed me he had not done so in writing, but had spoken to Gewirth verbally about the matter. The absence of a formal, published response by MacIntyre to Gewirth's critique may be telling. MacIntyre has not responded because he may be unable to surmount the objections Gewirth has posed to his virtue ethics. Scholarly protocol would at least seem to require a response to Gewirth, since MacIntyre initiated the critique. In my view, Gewirth has successfully reestablished the primacy of moral rules about rights and duties in relation to the content of the virtues. If we had more time, this point could be illustrated in relation to the moral philosophy of Thomas Aquinas and his derivation of the virtues from the principles of natural law, which is not to endorse *tout court* Aquinas's natural law theory as such. An irony of the present debate is that the concept of human rights that MacIntyre derides as a "fiction" has become the ground of the virtues in Gewirth's ethical theory. Whether or not MacIntyre's previous Marxism has influenced his critique of rights, if he had made human rights central to the virtues themselves, MacIntyre could have avoided some of the moral indeterminacy that mars how he relates the virtues to the practices, the telos of human life, and his conceptions of moral traditions and communities.

Second, even if we acknowledge the importance of the virtues and the place for the morality of law in MacIntyre's virtue ethics, MacIntyre must clarify what his professed "Augustinian Christianity,"[45] or "Thomistic Aristotelianism,"[46] entails for his understanding of the theological virtues in relation to the classical and Aristotlean virtues. What has Jerusalem to do with Athens? This question is pressing in view of MacIntyre's self-professed appropriation of the Thomistic tradition. In *Three Rival Versions of Moral Enquiry*, MacIntyre writes that

> on Aquinas's view the rights which are normative for human relationships are derived from and warranted only by divine law, apprehended by those without the resources afforded by God's self-revelation as the natural law. Law is

primary, rights are secondary. But for Enlightenment and post-Enlightenment modernity, human rights provide a standard prior to all law.[47]

This statement begs the question of how MacIntyre understands the natural and divine laws in relation to the theological virtues.[48] When I asked MacIntyre what role the theological virtues and divine law play, or ought to play, in his virtue ethics, especially given how the theological virtues complete and perfect the classical virtues for both Augustine and Aquinas, his response was, "I'm a philosopher, not a theologian!" If he can write that "the human good can be achieved only through a form of life in which the positive and negative precepts of the natural law are the norms governing our relationships,"[49] we still wonder how these norms are related to the theological virtues. Beyond his trilogy, we expect from MacIntyre an extended discussion of the theological virtues and the Biblical faith that informs his Thomistic tradition-constituted rationality and basis for critique of contemporary moral theories and practices. MacIntyre has written that hope "challenges any merely secular conception of reason" or "the belief of the Enlightenment that it is ignorance and irrationality alone that hinder us in our approach to the future, that the growth of scientific knowledge and understanding will save us."[50] But the question, "What may I hope?" was quite basic for Kant, despite his ethical formalism. The question of hope and Transcendence is also important for many contemporary philosophers who take their inspiration from a non-dogmatic and non-reductionist reading of the Enlightenment.[51]

Third, we may also ask some critical questions of Gewirth. For example, and setting aside the question of the possibility of a supreme moral principle,[52] does Gewirth's ethical rationalism completely avoid the moral indeterminacy he finds so problematic in MacIntyre's virtue ethics? I do not have in mind here the question of a determinate moral ground for Stage I of his argument to the PGC, since most commentators are willing to accept its validity.[53] Instead, I ask: Can Gewirth provide absolute moral determinacy with respect to the complex structure of rights and duties derived from the components of freedom and well-being? Gewirth argues the PGC has an invariant content, because it is derived from the generic features and necessary conditions of purposive action. The PGC provides for moral rules and determinate material contents that do not admit variability. The PGC's requirement that the agent act in accord with the generic rights, freedom, and well-being of his or her recipients is not contingent on what we happen to accept on variable self-interested desires or ideals. The PGC also requires duties relating to freedom and well-being. Well-being is of three kinds – basic, non-substractive, and additive. Basic well-being consists in having the essential preconditions of action such as life, physical integrity, and mental equilibrium. Non-substractive well-being consists in having the general abilities and conditions needed for maintaining a person's level of purpose-fulfillment and capacity for action. Additive well-being and goods consist in the abilities and conditions necessary to improve our levels of goods and increase our capacities and capabilities for action.[54] Now, according to Gewirth, the moral rights to these necessary goods of action are indeed determinate because of the invariance of their objects and, more generally, because they logically cannot involve the infringement of any person's rights except on the basis of the PGC's rational criteria for resolving the conflicts of rights.[55] Gewirth is concerned with both the "extrasystemic" and "intrasystemic" consistency of the PGC. The extrasystemic dimension concerns the conflicting duties that arise for persons independent of the PGC. The intrasystemic dimension concerns the conflicts that arise within the whole system of the PGC itself. Gewirth asks, "Are the requirements and other provisions it justifies always compatible with one another, or may conflicting requirements be derived from it? And since at least apparent conflicts of moral duties or requirements are found in the moral sphere, is the PGC able to resolve them?" If, in certain circumstances, the requirements of some moral rules justified by the PGC are overridden by the requirements of other rules, this does not remove the categoricalness of the PGC or its derivative rules. Thus, in the following conflicts between alternatives justified by the PGC, Gewirth believes he has shown that and why the alternative listed first must give way to the second alternative:

when the rule against killing human persons conflicts with the agent's acting in accord with his own generic rights where he is threatened with being killed by someone else (4.6); when one person's right to occurrent freedom conflicts with another person's right to basic well-being (4.11); when a person's right to occurrent freedom conflicts with his own right to basic well-being (4.20); when a person's right to basic well-being conflicts potentially over the long run with his own right to dispositional freedom (4.21); when a person's right to participate voluntarily or freely in transactions conflicts with his duty to obey procedurally justified social rules to which he has voluntarily or freely consented (5.5); when the rules against killing and restricting dispositional freedom of movement conflict with justified social rules requiring killing in war and punishment for crimes (4.6; 5.8); when social rules or arrangements of voluntary associations conflict with the right to well-being (5.6); when the right to occurrent freedom conflicts with the obligation to obey the criminal law (5.10); when the right to retain one's property conflicts with laws of the supportive state providing taxation to prevent basic harms such as starvation and to promote public goods (5.13,14); when the results of the method of consent, which has a necessary-procedural justification, conflict in extreme cases with the effective implementation of policies relieving starvation and other basic harms, policies that have a dynamic-instrumental justification (5.15); and when these results conflict with other important rights so that civil disobedience is justified (5.16).[56]

There are, of course, numerous substantive conflicts that are not identified in the above set. I have in mind conflicts of rights and duties related to the present information life-world. A positive right of access to electronic networks entails obligations on the part of governments or private corporations to fulfill the corresponding duty. This right of access incurs the difficulty that a positive right of access is inconsistent with liberty claims, or impracticable because of the overload of duties it entails, or because it fails various tests of universality. Access to information and information technology is a condition of possibility of human dignity in the information age.[57] Or, again, a corporation's claim-right to protection of intellectual property, whether by copyright, trade secret, patent, trademark, export law, or encryption, may conflict with claims to open access and privacy. Claims to freedom of speech are frequently in conflict with the government's claim to responsibly censor obscene and pornographic material or hate speech on the Internet, often in the interests of liberty or equality rights, or given a notion of democracy that includes gender equality. Traditional approaches to freedom of speech assume that the legal system can stop illegal speech, but networked communications have directly impacted how we morally and legally balance speech and other rights. Governmental claims to a right of access to medical records for the sake of epidemiological research, with a view to protecting the common good, conflict with assertions of privacy. Critics of the use of biometric encryption claim that finger scanning criminalizes welfare recipients, perpetuates the myth that economic problems are caused by the poor, and violates rights to privacy and freedom. Supporters, however, assert that finger scanning is less cumbersome than existing identification methods, helps to decrease welfare cheats from "double-dipping" and vendor fraud by professionals who provide government paid benefits to welfare recipients, and aids government agencies in their institutional obligations.

While these examples pose a challenge to Gewirth's theory of human rights, they are not, per se, an argument for Gewirthian moral indeterminacy within the parameters of his existing theory. The challenge is how the PGC is to be understood in relation to these substantive content areas, and how the criterion of the degrees of needfulness for action might apply, if at all. So if we must choose between MacIntyre and Gewirth on the problem of moral indeterminacy, Gewirth's ethical rationalism helps us derive substantive norms far more than does MacIntyre's virtue ethic. In a world of public policy, decision-making that bears directly on the up-building of the Reign of God in the *civitas terrena*, Gewirth's normative conclusions about economic and social rights and his realistic appraisal of economic power help us far more than MacIntyre's call for a return to a Benedictan Golden Age. Neither MacIntyre nor Gewirth offers much help with respect to understanding how the "already" of the Reign of God is related to the "not yet" of the *civitas eterna*. But this relation and the general question concerning Transcendence pose a host of further metaphysical questions.

Notes

1. Paul Ricoeur, "The Teleological and Deontological Structures of Action: Aristotle and/or Kant," *Archivio di filosofia* 55 (1987), pp. 205–217.

2. Alasdair MacIntyre, *After Virtue: A Study in Moral Theory* (Notre Dame, IN: University of Notre Dame Press, 2nd ed., 1988); Alan Gewirth, *Reason and Morality* (Chicago: University of Chicago Press, 1978).

3. MacIntyre, *After Virtue*, pp. 52–53.

4. Ibid., p. 54.

5. Aristotle, *Nicomachean Ethics* (1095a 16).

6. MacIntyre, *After Virtue*, p. 59.

7. Ibid.

8. MacIntyre, *After Virtue*, p. 68.

9. Ibid., p. 66, citing Gewirth, *Reason and Morality*, p. 63.

10. MacIntyre, *After Virtue*, p. 67.

11. Ibid., p. 67.

12. Ibid., pp. 66–67.

13. Ibid., p. 69.

14. Ibid., p. 69.

15. Alan Gewirth, "Rights and Virtues," *The Review of Metaphysics*, 38:4 (June 1985), pp.739–762.

16. Gewirth, *Reason and Morality*, p. 44.

17. Ibid., p. 135.

18. Ibid., pp. 26-42, 48-63.

19. Ibid., p. 48.

20. See Deryck Beyleveld, *The Dialectical Necessity of Morality: An Analysis and Defense of Alan Gewirth's Argument to the Principle of Generic Consistency* (Chicago: University of Chicago Press, 1991), p. 14.

21. Gewirth, *Reason and Morality*, pp. 22–63.

22. Ibid., pp. 63–103.

23. Ibid., pp. 104–198.

24. Gewirth, "Rights and Virtues," p. 744.

25. Ibid., p. 745; cf. Gewirth, *Reason and Morality*, pp. 77–78, 81–82.

26. Gewirth, *Reason and Morality*, p. 72.

27. Gewirth, "Rights and Virtues," p. 747; Gewirth, *Reason and Morality*, pp. 74-75.

28. Gewirth, *Reason and Morality*, pp. 100–101, 372–373, notes 19–26; see, Gregory J. Walters, "Is a Global Human Rights Community Possible?," *Confucianism and Human Rights*, ed. William Theodore de Bary and Tu Weiming (New York: Columbia University Press, 1998).

29. MacIntyre, *After Virtue*, p. 227.

30. Gewirth, "Rights and Virtues," p. 749.

31. Ibid., p. 750.

32. See, Gewirth, *Reason and Morality*, pp. 343–344, 346–349.

33. Alan Gewirth, *The Community of Rights* (Chicago: University of Chicago Press, 1996), pp. 45ff.

34. See, Gewirth, *Reason and Morality*, pp. 343-344; Gewirth, *The Community of Rights*, pp. 44–54; Douglas Husak, "Why There Are No Human Rights," *Social Theory and Practice*, 10 (1984), p. 140, n.15.

35. Gewirth, *Reason and Morality*, p. 332.

36. Gewirth, "Rights and Virtues," p. 752.

37. See *After MacIntyre: Critical Perspectives on the Work of Alasdair MacIntyre*, ed. John Horton and Susan Mendus (Notre Dame, IN: University of Notre Dame Press, 1994).

38. See Amy Gutmann, "Communitarian Critics of Liberalism," *Philosophy and Public Affairs*, 14 (Summer 1985), pp. 308–322.

39. Aristotle, *Politics*, VII.9, 1329a26; 10,1330a26ff.

40. J.B. Schneewind, "Virtue, Narrative and Community," *Journal of Philosophy*, 79 (November 1982), pp. 653–663.

41. Gewirth, "Rights and Virtues," p. 758.

42. Ibid., pp. 758–759.

43. Ibid., p. 760.

44. See Gewirth, *The Community of Rights*, pp. 26ff.

45. Alasdair MacIntyre, *Whose Justice? Which Rationality?* (Notre Dame, IN: University of Notre Dame Press, 1988).

46. Alasdair MacIntyre, "How Can We Learn What *Veritatis Splendor* Has to Teach?," *The Thomist*, 58:2 (April 1994), pp. 171–195.

47. Alasdair MacIntyre, *Three Rival Versions of Moral Enquiry: Encyclopedia, Genealogy and Tradition* (Notre Dame, IN: University of Notre Dame Press, 1990), p. 376.

48. This question is unanswered by MacIntyre in his "Community, Law and the Idiom and Rhetoric of Rights," *Listening,* 26:2 (Spring 1991), pp. 96–110.

49. MacIntyre, "How Can We Learn," p. 173.

50. Alasdair MacIntyre, "Seven Traits for the Future," *Hastings Center Report*, 9:1 (February 1979), pp. 5–7.

51. See Gregory J. Walters, *Karl Jaspers and the Role of "Conversion" in the Nuclear Age* (Lanham, MD: University Press of America, 1988), pp. 59ff.

52. See Renford Bambrough, "The Roots of Moral Reason," *Gewirth's Ethical Rationalism: Critical Essays with a Reply by Alan Gewirth*, ed. Edward Regis Jr. (Chicago: University of Chicago Press, 1984), pp. 39–51; see, *ibid.*, pp. 192–197.

53. Beyleveld, *The Dialectical Necessity of Morality*, p. 65.

54. Gewirth, *Reason and Morality*, pp. 58–63; Gewirth, "Community of Rights," pp. 278ff.

55. Gewirth, *Reason and Morality*, pp. 338–354.

56. Ibid., pp. 341–342.

57. Gregory J. Walters, "Canadian Information Highway Policy, the Right of Access to Information, and the Conditions of Human Action: Three Challenges to Moral Theology," *Science et esprit*, 49:2 (1997), pp. 193–229.

Thirteen

UNIVERSAL HUMAN RIGHTS, CONCEPTS OF OWNERSHIP, AND ABORIGINAL LAND CLAIMS

David Lea

Article 17 of the Universal Declaration of Human Rights states, "Everyone has a right to own property alone as well as in association with others." Though the UN has thrown its weight behind a universal right to property, the bare assertion of a right to property needs further clarification. This assertion certainly means that these rights should be recognized by all states, regardless of their conventions and local legislation. We can also say that this means such rights are independent of the established legislation ("positive law") of a particular country, in that these rights possess a legitimacy that is not derivative from the conventions and rules of any particular legal jurisdiction. Traditionally, philosophers have sought to express this view of rights by calling them "natural rights" – rights which transcend cultural and political boundaries, possess universal application, and constrain the legislation of political states to conform to their strictures.

In the following pages, I consider several important issues that arise when we attempt to apply these principles and reasoning to property rights to land. This discussion is apposite at a time when indigenous people throughout the world are reasserting ancient land claims, which they argue have priority over subsequent institutions and legal arrangements effected by the modern state. In Melanesia, people hold the powerful conviction that rights to land and ownership of land are enduring realities, which predate the creation of the state of Papua New Guinea and continue to require the protections and respect of the state. As the country develops, people feel that any development which affects lands held by traditional landowning groups requires the consent of these groups and monetary compensation for use and development of traditional lands. From a philosophical perspective, these views raise two questions. The first is, can discrete groups establish moral claims to land, which constrain conventions of ownership established by the state? Can groups establish natural rights to land, which command the respect and protection of the state according to the familiar Lockean formula? Second, what rights are established through these acts of original acquisitions, which must be respected by all parties including the state?

Having framed the central focus, I wish to initiate an historical perspective beginning with St. Augustine and St. Ambrose and moving forward chronologically to St. Thomas Aquinas and John Locke, the most prominent post-

Reformation thinker. My intent here is to present the views of those thinkers most influential in shaping our modern understanding of property rights. In the final section of the chapter, I will refer to certain contemporary work and offer my own conclusions.

1. Early Christian Writers and their Understanding of Ownership

In the early years of Christianity, and during much of the Middle Ages, the preponderant view was that the earth or the created world belonged to God and various forms of human ownership were conventional arrangements necessitated by humanity's fallen state.[1] In general, Patristic theory held that private property and the resulting differences in humanity's possessions were not natural. The earth and its products had been the common possession of humanity before the fall, but because of humanity's sinful state, social conditions now require this conventional institution of ownership.[2] Augustine, whose Christian thinking was a synthesis of prior Christian teaching and neo-Platonic ideas, held that people have possessions only by human right (*iure humano*), not divine right (*iure divino*), since the earth and its fullness belong to God. He goes on to say that kings and emperors determine human rights, including the right to property.[3] At times, Augustine says that property rights are limited by the use to which we put our possessions, and those who use their property badly have no real claim to it. *De jure*, property belongs to the good.[4] According to Augustine, the most admirable course is to renounce all ownership of the earth and its goods and hold in common the material things necessary to support life. And thus he tells us that renunciation of property in God's service is the higher calling, above ownership of wealth and property.[5]

Similarly, that other towering figure of the early Christian Church, Ambrose, whose thinking was also strongly influenced by Hellenic and neo-Platonic thought, emphasized humanity's non-proprietary relation to the created world and lack of dominant status. Ambrose taught that only God could have dominion over natural objects. Humanity could not have exclusive dominion because the criterion of dominion requires bringing something into being. Dominion was interpreted as exclusive control.[6] Aquinas softened this approach, arguing that dominion (*dominium*) was natural to God alone, but people could exercise a form of dominion in terms of their right to use these objects. Aquinas mentions that we may use something for the purpose of preservation or for convenience.[7] If we take Aquinas as the official authority on the teaching of the Catholic Church, then humanity could not have exclusive dominion over the created material world that belonged to God alone. However, within the material world, human rights were "of use" or "usufructs." With a use right "a man secures only daily and necessary advantage from another's property without impairing the substance."[8]

2. Seventeenth-Century Changes in Perspective

In the seventeenth century, the political writings of Hugo Grotius and Samuel Pufendorf offered arguments to support the view that individual forms of property must guarantee exclusive individual domination of the *res* or object of that right. They sought to demonstrate that humanity's rights over the earth and its creatures go beyond rights of usage, extending to the substance of the material thing. These rights are seen as equivalent to modern private rights of ownership, rights to exclude others from a person's holding (even when that person is not using it), and rights that approximate the modern right of capital, which includes, *inter alia*, the right of alienation and also the powers to waste or even destroy someone's holding.[9]

The departure from the traditional Thomistic teaching is obvious since Aquinas believed that the world belongs to humanity in common, not individually, and for everyone's use, but not for absolute dominion. In the eyes of Aquinas, private exclusive domination is not natural. In contrast, Grotius argued that this original common ownership was meaningless, as property implies occupation and occupation is only realized through private or individual property.[10] Pufendorf followed Grotius and denied that common ownership is a form of ownership, arguing the only form of property is private – property that arises from occupation and allows us to exclude others and alienate the holding. The writings of Grotius and Pufendorf were influential to the point that the equation of property with individual private property was completely accepted by the mid-eighteenth century. Blackstone's *Commentaries on the Laws of England*, written during that period, evidences this acceptance by stating that the "right of property" is "that sole and despotic dominion which one man claims and exercises over the external things of the world, in the total exclusion of the right of any other individual in the universe."[11]

However, the best-known theorist on property rights of that century and subsequent centuries was John Locke, whose views are extensively set out in the *Two Treatises of Government*.[12] With Locke, the great English theorist of property relations, private property can be seen as both a right and a moral duty. Following the humanist tradition, individual human beings could claim a right of private ownership based on human dominion over the material universe. But at the same time, Calvinism, and by extension Puritanism, had developed the idea that we are under an obligation to labor in the material world in order to fulfil functions of social usefulness. Max Weber said Calvinism took the ideals of the monastic life out of the monastery and placed them in the context of the daily struggle within this mundane reality.[13] Locke based his system of property on the command of God: "Everyone is bound to preserve himself and not to quit his station willfully; so by like reason when his own preservation comes not in competition, ought he as much as he can, to preserve the rest of mankind."[14] Locke saw that in order to effect this goal, individuals must have exclusive dominion over some part of the world's natural resources on which to apply their labors. This meant that each individual must have exclusive private holdings on some area of the earth's surface in order to work or labor. Thus, the imperatives of the divine plan required private property, and each individual was seen to be under a moral duty to acquire private property through labor in order to fulfill God's command.

But Locke's intellectual inheritance is difficult to pin down. Many have regarded Locke as the first libertarian who championed the freedom of the individual against tyranny and the encompassing power of government. Others, like C.B. Macpherson, saw Locke's position as a conceptual alteration resulting from the "new relations of the emergent capitalist society."[15] In this respect, Macpherson saw Locke as simply enlarging upon the direction initiated by Grotius and Pufendorf, which sees the right to property as private and absolute rather than inclusive and usufructuary. Macpherson saw Locke's concept of property as designed to enhance the individual's powers to acquire and accumulate wealth at the expense of the community. The extensive protections, which Locke extended to the individual against the state, were simply designed to set free a society of "possessive individualists." The product of such a society is individuals untouched by wider social obligations and exclusively motivated to unlimited acquisition of property through trade and commerce.

But Macpherson's view did not prove to be the final word on Locke. In the 1980s, James Tully produced a revisionist reading which, according to one author, sees Locke as the last medieval. According to Tully's 1980 view, Locke is a medieval in the Thomistic tradition, one who, throughout his writings, views the earth's surface as under the common dominion of mankind, but subject to the usufructuary rights of individuals.

According to Tully, the right of property amounts to an initial claim-right, which refers not to the earth itself, but to the man-made products useful to our lives: food, raiment, conveniences of life, meat, and drink.[16] What was originally granted to mankind, according to Tully, was not exclusive dominion over the earth, but the right to use the earth in order to create products useful to our lives.

Tully then explains that the exclusive right simply individuates the background "claim-right," in the same way that a right in the use of a seat on public transportation particularizes a prior right to use public transportation. Thus humans have a right to establish exclusive rights over land, only because they have a prior right to use the products of that land. For Tully, this is necessarily the case because the complementary natural inclusive and exclusive rights, respectively, refer to and inhere in the products of our labor.[17] Using Macpherson's terminology, Tully refers to the form of property right, which people like Filmer and Robert Nozick promote, as an "exclusive right." This right gives the proprietor the prerogative to exclude others from that to which the right refers (the *res*), in addition to other moral and legal powers over the *res* – that is, rights of abuse and alienation. In contrast, the rights assigned to humanity, in Tully's reading of Locke, are inclusive rights, because they invest a right not to be excluded from the use of that to which the right refers. Tully argues that while others have a duty to stay off the property to which Filmer's rights of private dominion or ownership refer, Locke envisions individuals as having a duty to move over and include other right-holders in the use of common property. Thus, for Locke, the idea of common dominion implies the inclusive right, which ultimately founds the exclusive right, and taken together, these juridical constructs are logical deductions from God's command. "Every one is *bound to preserve himself* and not to quit his station willfully; so by the like reason when his own Preservation comes not in competition, ought he, as much as he can, *to preserve the rest of mankind ...*"[18]

Tully asserts that this "unique construction" serves to establish Locke's main ideological conclusion, that fixed property in land does not have a natural foundation. In this light, the right to land is derived from the primary right to what is produced. The conclusion, Tully tells us, is that the common remains common and persons remain tenants in common, in accordance with God's original grant of common dominion.

These interpretations, which deny natural rights to land, are not convincing. The conclusion that rights to land have no natural foundation does not hold even given Tully's assumptions. The initial claim-right to the products necessary to survival is itself derived from prior duties to fulfil the command of the creator. Neither the claim-right nor the right to land is foundational, and duties, specifically duties to God, ground and give a basis to the natural rights and the form of political organization Locke proposed. We have a right to land because we have a claim-right to the products of the earth, but this right can only have moral force because I am obliged to follow God's command and ensure my survival. Even given Tully's interpretation of Locke, the right to property in land is still a natural right (a non-conventional moral right with universal application), no less than the claim-right to the products necessary for survival. It is simply the case that this universal natural right is not itself foundational, but like the claim-right, derives from primary obligations to the Creator.

But Tully's analysis is more interesting in its determination of the content of this natural right to land. According to Tully, the relation of individuals to the resources of the earth is essentially usufructuary. Given Locke's proviso against spoilage (that we are only entitled to that which we can use before it spoils), the condition that there be "enough and as good for others,"[19] and the notion of original common dominion by humanity, property rights appear to be essentially usufructuary, rather than approximations of the full-blown liberal concept of private ownership.[20]

3. Locke and Imperialism

Lockean scholarship has continued to grow in other directions. Locke, who at various times has been viewed as the first capitalist and at others as the last medieval, in the 1990s was seen as the first imperialist or, more properly, the first apologist for European imperialism. This view became popular on both sides of the Pacific, in North America as well as Australia. In Australia, the historian Henry Reynolds has been the most articulate scholarly defender of aboriginal land claims in the South Pacific region. Like many of the writers on that side of the Pacific, he recognizes that Locke's political writings offered a powerful rationalization for disregarding native ownership. In *The Law of the Land*, Reynolds criticizes both Locke's theory of ownership in *Two Treatises of Government* and its application to the Australian context. According to Locke, mixing individual labor with the soil, through agriculture, is the source of the natural right to personal ownership. Reynolds cannot accept this account of original acquisition because lack of aboriginal inclination towards agriculture would have rendered them propertyless, according to Locke's understanding of original acquisition of unowned objects.[21] He also points out that, *pace* Locke, English law was flexible enough to recognize different forms of property, for example, tenure over uncultivated land used exclusively for hunting and fishing and, in many cases, local customary rights.[22]

With increasing regularity, writers noted that Locke's emphasis on agriculture (especially the commercially viable form) as the legitimating mode of original acquisition meant aboriginal lands, which were not agriculturally developed, were essentially ownerless (*terra nullius*). Since indigenous people claimed territory that was not agriculturally developed, these territories were, in Lockean theory, empty or wasteland. Locke's argument could and was used to justify European expansion into these areas.[23]

Tully also has recently offered strong philosophical and historical arguments in support of aboriginal self-determination and territorial land rights in North America. Like Reynolds and many others, Tully now argues that Locke's emphasis on productive agriculture as legitimizing title worked to dispossess aboriginal title founded on different uses, for example, hunting and gathering. But most apologists for aboriginal land claims, like Reynolds, tend to leave the argument at this stage, having made the point that other customary forms of use can be equally legitimating. Tully, however, cannot follow suit because his previous work on Locke's political philosophy has committed him to the position that natural rights to land do not apply in a state of nature or pre-civil society. There, Tully pushed for a revisionist reading in which the formation of the state and the institution of civil society rightfully dissolves holdings acquired in the state of nature, empowering the state to substitute conventions of ownership projected towards the public good. Tully states:

A property in something is the completion of man's natural right to the means necessary to preserve and comfort himself and others. It is a paramount and remarkable feature of this initial claim right that it is not to the earth itself but to the manmade products useful to man's life.[24]

Naturally, if we believe the modern nation state is a European institution, then aboriginal land claims that pre date the formation of the state do not survive its formation. But Tully argues that aboriginal societies were sovereign nations with independent systems of property, traditions of thought, and international customary law developed over centuries of use.[25] Aboriginal property rights, therefore, were already enshrined within indigenous customary law and sanctioned by these sovereign nations. Features of aboriginal societies are said to obviate the extinction of these rights by the migration of representatives of European states who negotiated with and sometimes carried out international war against the natives. Tully asserts that by participating in negotiations and treaties, European powers recognized Indian nationhood. Indian nationhood was recognized by the European powers as evidenced by negotiating processes and treaties. Tully states, "Negotiations cannot extinguish the status of Aboriginal societies as nations with independent systems of property and traditions of thought, any more than negotiations can extinguish the equal status of the U.S. and Canada."[26] Furthermore, and most importantly, he maintains aboriginal societies did not lose this sovereignty, but remained independent nations under the fiduciary protection of the North American states. Bruce Morito and other scholars have developed the idea further and concluded that Amerindians are independent of European law. Morito argues that imposing European based legal procedure onto negotiations and treaty signing was itself a denial of the common ground that existed between nations.[27]

However, Tully's approach is difficult to apply to the South Pacific. Though the Polynesian communities in New Zealand, Hawaii, and Fiji possessed systems of cultural and political interaction that realized forms of sovereign nationhood, many indigenous settlements and communities in the rest of the South Pacific are not easily described as sovereign nations, especially in Melanesia. Several of these communities have a small territorial and linguistic base. Sovereign nationhood denotes a social, cultural, and political association that unites a large aggregate of families, clans, and tribes over an extended territory. In pre-colonial Papua New Guinea (P.N.G.), for example, there existed a relatively sparse population of dispersed settlements exhibiting great linguistic diversity. In P.N.G. we find over 800 language groups. In these circumstances, it is difficult to claim the existence of a political and social organization that was not merely local. Social interaction beyond the local level was constrained by these overwhelming obstacles of linguistic differences and geographical isolation. The relationships that tie together different and diverse groups require shared systems of commerce, political interaction, social coordination, as well as exchange of ideas.

Tully's view on aboriginal land rights is consistent with his previous work on Locke. Unlike Reynolds, he puts more emphasis on the organization of aboriginals into sovereign nation-states. Aboriginal land tenure does not constrain the state because these holdings were legitimately acquired independently and prior to the existence of the state. Instead, these holdings represent inviolable claims against the North American states because they reflect the sovereign territories of extant independent nations situated within their borders. Trenching upon Indian land implies denial of ownership, but only because these conventions are grounded in a more fundamental notion of national sovereignty.

4. "Control Ownership" and "Income Ownership"

The above difficulties should not lead us to conclude that many areas of the South Pacific lacked natural rights to land prior to the creation of the modern state. We have already shown that while Tully affirms that natural rights do not attach to land, his analysis can still be interpreted to support the claim that natural rights to land existed anterior to the formation of the nation-state. This is possible because in Locke's moral universe, all rights, including claim-rights to human products and rights to land, find their "natural" (non-conventional) foundation in our primary obligations to the creator. For those who are uncomfortable basing secular systems on divine commands, we recall *The Concept of Law*, where H.L.A. Hart attempts to give a secular basis to the notion of the natural law based on the universal natural motivation for survival.[28] We can leave the issue of the source of rights here, and accept that there are certain natural rights to property in land, based on the exigencies of survival, and which exist before the creation of the state. The question of the precise definition of these rights must still be answered.

The conservative view is that full-blown property rights, including rights to use, possess, destroy, transfer, and gain income from property, are originally acquired independently of the state and require the respect and protection of the state. This view was recently popularized by Richard Epstein, who sees any diminution of this bundle of rights as a fundamental violation of the right to property. Property, therefore, logically implies nothing less than the acquisition of the entire bundle of rights. This view has also received a sympathetic hearing from the U.S. Supreme Court.[29]

However, others like John Christman have argued that ownership is not a seamless package. Christman argues that the concept of ownership should be divided into control ownership and income ownership.[30] The first refers to the power to use and consume and involves possession of the ultimate authority over access to the item. The second deals with the right to exchange the holding with other willing parties and keep the proceeds from such trades. The right to income includes natural returns from trades, such as rent, interest, and profits. Christman states that income rights include not only rights to alienate holdings and exchange goods, but rights to all the economic rent available from those trades. Since full right to income provides owners with rights to all flows from market transactions, such transactions afford owners the right to economic rent.[31] Unlike Bruce Ackerman, who believes that control rights and income rights are incompatible perspectives on ownership, Christman maintains they represent two different modes of ownership.[32] Nevertheless, the two are separable, Christman claims, and one mode need not entail the other. Christman refers to both psychological and historical evidence to confirm this view. At this stage, we begin to see parallels with the distinction made by earlier Christian philosophers between rights to use and *dominium*, or absolute sovereignty over the object (or *res*) in question.

In any case, Christman's remarks raise the issue of whether or not indigenous customary rights, associated with a given territory, should be seen as encompassing both control ownership and income ownership. Obviously, if these customary ownership claims have meaning, they must include rights of access, use, and exclusion. Far less clear is the inclusion of rights of income, especially those associated with economic rent. Economic rent is any income from the trade of a good (factor), over and above the amount necessary to motivate the person controlling the factor to trade where the surplus is due to the fixed supply of the factor (its scarcity).[33] In indigenous societies, land was often regarded as inalienable, thus it could not be exchanged, sold, or given away because the people and their land were often seen as inseparable. However, Christman is not simply distinguishing rights of exchange from rights of control. Instead, he is saying that the right

> to use, possess, consume, destroy and alienate one's property – rights manifesting primary fundamental control (control rights) – can be meaningfully distinguished from the right to transfer title conditional upon receipt of goods in trade and the right to increased welfare and income from so doing.[34]

Christman is concerned with benefits of a monetary character, determined by market forces. He says that, unlike control rights, income rights are unequally conditional: "for while the right to income from trade or rent of an asset is itself fixed, the content of that right is not since this depends upon market factors over which one has no control or presumptive claim."[35]

The right to income can exist only in a cash-driven economy where relative scarcity and market factors determine a fluctuating flow of welfare and benefit from the exchange of holdings. Consequently, income rights regarding land exist only in a non-indigenous context and cannot normally be enlisted as customary ownership rights. The customary land of pre-colonial Australia, the Americas, Papua New Guinea, Fiji, and Tasmania was not rented, sold, or exchanged for increased levels of welfare or a continuing flow of monetary benefits. Only in the colonial and post-colonial period was customary land used in such a way.

This last observation raises several questions. First, we ask if the state is obligated to recognize income rights when ascribed to customary land, where such rights were not included in the original bundle of customary rights. If we adhere to the strict meaning of customary rights, then in many cases income rights would not be recognized as rights belonging to indigenous land tenure. However, liberal writers and even courts often do not state clearly that something other than customary rights is at issue when income rights are ascribed to these land claims.

Again, I would argue that there is a tacit but unproven assumption that these rights are logically continuous with the original customary claim (as well as the usually recognized rights to exclusive use and occupation).

Up to now, this chapter has proceeded at a high level of generalization and theory. What does the theory tell us about the practice of compensation for the use of customary land? The answer is that compensation claims for the use of customary land, calculated at a fixed or sliding rate of monetary return, cannot be made to follow from an original presumed natural right to the land. The natural rights, which attach to land, and were established through customary occupation and use, are properly described as modes of "control ownership." These rights include the rights to use and exclude, but would not have included the right to receive income from such property through transfer in a rental or sale agreement. The latter rights are more properly described as part of income ownership, since commercial dealing in traditional lands described as compensation payments cannot be given any moral foundation. Damage to the environment or life style of the people living close to these developments should be reflected in the compensation package. Failing evidence of such damage or inconvenience, no moral basis exists for claiming that a group is entitled to a greater share of the income from development. Of course, the traditional group will always retain the moral right to exclude others from their territory, but the right to be rewarded according to the valuation of the land set by market forces is not a right which can be derived from original customary association with the land base.

Notes

1. See A.J.A. Carlyle, *A History of Medieval Political Theory in the West*, Vol. I (London: William Blackwood and Sons, 1950), pp. 136–137.

2. See Herbert A. Deane, *The Political and Social Ideas of St. Augustine* (New York: Columbia University Press, 1963), p. 104.

3. Augustine, *In Ioannis Evangelium Tractatus CXXIV* (Turnhoti: Typographi Brepols Editores Pontificii, 1961), VI, pp. 25–26.

4. Augustine, *Corpus Scriptorum Ecclesiasticorum Latinorum*, ed. Alois Goldbacher (Vindobonae: F. Tempsky, 1895–1923), Vol. XLIV, pp. 426–427.

5. Ibid., XXXIV (2), p. 514.

6. Aquinas, *Summa theologica* (Ottawa: Commissio Piana, 1953), II–II, q. 66 a. 1.

7. Ibid., II–II, q. 62 a. 5.

8. Samuel Pufendorf, *On the duty of man and citizen according to natural law* [*De officio hominis et civis*], ed. James Tully, trans. Michael Silverthorne (Cambridge: Cambridge University Press, 1991), 4.8.8.

9. See A.M. Honore, "Ownership," *Oxford Essays in Jurisprudence*, ed. A.G. Guest, (London: Oxford University Press, 1964), pp. 107–147.

10. Francis De Pauw, *Grotius and the Law of the Sea* (Brussels: Editions de L'Institut de Sociologie, 1965).

11. See James Tully, *A Discourse on Property: John Locke and his Adversaries,* (Cambridge: Cambridge University Press, 1980), p. 73.

12. John Locke, *Two Treatises of Government,* ed. Peter. Lazlett (Cambridge: Cambridge University Press, 1967).

13. Tully, *A Discourse on Property,* p. 121.

14. Locke, *Two Treatises of Government,* Second Treatise, ch. 2, sec. 6.

15. C.B. Macpherson, *Democratic Theory* (Oxford: Clarendon Press, 1975).

16. Locke, *Two Treatises of Government,* First Treatise, ch. 4, sec. 41 ,Second Treatise, ch. 5, sec. 25.

17. Tully, *A Discourse on Property,* p. 122.

18. Locke, *Second Treatise,* para. 2:6.

19. Ibid., ch. 5, sec. 33.

20. See Honore, "Ownership."

21. Henry Reynolds, *The Law of the Land* (New York: Penguin, 1992), pp. 25–26.

22. Ibid., p. 20.

23. See Herman Lebovics, "The Uses of America in Locke's *Second Treatise of Government,*" *Journal of the History of Ideas,* 47 (1986), pp. 567–581; Thomas Flanagan, "The Agricultural Argument and Original Appropriation: Indian Lands and Political Philosophy," *Canadian Journal of Political Science,* 22 (1989), pp. 589–602; Barbara Arneil, "John Locke, Natural Law and Colonialism," *History of Political Thought,* 13 (1992), pp. 587–603; James Tully, "Aboriginal Property and Western Theory: Rediscovering a Middle Ground," *Social Philosophy and Policy* 11 (1994), pp. 153–180; see also "Rediscovering America: The *Two Treatises* and Aboriginal Rights," *Locke's Philosophy: Content and Context,* ed. G.A. Rogers (Oxford: Clarendon Press, 1994), pp. 165–196; Marilyn Holly, "The Persons of Nature versus the Power Pyramid: Locke, Land and America Indians," *International Studies in Philosophy,* 26 (1994), pp. 14–31; Mary L. Caldbick, "Wild Woods and Uncultivated Waste: Aboriginal versus Lockean Views of Land Ownership," unpublished paper presented to the Canadian Political Science Association (Brock University, June 1996).

24. Tully, *A Discourse on Property,* p. 122.

25. Tully, "Aboriginal Property and Western Theory," pp. 153–180; see also "Rediscovering America: The *Two Treatises* and Aboriginal Rights," pp. 165–196.

26. *Ibid.*

27. See also Bruce Morito, "Aboriginal Right: A Conciliatory Concept," *Journal of Applied Philosophy,* 13 (1996), pp. 123–140.

28. H.L.A. Hart, *Concept of Law* (New York: Oxford University Press, 1962).

29. See Richard Epstein, *Takings: Private Property and Eminent Domain* (Cambridge, MA: Harvard University Press, 1985).

30. John Christman, *The Myth of Property* (New York: Oxford University Press, 1994), p. 128.

31. See Ibid., pp. 31, 130, 169.

32. Ibid., p. 143.

33. Ibid., p. 31.

34. Ibid., p. 131.

35. Ibid.

Fourteen

SOLIDARITY AND HUMAN RIGHTS

William Sweet

1. Introduction

The word "solidarity" and the call to solidarity are familiar to us all. "Solidarity" reminds many of us of the trade union movement that arose in 1980 in opposition to the Polish government, whose leader Lech Walesa was awarded the Nobel Peace Prize in 1983 and whose actions were instrumental in the collapse of totalitarian regimes in Central and Eastern Europe. And for some four decades, the term "solidarity" and the call to be "in solidarity" have been uttered wherever we find those in need – the poor, the oppressed, and the marginalized.

Now, we might ask, how is it that people can respond to such a call? The fact is we live in a world that is home to a multiplicity of religions, creeds, forms of life, ethical standards, ethical practices, and discourses. And in recent years we have become deeply conscious of how these various creeds, practices, and discourses separate us from one another – and of how what others think, aim at, and wish for, and what they do, are sometimes entirely foreign to us. How is it possible to answer – or even hear – a call to solidarity in a radically pluralistic world?

We are faced with a similar situation when it comes to human rights. We have recently celebrated the fiftieth anniversary of the United Nations Universal Declaration of Human Rights – a Declaration that calls for "all peoples and all nations" to strive "to promote respect for these rights" which reflect the dignity of all members of the human family. Marginalized and dispossessed groups often appeal to such rights, and the term "human rights" is found not only in philosophical texts, but in social and political discourse throughout the world. But to talk about and, especially, to defend the concept of universal human rights these days is a far from easy task. The problem is not just the practical challenge, posed by diversity and pluralism, to the recognition of universal rights. There has been severe criticism of any talk about "rights." Skeptical philosophers, since the time of Jeremy Bentham, have written that natural human rights are nonsensical, anarchic, and dangerous. Some from developing countries, like Vinay Lal, see charters of rights and the discourse of human rights as a tool of oppression employed by "western" governments. And some "post-modern" philosophers, such as Richard Rorty, suggest that talk about human rights is irrelevant and adds nothing to our sentiments to see justice done and to help others.

This is not, however, the view of the French philosopher Jacques Maritain, who was well aware of the challenges of pluralism and skepticism, but who insisted human rights were necessary to justice and international development and cooperation, particularly in a world as culturally diverse as our own.[1]

Though he sometimes uses the term,[2] Maritain did not discuss "solidarity" at any length. Still, his views on human rights can help us to understand the moral obligation to be "in solidarity" with others, and to clarify how to act concretely in a way that promotes solidarity.

In this paper, I start with a standard description of solidarity and, after contrasting the term with a number of other concepts with which it may be associated, I consider what is supposed to be a radical criticism of this standard view – namely that found in the work of the philosopher and social critic, Richard Rorty. I will suggest that Rorty's analysis of the concept of solidarity has a number of serious problems, but also that some elements in his analysis can be used in the reconstruction of a more precise understanding of the notion. After sketching such a revised description, I will argue that Maritain's discussion of human rights is helpful in articulating how to act with solidarity, how to be in solidarity, why we should be in solidarity with others, and how a "sentimental education" promoting solidarity can be appropriate in our (post-) modern world.

a. A Definition of "Solidarity"

What is meant by "solidarity?" With whom are we called on to be "in solidarity?" What sorts of actions or activities fall under this category?

To help with at least this first question, let us consider a standard definition of the term.

The word "solidarity," which entered the English language in the middle of the nineteenth century, is derived from the French *solidarité*. It means a "relation among persons who recognize a community of interests, and which leads to the moral obligation not to harm one another and to come to one another's assistance" – cognate terms are "association," "mutual aid," "reciprocity," and even "companionship" and "fellowship." To be "in solidarity" is said of persons "who answer for one another and are committed to the same thing" and "who feel tied to one another by a common responsibility and interests." The antonyms of this concept are "independence" and "individualism."

From this description, we note the following features:

a) solidarity is, or involves, a relation; .
b) this relation is among persons;
c) the basis of this relation is a recognition by the persons concerned;
d) what is recognized is, at minimum, the existence of certain interests or responsibilities that are common or shared; and
e) the existence of this recognition – not just the existence of these common interests alone – leads to a moral obligation to act in certain ways.

We might also note the following: considering its connection with terms like "fellowship" and "companionship," this relation and this recognition involve emotions or, more broadly, affectivity.

The preceding description is simply a lexical definition and a set of synonyms for the word "solidarity." It has a prescriptive force for ordinary discourse, but lexical definitions are rarely conclusive in philosophical debate. Nevertheless, lexical accounts cannot be ignored either, and if we wish to speak of solidarity – or of rethinking solidarity – we must take common use into consideration.

How does solidarity come to exist? A moment's reflection suggests that it can arise in different ways. It may arise spontaneously, as it does in a family or community, or it may be something willed or commanded, or it may be something one chooses.[3] Still, knowing what can motivate solidarity does not tell us much about what solidarity is. We need to know about the nature or character of the "relation" that the persons involved recognize in one another. This is essential to understanding solidarity, but it can be deferred for a moment.

Generally, when we think about "solidarity," we regard it as roughly the same as "being just" or "doing justice," or "cooperation," or having a "fellow feeling" for others (*fraternité*), or "empathy" or "sympathy," or "the willingness to do good to another," or "loyalty," or "understanding," or "showing tolerance" for others. Yet the concept of solidarity is much richer than any of these.

For example, solidarity might seem to be much the same thing as "justice" or "being just." Solidarity, like justice, has both moral and political dimensions. Thus, when we think of the political side of "justice," we see it as focusing on institutional arrangements and relations – and these arrangements and procedures are also involved in defining the practical side or the mechanics or the procedures of solidarity. Still, this does not show that solidarity and justice are the same – but simply that both have a moral and political dimension.

Justice is clearly not the same as solidarity. In some situations solidarity requires more than "being just," and a person can act justly towards others without being in solidarity with them. We have all seen cases where "justice" is done "from above," or dispassionately, or is motivated solely by principle, not by regard for the other or "fellow interest" – whereas we would not think of solidarity as existing if these features were present. Solidarity implies, but goes beyond, acting justly.

Again, consider the notion of "fellow feeling" (what the French call *fraternité*). Here we see fellow citizens, or neighbors, or fellow human beings, as if they were our brothers or sisters. But the existence of "fellow feeling" doesn't mean that we must act to help our "fellows," or that failing to help them would be not only failing to do good, but failing in our duty, and wrong. We can have "fellow feeling" without being just – for example, where that sentiment leads us to break the law. Moreover, while "fellow feeling" reflects a feeling of closeness to another, common or shared interest need not be involved.

Nor is solidarity the same as acting in cooperation with others. A call to "cooperate" does not say anything about whether we have a duty or an obligation to cooperate; a person can cooperate in a project "out of the goodness of her heart," but would not be blamed if she refused to do so (unless, for example, refusing also entailed a violation of justice). Again, we can cooperate in something in which we do not have much interest, and we can "passively cooperate" – that is, refuse to stand in the way of another – which is far removed from the activism suggested by the concept of solidarity. People can cooperate in the realization of immoral ends; if we are tempted to describe such cases as instances of "solidarity," it is surely by analogy. What we really mean to speak of here is "collusion," rather than solidarity. As the description we started with and common usage imply, "solidarity" has a positive moral connotation.

Tolerance is not the same as solidarity. It generally involves characteristics almost opposite of being "in solidarity." Tolerance involves "accepting the other, where the other has a different – that is, not a common – interest with oneself," and it may require only a minimum of positive acts on our part – for example, simply the commitment not to impede others in the exercise of their actions. The concept of "tolerance" suggests the existence of important differences among individuals (as in the notion of religious tolerance), whereas solidarity implies that what differences exist among the individuals concerned are not important – that there is a recognition of common interests, and a willingness to engage in actions with others, even if it involves sacrifices on our part. Nor is solidarity the same as loyalty. Loyalty certainly may involve "acting justly," but it definitely need not. (Think of the loyalty of British football fans to their teams. And when our commitment to our family may, again, lead us to break the law, or to treat others in a way that we know to be wrong, we can describe that commitment as an instance of "loyalty," but not properly "solidarity.") While loyalty involves some kind of recognition of a relation with the another – the person or thing that is the object of our loyalty – the recognition need not be mutual, common or shared interest is not necessary, and neither is equality or parity among those involved in this relation. The loyalty of a soldier to her commander or a servant to his master is not a relation between equals.

Finally, we may have sympathy or empathy for another person, but solidarity is much more than this. Our sympathies are changeable, and can even be accidental, whereas the existence of solidarity would suggest a continuity over time and a relation to others that is not arbitrary. Moreover, we can meaningfully and legitimately say someone ought to be in solidarity with another, whereas it scarcely makes sense to say someone (morally) ought to "feel" sympathy. And most of all, the concept of empathy or sympathy does not imply such a sentiment is shared, or is based on a shared interest or mutual recognition – one simply has this "reaction."

While we could continue this contrast of solidarity with allied notions, perhaps it is not necessary. The central point here is that "solidarity" is both an important and a distinctive moral term. "Solidarity" goes beyond the characteristics of "being just," "cooperative," "tolerant," "fraternal," "loyal," "acting charitably," "doing good," and so on. Some of these activities may lead to the development of solidarity, but they do not necessarily lead to it, and they are still quite different from it. In solidarity, we show a recognition of a common interest and of others as equals, which "colors" the nature of the relation to them – it is a non-exploitative and non-disempowering relationship. Being "in solidarity" is not something that we can be casually. It involves acting or doing (or, at least, showing a firm and resolute willingness to act) and takes time, which is manifest in the notion of commitment or (as the French would say) *engagement*.

Finally, when we think about the concept of "solidarity," we see that it is not simply a "behavior,"[4] but a particular kind of behavior – a practice – and to speak of people being "in solidarity" with one another is to say that they are participants in a practice. What exactly this means is not fully spelled out in the definition we started with, though it is consistent with it, and it allows us to distinguish "solidarity" from a number of other ethical and quasi-ethical terms.

Now, the description I have been discussing does not specify with whom we should be "in solidarity" (assuming that this needs to be specified) or what exactly we should do. Some might say these details can be provided by referring to a general moral or normative theory. And no doubt this is precisely how these matters might have been resolved – at least, until relatively recently.

b. Rorty's Challenge

Today we see a widespread suspicion, if not a rejection, of the need for a general moral theory. Many doubt such a theory is even possible. One proponent of this view is Richard Rorty.[5] Rorty argues that to look for such a theory is a mistake, but that the absence of a general moral theory does not prevent us from talking about concepts such as "truth" and "solidarity."

In his essay on "Solidarity," Rorty describes two views of solidarity: one holds "that there is something within each of us – our essential humanity – which resonates to the presence of this same thing in other human beings"[6]; the other (that is, his own position) is that solidarity is a "sense"[7] or a "feeling" – though what kind of feeling is left unclear.

The former view, Rorty claims, hinges on an essentialist and universalist account of human nature – that something inherent in and common to all human beings does or should "resonate" or is recognized by other human beings. (Rorty says that this is "[t]he traditional philosophical way of spelling out what we mean by 'human solidarity'"[8] but he gives no reference to who, if anyone, actually holds this view.) And he says those who defend this view believe that it is on the basis of this (allegedly) essential property that we can speak of someone as being "human" or "one of us," and that is the foundation not only for an obligation of solidarity, but for moral obligation in general.

But, Rorty argues, no such essential property exists, and whatever property a defender of solidarity and human rights might appeal to as a "foundation" for them is contingently, if not somewhat arbitrarily, determined and provides no universal justification.[9] There could never be, then, any general or universal obligation to be in solidarity with others.

Rorty's own view is that solidarity is not something based on or the result of the intellectual recognition of the existence of certain properties in others. It exists on the affective level. He describes "solidarity" as a "self-doubt which has gradually ... been inculcated into inhabitants of democratic states"[10] – perhaps he means here "a feeling of guilt." But he also says solidarity is an "ability to see" differences between human beings "as unimportant"[11] or an "ability to notice, and identify with" the pain of others.[12] He holds that solidarity is something "made" or "produced," rather than something "found" or "recognized."[13]

Rorty thinks we must develop or "create"[14] this feeling or ability – to "try" (he says this three times on page 196 of his essay "Solidarity") to keep expanding the sense of "us" as far as we can. And he even proposes a means by which we can arouse this "imaginative identification"[15] with others, namely, what he calls "sentimental education."[16]

But if asked why we – by which Rorty means "we twentieth [and twenty-first] century liberals"[17] – should engage in such an activity, why we should "keep trying to expand our sense of 'us' as far as we can" and why we "should try to notice our similarities with others,"[18] Rorty's answer is that "there is nothing to back up such a request, nor need there be."[19] But he insists that even though people are or should be aware that the feeling or belief in solidarity "is caused by nothing deeper than historical circumstance," such a belief "can still regulate action and can still be thought worth dying for."[20]

Why, then, is it important that we engage in acts of solidarity? Rorty suggests that if we are to be consistent liberals, we are "dedicated" to this – that is, we know that we "should" engage in such actions – though the force of this "should" adds nothing to saying that we just want to be consistent liberals. For on Rorty's view there is no good "objective" reason to be a liberal; if one asked whether this "liberalism" is a better view than, say, Nazism or fascism, it seems that all he can say is that "it is, if you are a liberal" or, at worst, "it depends on where you are."

c. Why Rorty's Model Fails as an Account of Solidarity

Is Rorty's account a substantive view of solidarity? Does it capture what calls for solidarity are about? Rorty's "post-modern" view may give pause to the tendency some philosophers have for a highly rationalistic approach to morals – particularly concerning the relevance of appeals to the sentiments. Nevertheless, his account in general is seriously defective.

To begin with, Rorty's cure for the lack of solidarity in the world is definitely not philosophical or moral argument – he would see these as, at best, just "spinning one's philosophical wheels." The answer is, rather, a "sentimental education."[21]

This point is intuitively persuasive. Since the early modern period, there has been an emphasis on the role of (instrumental) reason and a suspicion, if not an outright exclusion, of the power of, and the data provided by, the passions or emotions. Now, such a rationalist approach, many people like Rorty have argued, provides too narrow and too limited a view of what sort of appeals are appropriate in philosophical argument; it ignores how people actually think and come to know. And, interestingly, this "rationalism" has not only been challenged by many contemporary philosophers, like Rorty, but would have been contested by Aristotle, Thomas Aquinas, and many others from "pre-modern" times. Even Plato would agree that it is often through some kind of non-rationalist education, rather than through philosophical argument, that individuals can come to see a point. (Think of the use of myth and "the noble lie" in his work.) It is quite plausible that if we can appreciate the suffering of others, we will be more likely to act in ways that show solidarity. So we can admit that Rorty is on to something when he writes that we need sentimental education.

Still, several points are troubling in Rorty's analysis. I cannot list them all here, but I will comment on three that bear on issues central to an adequate understanding of the nature of solidarity.

The first troubling point concerns Rorty's descriptions of "solidarity." Rorty's account of the "essentialist" view of solidarity is a caricature. Maybe there isn't any particular characteristic of a person that triggers some "resonance" in another and underlies the second person's sense of solidarity with the first. But (as suggested in the description of solidarity earlier in this paper) what is central to solidarity is not some particular natural characteristic; it is a recognition of the other and the possibility of a shared interest – and these recognitions underlie how the persons involved act and treat one another. When we act with others, we show that we see them as different, but also as like us, and that we are potential sharers in a common interest. We recognize the other as a being who has characteristics – which we may call "essential" – which make our recognition of that being as a person possible, and which actually lead to that recognition. In contrast, Rorty's description of solidarity is rather one-dimensional. It refers to someone who "acquires" a feeling of solidarity – but there is no "reciprocity," no recognition of a common interest, and no moral obligation. Rorty's description of "solidarity" looks the same as "just wanting to be helpful," whereas – on the account given earlier – it is much more than this.

A second troubling point concerns the justification of our sense of solidarity. Rorty argues that our feelings of solidarity are "contingently determined" and without justification. Now, if solidarity were just a feeling, he could be right – like any feeling, solidarity could have an explanation, but not a justification. But is Rorty right in describing solidarity as a feeling? Surely, to appreciate the suffering of others, it is not enough just to "feel" that suffering; we must also believe we must do something about it. At this point, providing a justification for being, and acting, "in solidarity" is demonstrably relevant.

Admittedly, Rorty asks what sort of justification could be provided here, and replies that we can give "no *neutral*, non-circular" one.[22] But is this what we must provide in order to give a justification? Why, for example, should we think a justification has to be "neutral"? ("Neutrality" is, in any case, a vague and ambiguous term.) Presumably, Rorty thinks that justifications have to have the form of foundationalist arguments – that is, that they have to be demonstrations from axiomatic principles. But even a philosopher as paradigmatically rationalist as Kant denied that moral action could be "deduced" from a moral standard. (Recall Kant's discussion, in chapter 2 of the *Groundwork of the Metaphysic of Morals*, on the distinction between "deriving" and "deducing" moral claims.[23]) And why think that, because our "beliefs" are "historically contingent,"[24] or have little "causal efficacy,"[25] they cannot have a "rational" justification? So we might reply that justification is important because truth is important, and the contingent fact that a certain belief has arisen in me is not sufficient to justify why I *ought* to hold that belief. Thus, Rorty's comments notwithstanding, we have no reason to imagine people blithely going to war, thinking their convictions were just one in a set of convictions, with nothing making them especially worthy, except that they are just those of which they and their fellows happen to be convinced.

Rorty's "pragmatic" view, of course, is that reasoning about moral matters usually doesn't work and that we can't prove that one way of acting is more moral than another. And so he concludes that reasoning isn't important and we should, instead, pursue a "sentimental education" to develop the feeling of solidarity.

Should we accept Rorty's "pragmatic" response on the issue of justifying our sense of solidarity, and his counter-proposal supporting "sentimental education"? Consider, for example, his claim that reasoning about moral matters usually does not work and that, as good pragmatists, we needn't focus on this in moral action. Certainly, if we want to convince someone to act in a certain way, or immediately to stop abusing or harming another person, articulating a grand moral theory does not often, if ever, work; on this point, Rorty is probably right. But it does not follow from the fact that sentimental education might lead us to certain humanistic views, that it is inappropriate to try to get to these views in some other way (for example, by reason and argument). Nor does it follow that we are right not to bother with arguments. Saying that sentimental education can get us to see a point or better appreciate the interests and needs of others is different from saying that this is all we need to defend our commitment to that point or to defend what we have come to appreciate. We might, then, come to hold a certain view after a "sentimental education," but this doesn't mean that we shouldn't try showing this view is true, or appropriate, or obligatory. For example, to teach children certain fundamental mathematical propositions, we may use apples or oranges or colored beads, but this does not mean we shouldn't be concerned with showing what makes these propositions true. We have no reason to hold, as Rorty does, that:

> If it seems that most of the work of changing moral intuitions is being done by manipulating our feelings rather than increasing our knowledge, that will be a

reason to think there is no knowledge of the sort which philosophers like Plato, Aquinas, and Kant hoped to acquire.[26]

There are other problems with Rorty's response to the view that solidarity needs a justification, and with his counter-proposal that we must have a "sentimental education" to develop the feeling of solidarity. To begin with, is Rorty's "sentimental education" an education? What is curious about his position is not that an education could be something "sentimental" – long ago, Hume, Smith, and Flaubert spoke of the education of the sentiments – but that Rorty calls it "education." This is not just a verbal point. To speak of "education" suggests that one is being led (*ducere*), not only to an end – which is a belief or a set of beliefs (something cognitive) that is in some way objectively good – but away from (*ex*) something that is, presumably, bad or ideological or parochial. Now Rorty would presumably admit that, in sentimental education, we are being led out of a narrow view to a broader, more comprehensive view. But since he believes values have no moral weight outside of their context, "sentimental education" is not an education towards a better view or set of beliefs, but is simply bringing it about that one's feelings are more consistent with (Rorty's) liberal ideals. Rorty's "education" is not an education informed by a model of "the good" or "the right." It is not clear how Rorty's understanding of "education" corresponds to education at all. Rorty says we may "tell some sad stories" to bring about solidarity, but he could say little, I think, against training, some gentle brainwashing, or indoctrination, and of course he speaks approvingly of "manipulating"[27] our views, which is far from the way in which "education" is usually understood.

A second difficulty in Rorty's counter-proposal of "sentimental education" concerns what he says is the point of sentimental education – it is to make us come to "notice"[28] that the differences of race, sex, and so on, are trivial compared to what we have in common, and he provides us with a series of examples.[29] But this remark puts Rorty at least dangerously close to inconsistency. For then the object of sentimental education is not (just) to get us to "feel" a certain way or to have a particular sense, but to get us to know or recognize something or to make us more aware – that is, to see the fact that these differences among people really are trivial.

Again, a genuine sentimental education must rest on some kind of knowledge or belief about those with whom we are in solidarity. If it is only a matter of "feeling," then can we ever assert, for example, that someone has been led to have the right feeling or reaction? And what basis would we have for saying that the appropriate response would be to treat others (with whom I am called to be in solidarity) as equals, and not simply as objects of pity? And even if we "feel" what the other feels – even if "I feel your pain" – what guarantees that the right response to this is a sense of solidarity? One response could be to show compassion; another could be indifference. It does make sense to speak of appropriate and inappropriate responses or feelings here, and this suggests that there is something objective and rational that underlies our responses.

A defense of solidarity, then, cannot be just, or primarily, a matter of feeling. If Rorty's weak account of solidarity and sentimental education were right, then there would be, for example, no reason why we could not speak of being in solidarity with animals or plants – and while we may have some sense of duty or obligation concerning animals and plants, how we can be in solidarity with them is by no means obvious. (Admittedly, we may want to do good for them but, again, unless we have common interests – assuming plants have interests – and at least the potential for reciprocal recognition, we cannot be in solidarity with them.) There must be something about other persons (though it needn't be the same thing in every case) that ultimately warrants not only a feeling of solidarity, but the obligation of solidarity, with them. The point of any sentimental education is not just that we should come to hold that the differences between one another should not be felt to be important – it is that we should see these differences as unimportant and, therefore, feel them to be so.

Thus, we can properly speak of having a "feeling" of solidarity with another, but solidarity is not just a feeling, and unless an appropriate basis and ground for that "feeling" exists, it is not one of solidarity. Consider the following question: Can I have a sense of solidarity with a person or a nation that treats me like a brute animal or as a member of an inferior race? My feelings might be manipulated so that I say "yes" – but this does not mean that we are in solidarity. A Christian slave might wish good things for her abusive master, but so long as she is enslaved and abused by him, and regardless of her feelings, it would be entirely inappropriate to say she was "in solidarity" with him.

The call to solidarity must have a rational justification. Reasons count, and giving reasons that should persuade others – even if these reasons do not succeed – is necessary if we are to take the call to solidarity seriously. For Rorty, we can give no reason for solidarity, and our acting in solidarity with others is not based on some particular property they have. But he forgets or fails to recognize that in solidarity, it matters whose pain and suffering (or, more generally, whose interests) are at stake. Thus, we agree that sad stories about mothers and children are relevant to the call to solidarity in a way that stories about cats and kittens are not. Arguably, the reason why Dickens moves us more than Descartes is not because we find Dickens's work better written, but because, as Dickens recognized, other human beings and their interests count, and this is why it is important to write passionately about – and to promote solidarity with – them. If sentimental education is to be sufficient, if it is to create solidarity, it must do something more than merely evoke a feeling. How Rorty's version of sentimental education will lead to genuine solidarity is simply not clear.

Finally, I want to note a third troubling point with Rorty's account. If Rorty is right about cultural differences and the impossibility of reasoning across cultures and across "final vocabularies," it is not clear how we can call on others outside our group, communicate with them, or ask them to engage in actions of solidarity with us. If Rorty's view is correct, how could others understand our calls to solidarity? There would be, after all, no common good, no common moral discourse, no shared vocabulary to which all can turn for guidance, and the calls to solidarity of one group would not amount to, or mean, the same as those of others. Yet the experience of ecumenism, cross-cultural dialogue, and practical financial and technical support to developing nations suggests there is and can be solidarity among members of different cultures, classes, religions, and so on.

Rorty's analysis of solidarity, and his method of sentimental education which he thinks will lead us to it, then, are seriously flawed. So is there any way in which we can find a basis for solidarity, a justification for encouraging solidarity, and a method for engaging in solidarity that addresses Rorty's concerns about the "over-rationalization" of ethics and the general inefficacy of argument?

2. An Alternative Model of Solidarity

Solidarity is not simply, and is certainly not primarily, a "sense" or "feeling," though people do feel or have a sense of solidarity with others. Rorty's description of it as an "ability" to see or empathize with another's pain is close – but again, falls short of what solidarity is.

What, then, is "solidarity" and what is it to be "in solidarity"?

To be "in solidarity," as suggested earlier in this paper, is to be a participant in a practice. By this, I mean (to use Alasdair MacIntyre's definition):

> any coherent and complex form of socially established cooperative human activity through which goods internal [and, I would add, external] to that form of activity are realized in the course of trying to achieve those standards of excellence which are appropriate to, and partially definitive of, that form of activity ...[30]

So, solidarity is an activity rather than just a sense or a feeling.

What kind of practice or activity is solidarity? It is one that involves promoting shared interests through the building of supportive relations among persons (what the French call *entraide*) and the respect of these relations. Specifically, it means aiming at the physical, intellectual, moral, and spiritual well-being of all concerned, by all concerned, to the best of their ability. (These "goods" are internal, and also external, to that practice.) What is also characteristic of this practice is that the matter of who contributes more or who benefits more is not of particular concern to the participants. There is, then, a parity or equality among the parties involved.

Now, when people engage in a practice, they acquire a disposition. Thus, solidarity indicates the existence of a tendency and a willingness by these persons to act to promote an interest they share, but it also indicates having already acted in a way that shows a recognition of such an interest and of one another. (Otherwise, we are talking simply of "doing good" – even if in a non-exploitative or non-disempowering way – or acting "charitably.") Thus, solidarity, in the sense of being "in solidarity," is best understood as an intentional or a dispositional notion or term in much the same way we say "courage" is a dispositional term. The acquisition of such a disposition is something that is, in the overwhelming majority of cases, voluntary – that is, people can choose to engage in actions that produce this character – although it can also occur (as Durkheim notes) "spontaneously."

To be "in solidarity" with others, then, is to have this disposition – which means being in an actively supportive relation with others, in view of a common interest. To be in solidarity also involves having a sense of commitment or *engagement* to the ends of the practice, and to the fact that these ends cannot be pursued except with the will and the commitment of others who seek the same end.

Dispositions are social, in the sense that practices do not exist, and the acquisition of dispositions does not occur, except through others. Dispositions require the presence of others, not only because we acquire our dispositions through acting with others, but because acting on the basis of a disposition always involves others. Solidarity also involves some level of mutual recognition (that is, recognition of the beings with whom we are in solidarity as beings like ourselves who in some way recognize us and who share an interest with us). This "recognition" need not be specific. Think of the work of Amnesty International. A prisoner of conscience might be aware of Amnesty being in solidarity with her, but this does not mean she is aware of each member or any particular member of that organization. Still, without some kind of mutual recognition, solidarity may end up being just "doing good," which runs the risk of making one of the parties a "do-gooder."

Other features of solidarity should be noted as well. First, while solidarity isn't based on sentiment, sentiment is involved. We care about the practice – we are *engagé* and committed to the end of the practice – but also care for those with whom we work. If we didn't care at all – if we were indifferent – then an observer would think there was no real solidarity. Second, when we act with solidarity, we not only act with others for the same interest, but in a way that is not disempowering or exploitative. For the relationship to the other is part of the interest to be realized. And this kind of activity is possible only among beings of a certain type (beings with self-consciousness and consciousness of others). Solidarity, then, is a relation among persons and involves a recognition of one another as persons.

Finally, solidarity is a moral practice. To be "in solidarity" – to have this disposition – is not only valuable and important, but a call to solidarity suggests that we may even have an obligation to act in a way appropriate to this end. Now, the source of this normative character is unclear. Is it just analytical – a feature of the existence of the disposition (that is, simply implied by one's *engagement* or willingness to act, or of one's commitment to the end), or is it a consequence of the recognition that there are common interests? Or is it that the existence of the relations with others and of the recognition of these relations is the *basis* for the claim that we ought to act in solidarity? This question of "moral foundation" is an important one, but it need not be answered quite yet.

(Before proceeding further, I wish to make a few side comments. First, an analysis of certain activities or practices as tending to or reflecting dispositions is nothing new. This is a matter discussed long ago by Aristotle and Thomas Aquinas, in their respective analyses of the virtues.

Second, a critic may wonder whether it makes any practical difference whether we are "in solidarity" with others or simply "do good" to them. I cannot go far into this matter here, though I would argue there is a difference both in approach and attitude in how we act, particularly because a policy of "doing good" alone might make us think the other person is the sole beneficiary of the good achieved. But building community, for example, requires solidarity, and not just doing good for another.

Third, the preceding description of solidarity is consistent with some of Rorty's comments on solidarity. Solidarity involves engaging in a certain social practice and exhibiting the disposition to continue to engage in this practice. Now what leads a person to engage in a practice and what develops a disposition is (almost always) not philosophical argument. Rorty's comment about the inefficacy of argument in leading a person to "solidarity" is often true. This still does not mean philosophical argument is irrelevant. It might show, for instance, how solidarity is consistent with other moral dispositions and with what we know of others.

Again, Rorty is right to draw our attention to the fact that solidarity requires "an ability to see" something about the other – though we must add that this involves not just the ability to recognize the other's pain but, more importantly, to see the other as one with whom we have (or can have) a common interest, to see what this interest is or can be, to see what the appropriate kind of actions would be to promote this interest and, most importantly, to see that we ought to do something in bringing about the realization of this interest.

Finally, Rorty is right to make the point that solidarity is not the "resonance" of "some *thing*" in us with the same "thing" in the other. We act in solidarity not because of some "resonance," but because we recognize the other as another person and because a common interest exists for both of us. As well, Rorty is right in describing solidarity as something "made." It usually involves not only doing or acting – that is, the building and maintenance of relations with others – but "building" a virtue or disposition. I would add that the kind of relations established, the interests promoted, and the disposition built are not arbitrary or purely contingent, but reflect basic needs and desires of human beings. This does not mean that any particular relations, interests, and dispositions are "necessary." It is not logically necessary that solidarity take a particular form or promote certain specific interests – assuming that such a notion of "logical necessity" can even coherently be applied here. Still, human beings do certain things to live and grow and develop (might this be a causal necessity?), and that they do do certain things is not "accidental." And so "solidarity" requires acting in a way that is consistent with how human beings live, grow, and develop. These are, however, side comments to the present argument, and are not essential to the position being defended here.)

In short, then, solidarity involves 1) the recognition of one another as beings who have common interests and who can engage in common action; 2) the existence of practices that enable the participants to begin to realize these common interests; 3) a decision to engage in these practices and to carry out certain actions that achieve these interests; 4) the actual engaging in these practices; and 5) the development of a disposition, or *habitus*, or virtue as a result of engaging in these practices – namely, that of being "in solidarity." And so, those who are "in solidarity" with others have a sense of commitment or *engagement* for the realization of a common interest, care for these others, and may be conscious of moral obligation to continue in such activities.

a. Maritain's Contribution

But what should we do, what practices should we engage in, and with whom should we engage in them, in order to have the disposition of being "in solidarity?" And is there any reason or justification for why we ought to be in solidarity with others?

Here the work of Jacques Maritain may be helpful. For many today, Maritain is a figure in the history of philosophy, rather than someone whose ideas must be engaged in philosophical debate. Yet many problems we currently face were known to him. Although most of his political writings date from the mid-1930s to the mid 1950s, he was well aware of the tensions and challenges involved in living in a culturally and ideologically diverse world. He was importantly influential in the drafting of the Universal Declaration of Human Rights in 1948[31] – a document that continues to have a central place in discussions of economic and social justice and political freedom. The rights and freedoms he called for are goals many still wish to realize today.

Bluntly put, Maritain would say people should respect human rights and actively engage in work that will promote these rights. In doing so, they promote the material, intellectual, social, and spiritual well-being of both themselves and others. When people engage in such activity with others, they develop a corresponding virtue or disposition – a disposition Maritain might have been willing to describe as being "in solidarity." Maritain's work also provides us with arguments why we should be "in solidarity" – though he is quite willing to admit that arguments do not generally make people moral, and so other forms of "knowing" or of "education" are required to encourage development of moral dispositions. Further, Maritain would claim to be able to show us that the differences among people are trivial. He would insist many of the natural differences among persons are morally irrelevant and that by recognizing this, we are not merely adopting a comfortable liberal view, but a view that is true.

Asked what engaging in the practice of solidarity concretely requires of us, Maritain would suggest it is the mutual recognition, and the united action to ensure the respect, of human rights – rights that concern all human beings. It is instructive to recall that the rights Maritain defends in his writings are not just the formal rights of freedom of conscience, speech, association, and private ownership of property. Maritain also defends rights to personal integrity, to participate actively in political life, to establish a constitution and decide the form of government, to associate with others and, particularly, to form or join political parties or movements, to an independent judiciary, and to equal access to public employment and open access to the professions. These rights would also include rights to choose one's work freely, to associate in professional associations or unions, to receive a just salary, to participate in the ownership and management of cooperative enterprises, to have access to social assistance (for example, unemployment insurance, sick benefits, and social security)[32] and, even, to proper food, clothing, and shelter.[33] Maritain's account of natural law and natural rights envisages a wide range of human rights and freedoms that, once we are aware of them and once we have the material means to realize them, cannot morally be ignored.

Thus, as we engage in activities that lead to a recognition and respect of these rights, we are not just getting them for others. Such rights are human rights, and so the defense of these rights as rights is a matter of common interest. If our work for the recognition of these rights is not for them as universal human rights, then no one has them as human rights. They would be, at best, morally justified powers to claim certain benefits or to act in certain ways. Moreover, Maritain would add that we should work for the recognition and respect of these rights, not just because we have a personal interest in them, but because we have an interest in that which respect for these rights will lead to – that is, the physical, intellectual, moral, and spiritual development of persons. For such reasons Maritain would hold that we should be in solidarity with others. If these rights are ever to be achieved or realized in a substantive way, we need a recognition of a shared interest and common action. Thus, in promoting and defending these rights as human rights, and in acting with others who struggle for these rights, we are "in solidarity" with one another.

(Incidentally, we share virtually none of these interests with non-human animals – it would seem that the only interest we might have in common with them is the interest not to experience pain or suffering. But it is doubtful this could ever be a shared interest, since it is unlikely that both we and animals could recognize this interest as common. This is not to say we have no duties or responsibilities to animals, but it does entail that we cannot be in solidarity with them.)

Admittedly, the rights enumerated by Maritain are general in form and give us only guidelines on how to act. Moreover, the simple decision to engage in the defense of human rights, and even the active pursuit of the recognition and respect of these rights, is only necessary, but obviously not sufficient for there to be solidarity. Maritain distinguishes a person who may do good things from a good person, and would distinguish between a person who acts in a way that is supportive of others and a person who is *"solidaire"* – that is, actually "in solidarity." Being "in solidarity" is not an attribute we can properly apply to someone based just on an observation at some isolated point in time or during some abstract time-slice. To have solidarity or to be in solidarity, we must intend to act in a certain way, with others, for a common end, and we must act in this way over time. It is for this reason that we can count on someone with whom we are "in solidarity."

How are people to be encouraged to act in this way and to develop such a disposition? Maritain would certainly concur with Rorty that sentimental education is appropriate – but he would understand it in a different way, and he would not say it is sufficient or the sole way of leading one to develop such a disposition. He would agree we can "see" some principles as true without having to be led to them through argument, and he would say the object of sentimental education is to get us to "see" or be aware of the other, our shared interests, and how we should regard one another.

Specifically, Maritain would say that, by drawing our attention (empathetically) to features of other human beings, we come to see (cognitively and morally) their essential characteristics. By means of an appeal to the sentiments, then, we acquire knowledge – insight – that not only is involved in, but even forms the basis for, the development of the disposition. And because such insights are truths and not just opinions, Maritain would argue that the means by which one leads another to the recognition of this is education – and not brainwashing or persuasion or manipulation. For Maritain, we must have more than sentiments in order to have solidarity; we must also know that what we are called to do is appropriate to human development and well-being. This is where, *pace* Rorty, philosophy comes in.

b. Foundations for Solidarity

A critic might object, saying that even if we allow that engaging in solidarity requires the recognition and respect of human rights, and even if we all have an interest in assuring these rights, is there any reason why we should be in solidarity with others? Is there any reason we should engage in activity in order to develop such a disposition? Could there be, for example, an objective, universal, moral obligation to be "in solidarity" – that is, a reason that is external to the practice of solidarity? Rorty's response is "No" – but this is not Maritain's view.

What would such a reason or argument look like? To begin with, this demand for foundations is a question that would have struck an "ancient" as somewhat odd. In the *Nicomachean Ethics*, for example, Aristotle was concerned not with proving we should be morally virtuous, but with showing how we could lead morally virtuous lives. Maritain would undoubtedly agree with Aristotle's approach, but this does not mean no reason can be given for acting in this way, and what this reason is does not have to be, as Rorty himself notes, one which would convince an egoist or a psychopath. Nor does it have to constitute a "neutral justification." For example, a Marxist would have just as much reason to defend solidarity as a Christian would – and would probably have many of the same reasons. Because of this, they might come to be in solidarity with one another.

If called on for a justification of the moral obligation to be "in solidarity" from outside the practice, Maritain would have no doubt drawn on an argument from natural law or, what is the same for him, from a general account of human nature.[34] But this is not the only defense of an obligation to be in solidarity that we can derive from his writings; there is also a "historical" defense. Given that some people find arguments from human nature and natural law problematic, here I will outline some of Maritain's "historical" arguments for why one should be "in solidarity."

Maritain notes that when human rights came to be recognized, they were not "deduced" from human nature or natural law, but were the product of an "awareness of an inclination" in human beings. The first instances of the "sudden awareness" of such rights occurred, Maritain notes, in the eighteenth century in Western and Central Europe.[35] While Maritain does not say so explicitly, when these rights "sprang into existence," they did so as a part of various practices – as activities of political, religious, and occupational association; as examples of political and religious expression; and as part of the pursuit of goods like property or conscience. The articulation of these rights reflected how people were already engaged in actions with others – and they reflected certain common interests and conceptions of the human person. Though the recognition of these rights was historical, though the practices that people engaged in varied, though these rights may have been expressed or understood in slightly different ways, and though the articulation of these rights evolved, these rights were not arbitrary. They arose out of concrete circumstances, they reflected features of persons which are not incidental but are connected with basic human needs, and they were a means by which these needs, and the respect for persons as persons, could be realized by those persons themselves. Human rights are themselves a "practice." As Jack Donnelly writes, "human rights [themselves] are a social practice that aims to realize a particular vision of human dignity and potential by institutionalizing these basic rights."[36] Moreover, the awareness of these rights was simultaneous with the awareness of them as prescriptive, and the awareness that we ought to work with others towards their recognition. There was no question of being engaged in these practices and later wondering whether one ought to be engaged in them. So, historically, there is no need for a separate justification of human rights. When they came into existence, they were recognized as having moral force. This does not mean a discourse of human rights or solidarity is by definition intrinsically prescriptive. Instead, our awareness of rights and of solidarity is concomitant with our awareness that we have to respond morally. (Thus, it is not obvious the burden of proving their moral weight is on the defender of such rights.)

Still, the appeal to a historical defense does not mean the obligations to respect and promote human rights, and to be in solidarity, cannot be justified in other ways. The rights that we have are the outcome of facts of human life and the practices we engage in. These rights may not be logically necessary, but many are causally necessary – that is, necessary for human beings to engage in the sorts of activities and practices relevant to human flourishing. Human rights and solidarity can be justified, given what human beings are. To ignore the call to be in solidarity and to ignore the demand to work for the realization of human rights is, then, to refuse to recognize that these interests are also needs, and that they reflect the needs, interests, and dignity of all human beings. And this, in turn, is to ignore facts about the world that are intimately connected with values manifest in social structures and institutions.

This argument does not claim that rights are "deduced" from human nature. Rights may grow and develop, and our obligation to promote them depends on a variety of contingent factors (about the recognition of others and about the material means at our disposal). Rights remain, however, related to our understanding of what it is to be a human person. Thus, even though the moral requirement of solidarity, and the mechanisms by which it may be achieved, have only come into being at a particular historical epoch, this obligation is not arbitrary.

If we are willing to accept Maritain's account of human rights as a concrete example of the object of – and the interests aimed at in – solidarity, and if a "historical" version of a defense of his views is plausible, then we have reasons to be "in solidarity." Such reasons may not be sufficient to move some people to act "in solidarity," but they are part of the explanation of why such actions, and the development of the corresponding dispositions, are appropriate and have moral weight.

3. Conclusion

The principal object of this paper was to argue for the importance of being able to justify a call to solidarity. I began by presenting a definition of "solidarity" and then attempted to show how it differs from a number of concepts with which it is often associated. Next, I outlined what has been held to be a radical critique of such an understanding of solidarity – that of Richard Rorty – and argued that Rorty's critique is either misdirected or inconsistent.

In the second part of this paper I maintained it is important to see solidarity both as a practice and as an intentional attitude or disposition to act. This acknowledges that the "post-modern" critique of solidarity and human rights – and of moral philosophy in general – has helped to remind us of a problem in modern philosophy, particularly its attitude towards the relevance of the sentiments and their place in the discussion of moral terms and in moral education. Nevertheless, a satisfactory account of solidarity requires moving beyond the "post-modern" view. In seeing solidarity as a practice and being "in solidarity" as a disposition, we can distinguish moments of acting to help others and isolated gestures of doing good from exhibiting a "way of being" that shows a sense of commitment or *engagement* to helping others, that is habitual and constant, and that has moral weight.

The value of Maritain to this project of describing and defending solidarity is that he gives us a concrete account of what solidarity amounts to, he suggests how it can be understood as a disposition, and he provides the basis for a justification of how it is obligatory – so that others can be called on to be "in solidarity." Maritain's account also has significant implications not only for general principles of economic justice, but for what are called "social" and "economic" rights. In respecting rights in the way that Maritain describes, then, we not only show solidarity but we are *"solidaire"* – in solidarity – with others.[37]

Notes

1. See Maritain's *Humanisme intégral: problèmes temporels et spirituals d'une nouvelle chrétienté* (Paris: Fernand Aubier, 1936). Two translations: *True humanism*, trans. M.R. Adamson (London: Bles, 1938), and *Integral Humanism: Temporal and Spiritual Problems of a New Christendom*, trans. Joseph W. Evans (New York: Charles Scribner's Sons, 1968); *Les droits de l'homme et la loi naturelle* (New York: Éditions de la Maison française, 1942), translated as *The Rights of Man and Natural Law*, trans. Doris C. Anson (New York: Charles Scribner's Sons, 1943); *Principes d'une politique humaniste* (New York: Éditions de la maison française, 1944); *Man and the State* (Chicago: University of Chicago Press, 1951), translated as *L'Homme et L'État*, trans. Robert and France Duval (Paris: Presses Universitaires de France, 1953); *La loi naturelle ou loi non écrite*: texte inédit, établi par Georges Brazzola (Fribourg, Switzerland: Éditions universitaires, 1986), translated as *Lectures on Natural Law*, trans. William Sweet, *The Collected Works of Jacques Maritain*, Vol. VI (Notre Dame, IN: University of Notre Dame Press, forthcoming); *Natural Law: reflections on theory and practice*, ed. William Sweet (South Bend, IN: St. Augustine's Press, 2001).

2. Maritain, Lecture plan for course of lectures on natural law, Princeton University (academic year 1949–50).

3. See Emile Durkheim, *De la division du travail social* (Paris: Presses universitaires de France, 1991), for a discussion of different types of solidarity.

4. See Durkheim's *De la division du travail social*, and François Ewald, "Solidarité," *Dictionnaire d'éthique et de philosophie morale*, ed. Monique Canto-Sperber (Paris: Presses universitaires de France, 1996), pp. 1433–1440.

5. See Rorty, "Solidarity," *Contingency, Irony and Solidarity* (Cambridge: Cambridge University Press, 1989), p. 189.

6. Ibid.

7. Ibid., pp. 191, 192, 195.

8. Ibid., p. 189.

9. Ibid., p. 194, n. 6.

10. Ibid., p. 198.

11. Ibid., p. 192.

12. Ibid., p. 193.

13. Ibid., p. 195.

14. Ibid., p. 196.

15. Ibid., p. 190.

16. See "Human Rights, Rationality and Sentimentality," *On Human Rights*, The Oxford Amnesty Lectures 1993, eds. S. Hurley and S. Shute (New York: Basic Books, 1993), pp. 111–134, at p. 122.

17. Rorty, "Solidarity," p. 196.

18. Ibid.

19. Ibid., p. 197.

20. Ibid., p. 189.

21. Rorty, "Human Rights, Rationality and Sentimentality," p. 122.

22. Rorty, "Solidarity," p. 197.

23. Kant, *Groundwork of the Metaphysics of Morals* [Akademie ed., p. 421] ed. H.J. Paton (New York: Harper and Row, 1964), p. 88.

24. Ibid.

25. Rorty, "Human Rights, Rationality and Sentimentality," p. 119.

26. Ibid., p. 118.

27. Ibid., p. 122.

28. Rorty, "Solidarity," p. 196.

29. Ibid., p. 192.

30. *After Virtue* (Notre Dame, IN: University of Notre Dame Press, 2nd ed., 1984), p. 187.

31. See René Mougel, "J. Maritain et la Déclaration universelle des droits de l'homme de 1948," *Cahiers Jacques Maritain*, 37 (1998), pp. 13–15.

32. See Maritain, *The Rights of Man and Natural Law*, pp. 60–61.

33. Maritain, *La loi naturelle ou loi non-écrite*, pp. 190–191.

34. See Maritain, *Man and the State*, pp. 85–89; *Natural Law: reflections on theory and practice*, pp. 27–31.

35. Maritain, *La loi naturelle*, p. 189.

36. Jack Donnelly, *Universal Human Rights in Theory and Practice* (Ithaca: Cornell University Press, 1989), p. 18, cited in David Duquette, "Philosophy, Anthropology and Universal Human Rights," *The Social Power of Ideas*, ed. Creighton Peden and Yeager Hudson (Lewiston, NY: Mellen Press, 1995), pp. 139–153, on p. 148.

37. I am grateful to Professor Philippe van Parijs, of the Université catholique de Louvain, for the hospitality of the Chaire Hoover d'éthique et d'économie sociale, where much of this paper was written and developed. Earlier versions of this paper were presented at the Université catholique de Louvain (Louvain-la-neuve, Belgium), the Ateneo de Manila University (Quezon City, Philippines), the University of Cape Town (South Africa), St. Paul's College (University of Manitoba, Winnipeg, Canada, as part of the Jesuit Speakers Series), and at the Canadian Jacques Maritain Association symposium "The Declaration of Human Rights: 50 years later ..." (University of Ottawa, Canada). I have benefitted from the questions and comments of those present. I am also grateful to the University Council for Research, St. Francis Xavier University, for a research grant that allowed me to undertake work on this topic.

CONTRIBUTORS

William Sweet is Professor of Philosophy at St Francis Xavier University, in Nova Scotia, Canada, and author of *Idealism and Rights* (1997) and, with Hendrik Hart, *Anti-foundationalism, Faith and Community* (2003). He has edited several collections of scholarly essays, including *La philosophie de la religion à la fin du vingtième siècle* (1993), *Religion, Modernity and Post Modernity* (1997), *God and Argument* (1999), *The Bases of Ethics* (2000), *Idealism, Metaphysics and Community* (2001), and, most recently, *Philosophy, Culture, and Pluralism* (2002). He is author of some one hundred scholarly articles, primarily in the history of idealist social and political thought, is a co-editor of a new edition of Bernard Bosanquet's *The Philosophical Theory of the State* (2001, with Gerald F. Gaus), and edited the 20-volume *Collected Works of Bernard Bosanquet* (1999). He is the Secretary-General of the World Union of Catholic Philosophical Societies, Vice President of the Istituto Internazionale Jacques Maritain (Rome), and President of the Canadian Jacques Maritain Association.

Leslie Armour is Professor Emeritus of Philosophy at the University of Ottawa and author of *"Infini Rien": Pascal's Wager and the Human Paradox* (1993), *Being and Idea: Developments of Some Themes in Spinoza and Hegel* (1992), *The Idea of Canada and the Crisis of Community* (1981), *The Faces of Reason: An Essay on Philosophy and Culture in English Canada, 1850–1950* (1981, with Elizabeth Trott), *The Conceptualization of the Inner Life* (1980, with Edward T. Bartlett), *Logic and Reality: An Investigation into the Idea of a Dialectical System* (1972), *The Concept of Truth* (1969), and *The Rational and the Real: An Essay in Metaphysics* (1962). He is a Fellow of the Royal Society of Canada.

Mostafa Faghfoury lectures in philosophy at Heritage College, Hull, Québec, Canada. He is editor of *Analytic Philosophy of Religion in Canada* (1983) and has published in *De Philosophia, The Southern Journal of Philosophy, Philosophy Research Archives*, and other journals.

Paul Groarke is an Assistant Professor in the Criminal Justice Program at St. Thomas University, Fredericton, Canada. He is also a practicing lawyer and a member of the Canadian Human Rights Tribunal. He has published in *The South Pacific Journal of Philosophy and Culture*, the *Canadian Journal of Political Science, Philosophy in Review*, and *Dialogue*.

Sarah Hutton is Reader in Renaissance and Seventeenth-Century Studies at Middlesex University, England. Her publications include *Platonism and the English Imagination*, edited with Anna Baldwin (1994), *Women Science and Medicine 1550–1700*, edited with Lynette Hunter (1997), a new edition of Ralph

Cudworth's *Treatise Concerning Eternal and Immutable Morality* (1996), and a revised edition of *The Conway Letters: the correspondence of Anne, Viscountess Conway, Henry More, and their friends, 1642-1684* (1992). She is Director of the *International Archives in the History of Ideas / Archives Internationales d'Histoire des Idées*, a member of the editorial board of *The British Journal for the History of Philosophy*, and is currently President of the British Society for the History of Philosophy.

Jack Iwanicki was, until his recent retirement, Professor of Philosophy at the University of New Brunswick, Canada. He studied philosophy and law at the University of Toronto, and law at Indiana University. He is the author of several articles in the philosophy of law, including "Necessity" in *The Philosophy of Law: An Encyclopedia* (1999).

Thomas Jeannot is Associate Professor of Philosophy at Gonzaga University in Spokane, Washington. His interests include Marxism and critical theory, hermeneutics, classical American philosophy, and ethics. He has published in the *International Philosophical Quarterly*, *The New Scholasticism*, *Transactions of the Charles S. Peirce Society*, *Journal of Speculative Philosophy*, *Radical Philosophy Review*, *International Journal of Social Economics*, *Logos* (USA), and other journals.

Howard P. Kainz is Professor of Philosophy at Marquette University, Milwaukee, Wisconsin. He is the author of *G.W.F. Hegel* (1996), *An Introduction to Hegel: The Stages of Modern Philosophy* (1996), *Democracy and the Kingdom of God* (1993, 1995), *Ethics in Context: Towards the Definition and Differentiation of the Morally Good* (1988), *Paradox, Dialectic, and System: A Contemporary Reconstruction of the Hegelian Problematic* (1988), *Hegel's Phenomenology, Part I: analysis and commentary* (1976), *Hegel's Phenomenology, Part II : the evolution of ethical and religious consciousness to the absolute standpoint* (1983), *Democracy, East and West: A Philosophical Overview* (1984), *Philosophical Perspectives on Peace: An Anthology of Classical and Modern Sources* (1987), *The Philosophy of Man: A New Introduction to Some Perennial Issues* (1981, 1989), *Wittenberg, Revisited: A Polymorphous Critique of Religion and Theology* (1981), *The Unbinding of Prometheus: Towards a Philosophy of Revolution* (1976), *Ethica dialectica: A Study of Ethical Oppositions* (1979), and *Active and Passive Potency in Thomistic Angelology* (1972). He has published in such journals as *Metaphilosophy*, *The Monist*, the *International Journal of the Philosophy of Religion*, *The Journal of Philosophy*, and *The Review of Metaphysics*.

David Lea is Senior Lecturer in Philosophy and Acting Dean of Humanities at the University of Papua New Guinea. He is author of *Melanesian Land Tenure in a Contemporary and Philosophical Context* (1997), and has published in *The Journal* *of Applied Philosophy, Alternatives, Business Ethics: A European Review, History of European Ideas, Sophia, Reason Papers, The Journal of Social Philosophy, Dialectica: Revista de Filosofia, Cientas Sociales, Literatura y Cultura,* and other journals.

Philip Lancaster completed a Ph.D. in philosophy at the University of Ottawa. While serving in the Canadian Armed Forces, he was an aide to Canadian General Romeo Dallaire in Rwanda, as part of the United Nations Observer Mission: Uganda and Rwanda (UNAMIR) in 1993–1994. His paper in this volume was completed while he was working as Resident Programme Officer, Juba (UNICEF) in the war zone in the Sudan. He has published in *Études maritainiennes.*

Rex Martin, is Professor of Philosophy at University of Kansas, holds a personal chair in the Department of Politics in the University of Wales, Swansea, and has held visiting appointments at the University of Auckland and at the Faculty of Law, University of Sydney (Australia). He is a Vice President and member of the executive committee of the International Association for Philosophy of Law and Social Philosophy (IVR) and was President of its American Section (1993–95). He is the author of *Historical Explanation* (1977), *Rawls and Rights* (1985), and *A System of Rights* (1993), and edited *G.C. MacCallum's Legislative Intent and Other Essays on Law, Politics and Morality* (with Mark Singer, 1993). He is currently preparing a revised edition of *R.G. Collingwood, An Essay on Metaphysics* (for the Clarendon Press). He has published in several journals, including *American Philosophical Quarterly, Review of Metaphysics, Journal of the History of Ideas, Philosophy, Ethics,* and *History of Political Thought.*

Bradley Munro worked in the Department of the Secretary of State, Canada, and is currently a researcher in human rights policy in Ottawa. He completed a Ph.D. in Philosophy at the University of Waterloo. He has published in *Idealism, Metaphysics, and Community.*

Ralph Nelson is Professor Emeritus of Political Science at the University of Windsor, Canada, and editor and translator of a number of works by Yves Simon for Fordham University Press (*Prévoir et savoir [Foresight and Knowledge],* 1996) and for *The Thomist* and the *International Philosophical Quarterly.* He is also author of numerous studies and reviews, published in *Papers in Public Law, Public Legal History, Natural Law, and Political Thought: estudios en homenaje al professor Jesus Lalinde Abadia, From Twilight to Dawn: The Cultural Vision of Jacques Maritain, Freedom in the Modern World, THÈMES, la revue de la B.P.C. Proceedings of the American Catholic Philosophical Association, Études maritainiennes, Acquaintance with the Absolute: The Philosophy of Yves Simon,* and *Jacques Maritain: a Philosopher.* He is editing Volume 14 of the *Collected Works of Jacques Maritain.*

J.L.A. West is a doctoral candidate in philosophy at the University of Waterloo, Canada. His principal interests are in mediaeval philosophy, and he has published in a collection of essays on *God and Argument*, and in such journals as *Études maritainiennes*, *Polis*, *Eidos*, and *Philosophical Forum*.

Gregory J. Walters is Professor of Theology at Saint Paul University, Ottawa, Canada. He is author of *Human Rights in Theory and Practice: a selected and annotated bibliography* (1994), *Karl Jaspers and the role of "conversion" in the nuclear age* (1988), *Equal Access: Safeguarding Disability Rights* (1992) and, most recently, *Human Rights in an Information Age: a philosophical analysis* (2001). He is editor of *The Tasks of Truth: Essays on Karl Jaspers's Idea of the University* (1996), and has also published in *International Philosophical Quarterly*, *Jahrbuch der Österreichischen Karl Jaspers Gesellschaft / Yearbook of the Austrian Karl Jaspers Society*, *Violence et Coexistence Humaine / Violence and Human Coexistence*, *Great Events from History II: Human Rights*, and *Science et esprit*.

INDEX

Aboriginal, 13, 201, 206, 207
Ackerman, Bruce, 208
Adler, Mortimer, 171
Akayesu, Jean-Paul, 118
Ambrose, Saint, 201
Amyraut, M., 54, 56-61
Anti-voluntarism, 29, 31, 34, 36, 37
Aquinas, St. Thomas, 3, 10, 12, 13, 20, 21-25, 43, 60-63, 91, 92, 104, 113, 115-117, 119, 123, 145, 155, 158-164, 171, 184, 193, 195, 196, 201-203, 219, 221
Arbour, Louise, 119, 120
Aristotelian, 20, 23, 25, 44, 160, 184, 195
Aristotle, 20, 84, 86, 91, 92, 159, 177, 183-185, 193, 219, 228
Armour, Leslie, 10, 233
Armstrong, Brian Gary, 58
Aron, Raymond, 4, 172-175, 177
Augustine, Saint, 158, 159, 195, 196, 201, 202
Austin, John, 163
Authority, 76, 104, 105, 136, 138, 139, 149, 157, 159, 163, 168, 185, 186, 208
Autonomy, 84, 92, 94, 156
Axworthy, Lloyd, 128

Bacon, Roger, 46
Barclay, Robert, 55, 56
Baroody, Jamil, 105
Bauer, Bruno, 85
Baxter, Richard, 54
Beetz, Justice, 135
Bentham, 2, 4, 22, 87, 88, 175, 186, 213
Berdyaev, 89
Berlin, Isaiah, 42, 56, 175
Bérulle, Pierre de, 59

Birthright, 33
Blackstone, W.T., 175, 203
Bolingbroke, Viscount, 30, 31
Bonaparte, Napoleon, 44
Bosanquet, Bernard, 5, 233
Bossuet, 55
Bradwardine, Thomas, 46
Burke, Edmund, 2, 4, 35

Caird, Edward, 54
Cameron, John, 54-59
Cantor, 62
Capitalism, 49, 51, 52, 59, 83, 86, 87, 89-92, 177, 203, 205
Cassin, R., 104, 122
Catholic, 59, 60, 83, 84, 89, 90, 94, 119, 123, 155, 184, 185
Chang, Peng-Chun, 104, 110
Charter of Rights, 12, 79, 127-139, 162, 164-166, 168, 171, 179
China, 8, 30, 100, 113, 117, 118
Chrétien, Jean, 133
Christman, John, 208, 209
Churchill, Winston, 101
Cicero, 158
Clarke, Samuel, 10, 36, 37
Clinton, W., 41
Coercion, 148, 151
Coleridge, 54
Collectivist, 91, 104
Columbus, 100
Common good, 11, 13, 15, 71-73, 75-77, 79, 92, 145, 155, 156, 158-166, 171, 172, 175, 176, 223
Communism, 83, 85-87, 89, 93, 104
Communitarian, 11-13, 76, 84, 94, 157, 158, 160, 162, 171, 177
Connatural, 116, 117, 119
Constitution (U.S.), 156, 157, 161, 162

Cory, Justice, 131-133
Cranston, Maurice, 171, 174
Cudworth, Ralph, 10, 28, 29, 36-38,
    233
Cumberland, Richard, 33
Cuneo, Michele de, 100, 101

Democracy/democratic, 6, 8, 11, 50,
    53, 63, 66, 75-77, 79, 84, 89, 90,
    92, 93, 102, 107, 111, 112,
    117-119, 156, 158, 172, 173,
    177, 178, 179, 198, 218
Deontological, 36, 183, 184, 186
Descartes, 10, 42, 54, 60, 62, 222
Dewey, John, 11, 46, 83-86, 88-94,
    171, 174
Dickens, 222
Dickson, Brian, Chief Justice, 130,
    135-139, 163-165
Dignity, 1, 2, 6, 7, 14, 15, 47, 63, 91,
    92, 101, 107, 109, 120, 122, 124,
    133, 198, 213, 229
Disobedience, civil, 197
Donagan, Alan, 183, 192
Donnelly, Jack, 5
Dostoyevsky, 87
Duns Scotus, 43
Duplessis, Maurice, 41
Durkheim, 224
Duty/duties, 7, 13-15, 19, 20, 22, 24,
    25, 36, 47, 66, 129, 146, 171,
    175, 178, 197, 204, 205, 215,
    227
Dworkin, Ronald, 4, 87, 175

Eliot, T.S., 92
Engels, F., 48
Epictetus, 20
Epstein, Richard, 208
Equality, 1, 2, 5, 20, 27, 29-32, 34,
    63, 65, 87, 88, 112, 130, 156,
    159, 160, 162, 163, 166-168,
    173, 198, 206, 216, 223

Erasmus, 101
Estey, Justice, 134

Fairness, 27, 101, 130
Falwell, Jerry, 91
Family, 20, 23-25, 28, 131
Fichte, 102
Filmer, 204, 205
Finnis, John, 4, 10, 13, 19, 21-23,
    25, 156, 175-177
Flaubert, 221

Gadamer, Hans-Georg, 83
Gauthier, David, 52
Gellner, Ernest, 50
Genocide, 12, 100, 118, 119, 121,
    131, 145, 147-150
Gert, Bernard, 183, 192
Gewirth, Alan, 4, 13, 176-178,
    183-198
Glendon, Mary Ann, 178
Gonthier, Justice, 133, 134
Green, T.H., 5, 11, 42, 71-80
Grisez, Germain, 21, 22
Grotius, Hugo, 171, 203

Hart, H.L.A., 4, 22, 25, 208
Havel, Vaclav, 107
Hegel, 4, 19, 44, 46, 51, 84, 85, 233,
    234
Herder, J.G., 102
Hill, Bridget, 30
Hitler, 193
Hobbes, 3, 10, 19, 45, 52, 71, 87,
    120, 145, 155, 156
Hodgson, Colonel, 111
Hook, Sidney, 84, 92, 93, 174, 175
Huisseau, Isaac d', 54, 56, 59, 60
Hume, David, 10, 21, 184, 185, 221
Humphrey, John, 104, 110, 111
Hurka, Thomas, 73, 74

Ibn Roschd, 184

Inflation (in rights), 1, 12, 13
Interests, 1, 72, 73, 76, 88, 144, 161
Iwanicki, Jack, 12, 127-142, 234

Jeannot, Thomas, 11, 83-95, 234
Jefferson, Thomas, 20, 103
Jesus, 99, 100
ji-yu, 7
Joad, C.E.M. , 45
John Paul II, Pope, 171

Kades, Lt. Col. C. L., 7
Kant, 4, 22, 101, 102, 113, 143, 145-147, 150, 172, 183, 184, 186, 194, 196, 220, 221
Kierkegaard, S., 184
Kindler v. Canada, 131, 133
King, Martin Luther. Jr. , 107
Koretsky, Vladimir, 104, 110

La Forest, Justice, 128-131, 134
Lal, Vinay, 213
Lamer, Chief Justice, 133
Law of nations, 119
Law Society of B.C. v. Andrews, 168
Le Dain, Justice, 135, 136
League of Nations, 103
Leibniz, 114
Lenin, 45
L'Hereux-Dubé, Justice, 130
Libertarian, 14, 35
Lisska, Anthony, 22
Locke, John, 3, 10, 19, 28, 29, 36, 42, 120, 155, 201, 203-207
Loyalty, 177, 215, 216

MacArthur, General Douglas, 7
Macaulay, Catherine, 10, 28-32, 35-38
Machan, Tibor, 4
MacIntyre, Alasdair, 4, 13, 158, 183-198, 223

Macpherson, C.B., 156, 204
Maimonides, 184
Malik, Charles H. , 104
Mandela, Nelson, 107
Maritain, Jacques, 1, 2, 11, 13, 43, 60, 62, 83-94, 101, 109-124, 156, 161, 171, 172, 177, 213, 214, 226-231, 233, 235
Maritain's piano analogy, 114
Marx, 2, 4, 11, 42, 44, 48, 49, 51, 83-94
Marxist, 43-46, 48-51, 53, 84, 85, 87, 92, 123, 157, 173, 174, 195, 229
Masaryk, Thomas, 102
Masham, Lady, 10, 28-30, 32, 37, 38
Maximus, Valerius, 161
McInerny, Ralph, 22
McIntyre, Justice, 136, 168
Michener, Norah, 62
Mill, J.S., 106, 186
Milne v. Canada, 134, 139
Mirandola, Pico della, 101
Miron and Valliere v. Trudel et al, 133
Moore, G. E., 186
More, Thomas, 101
Morgentaler, Henry, 130
Moses, 57, 87
Mounier, 89

Nationalism, 59, 102
Natural law, 3, 9, 10, 14, 15, 19-25, 30, 31, 33, 113-123, 156, 171, 172, 175, 195, 208, 227, 229
Need, 89, 122, 123, 192, 229
Nelson, Ralph, 12, 171-181, 235
Nickel, James, 105
Nietzsche, 87
Norris, John, 56
Nozick, Robert, 4, 87, 90, 192, 193, 204

Okali, 118

Pagels, Elaine, 155, 156, 158
Paine, Thomas, 27, 32
Pascal, Blaise, 113, 184, 185, 233
Paul, Daniel, 106
Paul, St., 46
Peacock, Reginald, 43
Pearson, Lester, 104
Peng, Li, 117
Penn, William, 54-57, 60
Perfection, 57, 72, 115
Person, 1, 2, 4, 6, 14, 20, 24, 85, 91,
    100, 107, 113, 117, 132, 133,
    156, 161, 166, 167, 185, 214,
    224, 229, 230
Personalism, 89, 90, 92, 93, 172
Plato, 20, 47, 219, 221
Platonism, 35, 37
Pluralism, 55, 56, 91, 92, 175, 213
Popper, Sir Karl, 102
Pragmatism, 5, 83, 84, 92, 186, 220
Price, Richard, 10, 35-38
Principle of Generic Consistency
    (PGC), 184, 186, 189, 190, 192,
    193, 196-198

Property, 4, 13, 20, 24, 27, 31, 85,
    87, 88, 173, 201-210, 229
Prospective Purposive Agent (PPA),
    188-190
Pufendorf, Samuel, 202, 203
Purchas, Samuel, 100

R. v. Butler, 165
R. v. Keegstra, 165
R. v. Oakes, 129-131
R. v. O'Connor, 130
R. v. Ward, 128, 129, 139
Rapaport, Anatol, 144
Raphael, D.D., 36
Rationalist, 36, 38, 112-116, 196,
    198, 218, 219

Rawls, John, 47, 87, 90, 106, 144,
    175, 183, 192, 193
Reagan, Ronald, 90
Rebel, 118
Recognition, 5-7, 11, 63, 71, 78, 79,
    107, 214, 215, 222-229
Relativism, 30, 53, 56, 105, 119, 173
Respect, 12, 15, 65, 105, 106, 173,
    191, 230
Responsibility, 7, 10, 22, 23
Reynolds, Henry, 206
Richelieu, Cardinal, 45, 59
Robb, James H., 62
Robertson, Pat, 91
Rockefeller, Steven C., 91
Roe v. Wade, 130
Roosevelt, Mrs. Eleanor, 103, 110
Rorty, Richard, 4, 13, 87, 92, 213,
    214, 217-223, 225, 228-231
Rousseau, 4, 36, 113, 123

Saint John, Henry, 30
Santa Cruz, Hernan, 104, 110
Sartre, Jean-Paul, 25, 41
Secularism, 84, 85, 88, 89
Seville, Isidore of, Saint, 160
Sheena B., Re, 133
Sidgwick, H., 186
Simon, Yves, 13, 172, 177, 235
Smith, Adam, 221
Solidarity, 13, 177, 213-231
Song, Robert, 62
Sorel, 89
Spencer, Herbert, 4
Spinoza, 71, 233
Stalin, 84, 89, 93, 193
Strauss, Leo, 156
Suarez, Francisco, 155, 156
Suharto, 53
Swaggart, Jimmy, 91
Sweet, William, 1-16, 68, 81, 117,
    213-233

Taylor, Charles, 105
Telos/teleology, 3, 15, 23, 183-186, 193, 194
Testard, Paul, 57
Thatcher, Margaret, 90
Theology, 31, 35, 36, 38, 85, 86, 92, 94, 184, 195, 196
Tolerance, 216
Toleration, 4, 53, 57
Tomaselli, Sylvana, 31
Tully, J., 156, 203-208

Van Stam, F.P., 57
Veatch, Henry, 22
Virtue, 13, 28, 32, 36, 147, 183, 184, 192-196, 198, 225, 226, 228
Vishinsky, 105
Vitoria, Francisco de, 156

Walesa, Lech, 107, 213
Watson, John, 54
Weber, Max, 59, 143, 203
Welfare, 3, 23, 52, 64, 90, 198, 209
Whitehead, George, 55
Wilson, Geoffrey, 104
Wilson, Justice, 130, 135
Wilson, Woodrow, 102
Winston, Morton, 158
Wollstonecraft, Mary, 4, 10, 27, 31-38
Wyclif, 43

Yoshida, Shigeru, 7

Zamuddin, Tum Daim, 110, 112
Zemin, Jiang, 117